The Patrimonial Foundations
of the Brazilian Bureaucratic State

The Patrimonial Foundations of the Brazilian Bureaucratic State

FERNANDO URICOECHEA

UNIVERSITY OF CALIFORNIA PRESS

Berkeley • Los Angeles • London

University of California Press
Berkeley and Los Angeles, California
University of California Press, Ltd.
London, England
Copyright © 1980 by
The Regents of the University of California

Library of Congress Cataloging in Publication Data
Uricoechea, Fernando.
    The patrimonial foundations of the Brazilian bureaucratic state.

    Revision of the author's thesis, University of California, Berkeley, 1976, which was published in 1978 under title: O minotauro imperial.
    Includes bibliographical references and index.
    1. Brazil—Politics and government.
2. Bureaucracy—Brazil—History.
3. Brazil. Guarda Nacional—History. I. Title.
JL2424.U74   1980   301.5'92'0981   78-66010
ISBN 0-520-03853-3

Printed in the United States of America

1 2 3 4 5 6 7 8 9

To María Cristina

Contents

Tables

Abbreviations
Used in the References

act:	acting
AEB:	Arquivo Histórico do Estado da Bahia
AHRGS:	Arquivo Histórico do Rio Grande do Sul
AN:	Arquivo Nacional
APM:	Arquivo Público do Estado de Minas Gerais
BPER:	Arquivo da Biblioteca Pública do Estado do Rio de Janeiro
bat:	battalion
cs:	*comandante superior* (commander-in-chief)
cap:	captain
cav:	cavalry
cod:	*códice:* manuscript volume
col:	colonel
com:	commander
comp:	company
ch:	Chief
G.N:	*Guarda Nacional*
j.p:	*juiz de paz* (justice of the peace)
leg:	legion
lieut:	lieutenant
loc:	local
MJ:	Ministry of Justice or Minister of Justice

ms:	manuscript
off. let:	official letter, dispatch
pp:	president of province
pac:	*pacote* (parcel). Together with *caixa, maço,* and *lata, pacote* represent the units of archival reference. An average parcel contains 200 to 400 manuscripts.
sect:	section of a company
vice-p:	vice-president of a province

Author's Note

A few words with regard to the quotation and transcription of original sources:

From Chapter 3 onward, and on those occasions when a series of quotations is introduced in the text, reference to the sources ordinarily comes only after the last quotation of the series. The references from which the quotations are drawn are given in the same order in which the sources are quoted. Consequently, the archival reference to a quotation will be found in the footnote at the end of the last quotation of the series.

Capitals, obsolete in modern usage, have been preserved with the hope, perhaps not vain, that the emphasis behind the use of capitals might teach us something about what nineteenth-century Brazilian patrimonial officers and bureaucratic officials considered valuable.

Preface

An earlier version of this book was written and submitted in 1976 as a doctoral dissertation for the degree in sociology at the University of California, Berkeley, and published in 1978 in Portuguese with the title *O minotauro imperial*, DIFEL:Rio de Janeiro. I am indebted to the Ford Foundation for a research grant that enabled me to visit the regional archives and to obtain research assistance for this work. Access to archival sources was greatly facilitated by the kind help of the personnel of the different archives, and I want to thank those who were particularly instrumental: Aclair Ramos de Oliveira, Maria de la Encarnacion Espana Iglesias, Maria Luisa Fernandes de Carvalho, and José Gabriel Costa Pinto at the Arquivo Nacional in Rio de Janeiro. The latter was particularly helpful in helping me decipher otherwise illegible manuscripts. Equally helpful in this task was the Director of the Arquivo Historico de Rio Grande do Sul, Cel. Moacir Domingues, who, together with Suzana Schunk Brochado, provided valuable cooperation that speeded up the process of data gathering. The people at the Arquivo do Estado da Bahia were also extremely kind and cooperative. The acting Director of that regional archive, Wilson Sampaio do Prado Pinto, was most generous with his assistance, as were the other members of the archive, particularly Neusa Rodrigues Esteves, Adir de Souza Chaves, and Tereza Maria dos Santos.

I am indebted for my access to the Archive of the Biblioteca Publica do Estado do Rio de Janeiro at Niteroi, to Yeda Gappo Viana de Brito. All the above persons considerably eased a process that would otherwise have taken much longer. I would like to give my special thanks to Rui Vieira da Cunha, who belongs, together with José Gabriel Costa Pinto, to the research section of the Arquivo Nacional at Rio de Janeiro. My talks with him encouraged me to enquire further into the role of the *Guarda Nacional* in Brazilian institutional life at a time when I had only a vague intuition of its importance.

My work was also helped by the generous research assistance provided by Maria da Graça Salgado, whose enthusiastic and intelligent cooperation was a permanent source of stimulation. Maria Margarita Uricoechea and Luiz Henrique Nunes Bahia also were helpful in the statistical handling of some data.

For several years I have been associated with the Instituto Universitario de Pesquisas do Rio de Janeiro. It was there that I had the opportunity to familiarize myself with, and draw on, the Brazilian versions of an intellectual debate that I had first encountered during my graduate years in Berkeley. I am very grateful to the Institute for the time and resources it has generously put at my disposal. I have greatly benefited from the seminars and lectures I have conducted there as a faculty member, and from the comments and criticisms of colleagues and friends on different portions of a previous version of this book. I am grateful to Simon Schwartzman, Carlos Hasenbalg, and Olavo Brasil de Lima, Jr. for their helpful criticisms, and to Cesar Guimarães, for his opportune encouragement. Rafael Bayce, Vicente Barretto, and Ron Seckinger also made comments from which I benefited. Neil J. Smelser, Arthur L. Stinchcombe, and Tulio Halperin, the members of my dissertation committee, were a challenging source of scholarship that I have tried to emulate. The influence of Max Weber on my thought will become evident in the first chapters. I came to study Weber for the first time thanks to an old friendship with Dario Mesa. To all these friends and colleagues, as well as to those others whom I have inadvertently omitted, my gratitude.

Rachel Barreto, Suellen Huntington, Douglas Aley, and Charlie Silver provided valuable editing assistance on different chapters of the first version of this book. Subsequent editing was done by Hilary Lager thanks to a generous grant from Candido Mendes, President of the Sociedade Brasileira de Instrução. This final version owes much to the efficient and skillful cooperation of Diane Sipes, the copy editor. Whatever Spanglish has remained must be attributed exclusively to my own sense of style.

Convention has it that I declare none of the above mentioned individuals is to be held accountable for any errors in the subsequent pages. This is conventionally correct. But my wife of many years, María Cristina Iriarte, should share the credit for whatever plaudits the book may receive. Her encouragement, her criticisms, and her love have much to do with what I here present. In a way, then, this work is as much hers as mine. I dedicate it to her as an expression of my deep, ineffable debt.

Introduction

Contingency is rooted in infinity.

Leibnitz *apud* Eduard Bodemann,
Die Leibniz-Handschriften

Knowledge deals with contingency. There are, however, different methods of treating contingency. The above statement by Leibnitz was designed to provide a firm grounding for the satisfactory explanation of this concept, but a critical reading of it provokes a sense of epistemological vertigo. In fact, Kant's *Critique of Pure Reason* is in part intended to demonstrate the futility of trying to overcome this vertigo through the notion of a necessary being. Sociological reason, less aesthetic and architectonic than transcendental reason, overcomes it by means of its recourse to *history*.[1]

Historical knowledge is thus the only scientific means of escape from the perturbing notion of an infinite regression of causes. Nevertheless, the sociological view of *necessity* as historical rather than metaphysical has not always been accompanied by the equally critical idea that the *principle of knowledge* of that necessity is, likewise, to be found in history and not in metaphysics. The pertinacity of evolutionary schemata in historical thought, for instance, attests to the relevance of the above distinction.

Two major strands of thought have consistently upheld both necessity and the knowledge of necessity in history. The first, the systematic strand, of course proceeds from Karl Marx; the second, the rhapsodic strand, was developed by Max Weber.

This work is an exercise in historical synthesis with the aid of Weber's sociological categories; it attempts to interpret

1

the historical experience of the Brazilian political community during the Imperial period, in terms of the ideal-typical notion of patrimonial bureaucracy.* The major object of research may be stated as follows: how did patrimonial bureaucratic rule develop in Imperial Brazil, and, in particular, what role did patrimonialism play in the process of development of the modern bureaucratic state?

The notion of patrimonial bureaucracy, however, is viewed in a particular light from the perspective of an ideal-typical methodology. In fact, most of Weber's ideal types are created from the standpoint of a single regulative principle, which gives them a typically one-sided accentuation and purity. The notion of patrimonial bureaucracy, however, is a hybrid one, since two opposed regulative principles are accented simultaneously: rational and traditional authority. This is an exceptional strategy that Weber felt forced to employ, against his own methodological injunctions to the contrary, because of the significance of these structures for the analysis of the processes of change. In fact, after a discussion of his ideal types of authority, Weber adds:

> We shall be compelled again and again to form expressions like 'patrimonial bureaucracy' in order to make the point that the characteristic traits of the respective phenomenon belong in part to the rational form of domination, whereas other traits belong to a traditionalist form of domination.[2]

With the help of this dynamic pattern of authority I propose to reconstruct the historical synthesis of nineteenth-cen-

---

*Ideal types or ideal-typical notions are synthetic concepts built by means of the one-sided accentuation of analytical aspects for the rational understanding of multifarious phenomena. Out of a manifold historical reality, ideal types select those aspects which fit into a theroretically meaningful historical construction. As such, ideal types are regulative concepts—utopian syntheses that neglect empirical elements which are not typical and therefore theoretically residual. Patrimonial bureaucracy is a concept belonging to such a class. It is a synthetic construction that accentuates the coexistence, within one pattern of political rule, of the universalistic and legal-rational elements at the center of the power structure and the particularistic and traditional elements at the periphery of the power structure. Any historically concrete structure may thus be approximated with the help of this notion, the usefulness of the approximation depending, of course, on the contrasts and continuities established between the historical object and the conceptual pattern.

tury Brazil in terms of a configuration of political authority made up of an inherent structural tension: on the one hand, the existence of an administrative apparatus bureaucratically controlled by the state, pushing for the overall bureaucratization of government, and on the other hand, the parallel existence of an administrative apparatus patrimonially controlled by the local classes and pressing for the prebendalization* of office.[3]

This work attempts to reexamine the Brazilian nineteenth-century political organization in terms of the vicissitudes and tensions between these two structures of government. The major monographic section will focus on a thorough analysis of a hitherto neglected association, the *Guarda Nacional*, a status association of freemen which made possible the most systematic and extensive experiment in patrimonial domination in nineteenth-century Latin America.

I first propose to examine systematically the genesis of patrimonial bureaucratic administration during the colonial period (1500–1822) and the societal and institutional context within which it emerged. In this period two major social groups emerged that became important in the organization of a patrimonial administration—the landlord group and the professional military.

In order for a patrimonial administrative order to be set up, however, it is also necessary that the notions of status and of administrative obligation determined by status toward the prince (liturgies,** in other words) be institutionalized. In fact, the existence of such a status order† permits the cre-

*By prebendalization of office I mean the process whereby an office is appropriated by its incumbent as an object of personal right, thereby negating the public and impersonal nature of office. The organic link between prebendalization and patrimonialism is apparent: prebendalization is a traditional form of political organization not checked by impersonal administrative canons, and patrimonial officers depending on prebends do their utmost to control access to office and to transform the prebend into a hereditary possession. The word "prebend" will be used throughout to denote benefices awarded by the state in exchange for administrative services. In Brazil, these benefices ordinarily took the form of land grants.

**Liturgies are here understood to be negative privileges in the form of administrative services that members of corporate and privileged groups were obliged to provide.

†A status order is here understood to be a social order in which rights and obligations are allocated primarily according to status group.

ation of an administration of dilettantes. I propose, consequently, to inquire into the structural conditions during the colonial period that favored such an outcome.

Brazilian colonial society had already created some of the initial conditions for a wide-ranging patrimonial bureaucratic structure. Yet only in the second quarter of the nineteenth century was this pattern of state organization transformed into a systematic and institutionalized arrangement. It was then that the prince and the state systematically made use of the population of freemen and agrarian notables by means of the *Guarda Nacional*, an organization especially designed for that purpose.

By focusing our attention on this militarized corporation, and by examining the structural conditions behind its liturgical administration of the patrimonial bureaucratic state, I hope to be able to cast some light on the process of statebuilding and the development of bureaucratic authority in Brazil in the last century. This focus, moreover, will permit us to take an empirical look at the intellectual controversy that lies behind this work, namely, the power relations between the central state and local society in agrarian Brazil.

A brief outline of the work will help to set the chapters in proper perspective and to bring out their substantive continuity. Chapter 1 contains a general introduction to the structural and institutional background of Imperial Brazil, that is, to its colonial society. Here the basic political, economic, and administrative aspects of its social organization are introduced. Chapter 2 examines the bureaucratic state during the Empire and its patrimonial context. Chapter 3 briefly discusses the militarized character of Brazilian society at the time of the creation of the *Guarda Nacional*, and its formal structure as an instrument of patrimonial administration. In the next two chapters, the problematic materialization of the patrimonial program and its perversion are discussed. Chapter 6 is devoted to an examination of the peculiarly regional expression that the corporation assumed in the frontier society of the south. Finally, Chapter 7 concludes the discussion begun in Chapter 2 on the development of the modern bureaucratic state, but this time from the perspective of the changes and continuities in the normative canons orienting the administrative apparatus of the legal rational state.

A few words with regard to the question of method are in order here. This work is primarily historical rather than demonstrative, and more inductive than deductive. It does not, in consequence, proceed with the elegance of an hypotetico-deductive and nomological model that aims at the explanation of a given historical pattern of events. The method is interpretative; the goal is to interpret, by the use of ideal-typical concepts, important aspects of the Brazilian past that would otherwise stand dissociated from one another. The meaningful and "necessary" connections between those aspects are revealed by the use of Weberian concepts. As such, this research cannot be said to be guided as much by a systematic and general theory, as by the imaginative use of those problematical concepts that permit the construction of meaningful patterns of historical intepretation.

It can be seen now, in view of these objectives and strategies, that the nature of the evidence may be problematical, a point that is of particular importance for research such as this, based on a one-sided interpretation of a considerable number of manuscripts from the last century. The major body of research, in fact, is based on the analysis of the official correspondence between patrimonial commanders and bureaucratic officials, specifically between local commanders and commanders-in-chief, between commanders-in-chief and provincial commanders, between provincial commanders and provincial presidents, between provincial commanders and the Court bureaucracy, and between provincial presidents and the Court bureaucracy. Needless to say, such a large amount of documentation may be interpreted in a variety of ways. The unequivocal and unambiguous significance of a determinate fact as a scientific datum might be indispensable if this research consisted of nomological explanations. But ideographic interpretations of the kind executed in this monograph operate differently; lability of meaning is an integral part of the structure and core of the historical material. In this context, the strictly unambiguous translation of established facts into relevant data is, to say the least, chimerical. The rational meaning of a fact does not inhere in the fact itself but in the theoretical perspective that serves as its frame. It is thus entirely legitimate to transform a single fact into a plurality of data—not necessarily compatible—according to the

theoretical formulae assumed, without doing the least violence to the fact itself.

This general consideration with regard to the admissible
plurality of interpretations of empirical facts should not be
construed as a weakness of interpretative sociology. It is, in
the first place, an indication that adequate explanatory understanding does not so much depend on crucial experiments
as on the scope of meaning that is gained by the use of such
patterns. Secondly, one cannot argue against the validity of
a single interpretation simply because a plurality of interpretations exist, all of which are consistent with the facts. While
not "falsifiable," an interpretation is scientifically adequate
according to the degree to which it successfully establishes
meaning for the widest possible scope of relevant phenomena by illustrating their internal relations. The question of
evidence and falsification turns here into the question of internal coherence and the meaningfulness of the proposed
pattern.

This work has been guided by two convictions: one, that
social values are effective principles of social action and, two,
that the "pragmatic" writing of history is sociologically unsatisfactory. The widespread disregard of values as ingredi-
ents of social action has ordinarily been brought about by a
failure to grasp the collective, social nature of values, and by
the mistaken belief that they are individual preferences subject to utilitarian, arbitrary, and contingent choice. This is not
the place to show how poor a representation of society as a
moral order results from such negligence. In view of the
above considerations, the method I have used always attempts, as far as possible, to examine the normative orientations and "professions" of the relevant actors.

While the expression, "pragmatic history," was applied
by Hegel to the interpretation of great historical characters
only, there is no reason for not applying it to analyze the
action of ordinary, prosaic social actors.

> The pragmatic historian fancies himself justified and even
> obliged to trace the supposed secret motives that lie behind
> the open facts of the record. . . . To make these pragmat-
> ical researches in history easier, it is usual to recommend

the study of psychology, which is supposed to make us acquainted with the real motives of human actions. . . . A pragmatical psychology ought at least to leave the historian, who investigates the motives at the ground of great actions, a choice between the 'substantial' interests of patriotism, justice, religious truth and the like, on the one hand, and the subjective and 'formal' interests of vanity, ambition, avarice and the like, on the other. The latter, however, are the motives which must be viewed by the pragmatist as really efficient, otherwise the assumption of a contrast between the inward (the disposition of the agent) and the outward (the import of the action) would fall to the ground. But inward and outward have in truth the same content; and the right doctrine is the very reverse of this pedantic judiciality. If the heroes of history had been actuated by subjective and formal interests alone, they would never have accomplished what they have. And if we have due regard to the unity between the inner and the outer, we must own that great men willed what they did, and did what they willed.[4]

This is probably the best method of preserving the integrity of the thousands of dispatches from Brazilian patrimonial servants and bureaucrats on which this work of research is largely based.

1

The Genesis of the Patrimonial Context

Historically, the dominant classes and political institutions of Brazil have had a texture and a quality as singular as the society to which they belonged. This society helped to shape their identity, and in so doing left its imprint on their typical behavior, organization, and culture.

Thus, their genesis is not fortuitous, but has a long, protracted, secular, and necessary history, namely, the colonial history preceding nineteenth-century monarchical Brazil, the indigenous roots of which date back as far as the 1520s.

The Colonial Enterprise

Brazil, discovered by the Portuguese in 1500, remained a colony of that nation until 1822, when it broke away to become an independent state under a descendant of the Portuguese royal house, Pedro I. The years 1500–1822 are known as the colonial period, those 1822–1889 as the Empire years, and the period from 1889 to the present day is known as the Republican era.

In this chapter, I will briefly touch on the colonial period, in as far as it was relevant to the object of our interest—the nineteenth-century militia known as the *Guarda Nacional*.

Early nineteenth-century Brazil—the starting point of our story—was notably different in a material sense from the

8

Brazil of the early sixteenth-century *capitanias* (captaincies), although its constitutive principles and the form of its organization were basically the same. There is no doubt that three centuries of continuous, if spasmodic, colonization and settlement modified the scale of Brazilian society, but its basic form and general profile remained appreciably intact until the end of the first half of the nineteenth century.

The Portuguese colonization of Brazil took place as a result of the Dutch supremacy in Asian trade, which caused the Portuguese to turn their attention to their recently acquired possessions in South America. In the beginning, the Portuguese settlements were limited to a narrow coastal strip. They were by nature commercial rather than agrarian, and their purpose was the organization of production and trade, based on the exploitation of natural resources.

The occupancy of the *litoral* (the narrow coastal strip running from Pernambuco in the north through Bahia to Rio de Janeiro in the south) began in 1530 with the establishment of sugar plantations geared to produce for the European markets. Until 1650—during the period known as the sugar cycle— the *litoral* was the only part of Brazil that was colonized. In the middle of the seventeenth century, however, settlement shifted from the north southward and westward, from the coast to the hinterland, from sugar-planting to diamond and gold mining.

In the meantime, because the southern and central parts of Brazil were easier to penetrate than the formidable *sertão* (backlands) in the north, the inhabitants of São Paulo early in the seventeenth century settled a region that became a marginal economic area bound by loose ties to the developing plantation economy of the north. The *Paulistas* raided the interior in *bandeiras*, which were private expeditions formed under the leadership of war lords in search of gold and Indians for slaves. These ventures were sometimes commissioned directly by the Crown, with a view to establishing villages and agents of patrimonial authority in exchange for prebends. Another *bandeira* movement, less feverish in nature, pushed inland along the courses of the Rio São Francisco and its tributary, the Rio das Velhas, in the north.

The discovery of gold and diamonds in the 1690s greatly stimulated the degree, pace, and intensity of migration. Settlement became so rapid that the new settlers often arrived before the metropolitan representatives of authority. The mining cycle, which lasted from the end of the seventeenth century to the middle of the eighteenth, greatly increased a population that in 1615 had numbered 3,000 Portuguese[1] and 400,000[2] natives; thus the mining cycle was decisive in the colonization process.

The successive migratory waves of *emboabas* (Portuguese and foreign gold explorers) and *sertanistas* from São Paulo into the interior ceased with the exhaustion of the mines in the 1750s, after which settlement was again concentrated on the coastal regions. This initiated the third major agricultural cycle, that of coffee cultivation.

The pastoral economy that organized and populated the southern lands was less spectacular but more uniform and lasting in its effects than the sugar and mining economies mentioned above.

> Agriculture alone would not have led to the colonizing of the hinterland; that is why until the seventeenth century the Portuguese were still clinging like crabs to the coastline. It was mining and cattle-raising that made possible and stimulated the advance; the former for obvious reasons: the considerable value of gold and diamonds, in value and weight, solved the problem of transportation. The latter . . . 'because herds need not be carried; they themselves support with the weight of their own bodies the long journeys. . . .'[3]

Ranching units—the *fazenda* and the *estancia*—gradually scattered themselves over the lowlands and plains of Brazil. At the turn of the eighteenth century, cattle-breeding had grown into a fully developed economy in the hinterland of Minas Gerais and Bahia, and in the southernmost Brazilian state, Rio Grande do Sul, where the first *estancias* appeared in 1715[4] at least two decades before the official systematic launching of colonization in that area. The ranching industry took firm hold of the local economy there during the last quarter of the eighteenth century.[5]

Although the cattle industry at no time held economic leadership during the colonial period, its impact was at least as great as that of mining and sugar-planting, for, spread over large areas and better cushioned against economic crises and recession than large scale agricultural undertakings, the pastoral economy of necessity became the most influential instrument of colonization. Besides, although cattle-breeding was operated as an adjunct economy to the northern economies to which it supplied meat, it also served them in another way, since they depended on it for the process of extraction in the case of mining, and for the transportation of settlers in the case of agriculture.

Thus, once begun, the process of population and settlement of the country received some degree of ongoing stimulation, regardless of the level of prosperity or stagnation of the economy, throughout the colonial period. Also, the overall pattern of settlement of the territory gained a more or less stable form in the latter part of the eighteenth century.[6] Minor shifts were to take place later on, particularly with the development of the coffee industry, but on the whole, the above profile is substantially accurate and provides a background for Imperial Brazil in the nineteenth century.

The Pattern of Colonization

On the question of who in fact directed the process of colonization, there are two schools of thought. One, the patrimonial school, upheld by Faoro,[7] maintains that the king and his organs of monarchical administration were responsible; the other, the feudal school, to which Nestor Duarte adheres,[8] claims that private groups took the initiative and had the major thrust.

But what about the colonizing process itself? Did it actually adopt the neat characterization claimed by both schools of interpretation, or is such a characterization so abstract in both cases that in the end it impoverishes and severely misrepresents the historical settlement process?

There is no denying that the commercial and colonial enterprises in general were directed by the Portuguese Crown, and that the Crown at the same time significantly stimulated a dispersive and increasingly momentous territorial settlement. Nonetheless, the economic organization of sugar production and its subsidiary ranching industry resulted in the further appropriation of land and, consequently, the continuous contraction of the frontier. As recent research by Stuart Schwartz has shown,[9] the function of the private *engenho* (the sugar plantation and mill) as a frontier institution in colonial Brazil was recognized from an early date. Not only was this frontier institution a factor in the concentration of urban functions, but it was also an effective substitute for urban growth.[10] Therefore, the process of colonization was actually affected by the joint influence of metropolitan policy (particularly strong during the initial stages of settlement) and the spontaneous intervention of the economic institutions of civil society, aided at times by the Crown's own encouragement of privatization as an expedient means of settling the southern areas.[11]

Rather than a completely private or public pattern of settlement and colonization, what emerged was a complex pattern of active participation by both protagonists. The Crown and its colonial representatives directly encouraged the civil organization of armed incursions to establish towns in return for royal favor and prebends (land grants and the like), while a simultaneous and entirely civil movement was actively intent on acquiring land, Indian slaves, and gold. This dual initiative was to mark all of Brazil's early history, and it is highly relevant to the period of our special interest, the nineteenth century.

It was quite natural, then, that the economic penetration of the interior, which also expanded the frontier, left behind the process of administrative and political institutionalization. This was also the case in the Argentinian hinterland of Misiones for instance, according to Halperin Donghi's account.[12] The clogged moroseness of the Portuguese patrimonial bureaucracy[13] was certainly no match for the voracious land hunger of the adventurers and landlords in their continuous movement toward the frontier.[14]

The extensive and largely privatized nature of settlement left formidable imprints on the institutional life of the colony in two major areas, the *engenho* and the *sesmaria* (land grants).

Administration and Prebendalism

> When differences weakened family ties
> Came benevolent fathers and dutiful sons;
> And when lands were disrupted and misgoverned
> Came ministers commended as loyal.
>
> Lao-Tzu, *The Way of Life*

At the same time the prebendalization of the royal administration of the South American territory reinforced this process. The joint influence of the pattern of land settlement and the pattern of administration distinguished the political organization of the Portuguese territories in America.

Soon after the discovery of Brazil, and after a brief and unsuccessful state exploitation of dyewood, the colony was divided into twelve *capitanias*, each held by a *capitão-mor* (captain-major) who possessed the hereditary right to possession and usufruct of the land, while the king retained his title to it. The *capitão-mor* was entitled to distribute land in the form of *sesmarias*, which were granted to landlords who became patrimonial retainers. Thus the king obtained, at a low cost and very little risk to himself, the administrative services of the captain-majors, who benefited in turn from the fact that they were the highest military, civil, and fiscal authorities within their captaincies. Under this system, the technical monopoly of the means of administration and power and the hereditary appropriation of the means of economic production were held by a class of *fidalgos* (noblemen).

In 1584, organization became more centralized. The captain-majors were replaced by governors subordinated to a *governador-geral* (captain-general),whose job it was to coordinate the network of captaincies, which were now no longer independent of one another. Fearing the dispersion of too much power, the *governo-geral* at Bahia withdrew many of the political privileges from the former decentralized organization. Although the administrative jurisdictions of the captaincies were curtailed, the governors of the *capitanias* still maintained their function as military commanders and, as such, built up a series of fortifications in an almost prophetic attempt to guard against invasion. Moreover, the reorganization still left the patrimonial management of the *capitanias* and its prebendal nature intact. On the whole, however, the more elementary and schematic pattern of patrimonial administration gave way to an incipient but still tepid process of bureaucratic organization.

The *governo-geral* system of administration continued throughout the remainder of the colonial period, with occasional minor modifications, and survived the shifting of its seat to Rio de Janeiro. Even though the few initial bureaucratic strokes gradually became more precise and more important in defining the shape of the colonial edifice, they continued to be insufficient for the administration of so vast a land without the aid of the inefficient, but nevertheless cheaper, cooperation of prebendaries and *honoratiores*.* While public office would, of course, continue to be the fruit of royal favor, the earlier provision of offices as prebends in perpetuity led to the creation of temporary prebends.

The technical exigencies required for the efficient performance of certain administrative functions encouraged a piecemeal professionalization of some patrimonial organs and a rather systematic regulation of promotions, transfers, retirements, etc.[15] This was especially true of the judiciary, as the proper adjudication of justice demanded that the judge be familiar with a set of procedures and technicalities that, not infrequently, favored the transformation of professional practice into an esoteric exercise restricted to a few. Under these circumstances, it is astonishing to observe the weakness and atrophy of corporative consciousness in the judiciary, as compared to its development in other patrimonial societies such as Tudor England. Not even the highest rank of the colonial magistracy, the judges of the High Court of Bahia, showed corporative action.[16] The High Court was, to all intents and purposes, a docile instrument of the lord paramount.

Another sector whose functions tended to be professionalized, although to a less pronounced degree, was the *Fazenda Real* (Royal Exchequer). Indeed, the technical requirements for defending the Crown's interests must have been very much needed in Brazil, especially considering the character-

---

Honoratiores is here understood to be a group or stratum of local notables, a rural "patriciate" with virtual monopoly of power and status.

istic fiscalism of the Portuguese Crown. Moreover, if we bear in mind the typical connection between fiscal administration and early bureaucratization, which Weber has pointed out, it becomes easier to understand how the process of professionalization evolved.[17]

The patrimonial origin of this fiscal orientation was thus an indirect means for the progressive bureaucratization of government. The patrimonial structure stood more firmly in the intermediate and peripheral ranks of the administrative machine, royal favor being notably visible in the municipal and local provision of office, probably given largely as military prebends with police and judiciary obligations attached. Yet, the more bureaucratic the monarchical administration became (through the pragmatic spurs of reorganization, correction, and redefinition of the hierarchical order of royal officials and their structural niches and jurisdictional competences), the more labyrinthine grew its meddling in the usage-sanctioned maxims of prebendal administration.

The development of rational bureaucratic administration would have been in any case as exotic as the spontaneous extinction of privilege and personal discretion. A bureaucratic principle of social coordination, with its insistence on objectivity and universality, could only have flourished in a society familiar with institutional mediation by contractual organizations of a capitalist nature and concerned with rational calculus. As an effective ideology, such a bureaucratic principle would have had to be a normative projection of social relations substantively based on contract. The colonial world, however, with its subjective and particularized social relations, was too fraught with—and enmeshed in—the immediacy of privatized patriarchal experience to be able to conceive of impersonal forms alive enough to permit the objective and institutionalized ordering of that very experience. The colonial world simply did not provide the basis for the bureaucratic principle to become a constitutive element of social relations.

It was no coincidence that the sectors more exposed to bureaucratic rationalization were the central sectors of the royal bureaucracy itself. All the same, a rational bureaucratic administration composed of salaried officials was not to emerge until the nineteenth century, when functions were no longer defined by pragmatic considerations created by eventualities and contingencies, but were derived systematically from a set of substantive canons of organization. What pre-nineteenth-century Brazil lacked was not a bureaucratic elan—quite the contrary—but an objective canon for the technical division of administrative duties.

It would be inadequate to attribute this lack to the prebendalization of the vast administrative areas, in particular of the peripheral areas extending into the rural society of the backlands. A more plausible explanation would be the absence of a vigorous domestic group intent on an objective and impersonal regulation of social intercourse based on contract, work, and the adjudication of justice. The languid—too languid—essence of municipal life that Oliveira Vianna has so thoroughly described for us, the apathetic pace of the urban centers, the paucity of bourgeois culture and interest associations, and the formidable contraction of market institutions generated by the presence of slavery were all conditions that together delayed the emergence of a rational bureaucratic order.

The Agrarian Context

> in fact, they regarded the household
> as a miniature republic.
>
> Seneca, *Letters from a Stoic: Epistulae
> Morales ad Lucilium,* letter xlvii

Thus far we have examined the effects of the patterns of land settlement and the administration of government on the privatization of local power. If those patterns facilitated the presence of private groups in the process of state-building, the colonial latifundium was, in its turn, the agent that stereotyped and invigorated that presence. We have already described how the royal grants of latifundia, *sesmarias,* to patrimonial retainers emerged as the typical form of administration of the new Portuguese territory. In exchange for their prebends, they were obliged to cultivate the soil and establish settlement. The *engenho* and the *fazenda* became the basic cells that would contribute to establishing a characteristic physiognomy of colonial society. The *engenho* (the sugar cane plantations and mills) stayed close to the cities as these provided transportation facilities, while the *fazenda* (more general farms) penetrated farther into the interior. The *engenho* was the more typical manifestation of the general orientation of the economy and society of the time, because its economic articulation with the commercial-circuit of colonial capitalism was direct, constant, and uniform. The *fazenda*, though occasionally acting as a tributary to this circuit, not infrequently produced commodities for a local market only. Furthermore, in that the *engenho* used extensive slave labor, whereas the *fazenda* frequently employed *caboclos* (free Brazilian-born men, usually of mixed blood), the *engenho* contributed directly to the creation and maintenance of the most characteristic institutional relationship of colonial Brazil, the landlord-slave complex. Therefore, from the point of view of the predominant patriarchalism of domestic society and the production of commodities for export and the employment of slave labor, the sugar cane mill was Brazil's most typical institution throughout the mercantile and colonial epoch.

Notwithstanding their differences, both the *engenho* and the *fazenda* were the most powerful enclaves for the organization and development of civil society during the centuries of Portuguese rule. Their influence on the destinies of lord and peasant alike was so encompassing that it is correct to characterize them, with Erving Goffman, as total institutions, that is, as social establishments operating "as a place of residence and work where a large number of like-situated individuals, cut off from wider society for an appreciable period of time, together lead an enclosed, formally administered round of life."[18] That institutional aspect was not as striking in the *fazenda* as in the *engenho*, but both shared characteristic institutional isolation, being self-contained in that they possessed the essential economic, political, and social elements of the larger community[19] and relative autonomy vis-à-vis broader society.[20]

The Portuguese Crown permitted a greater degree of land-granting in the local administration of government than did the Spanish patrimonial bureaucracy;[21] indeed land was a prominent instrument for granting royal favors to patrimonial retainers, taking the place of salaries. This was because of the Crown's lack of revenue, and because the lack of a sedentary population meant a scarcity of taxpayers on whom the Crown could draw in order to support local officials. The discovery of the mines and the subsequent inflow of precious metals into the Portuguese Royal Exchequer was responsible for the reduction and curtailment of land prebendalization in Brazil, reductions being effected by a decree in 1695 and other more drastic ones in 1697 and 1699.[22]

One of the consequences of the obduracy of the system of office prebendalism was to delay the formation of a modern state in Brazil, because prebendalism retarded the shift from patrimonial to bureaucratic administration. Another consequence was to help accelerate the transformation of the latifundia into a springboard for local power.

Consequently, from Brazil's earliest days as a colonial nation, the latifundium became the locus of both economic enterprise and local government. The prominence of private landlordism was further enhanced by the military character of the latifundial organization. This militarization was not simply the result of the military competence exercised by the local landlord in his capacity as a patrimonial royal official; it was also encouraged during the first 200 years of colonization by the need to protect the *engenhos* and *fazendas* of the hinterland against the continual danger of Indian raids.[23]

The patterns of privatization of authority and of militarization, produced by the style of settlement and the administration of Brazil, are, in the agrarian context, reenacted and stereotyped, thanks to the form of organization of local institutions. Pervasive patriarchalism, unfolding hand in hand with these patterns, was probably one of the more notorious signs of the far-reaching influence of domestic society on public life and its political institutions. This patriarchalism, produced by the internal characteristics of the *engenho* and the *fazenda*, was further exacerbated by the exiguity and weakness of countervailing municipal institutions of a wider scope. Inevitably, the patriarchalism of the *senhor de terras e escravos* (lord of land and slaves) asserted its arbitrary presence beyond the confines—however broad—of his personal domain. The stunted growth of urban life and municipal institutions, brought about by the Crown's suffocation of indigenous industry and by slavery's inhibition of guild and market, accounts to a very large extent for the pervasiveness of patriarchalism.[24]

The forms of solidarity to be found in Brazilian society at the time are explained by the brutal contractions of communal forms of solidarity brought about by the latifundium and its slave-based organization. Typical processes of *Vergemeinschaftung* and solidarity formation were thus generally restricted to the small world of the latifundium. Throughout the colonial period, the sole focus of life and organization resided within the confines of these "seigneurial" estates, which enjoyed a remarkable degree of independence and developed an elaborate organization of self-sufficient production. Except for certain items that the estate was unable to produce, such as salt, powder, iron, and lead, everything was produced by servants or slaves in the *oikos* (a specialized industrial establishment for the satisfaction of the lord's material needs) of the lord, or in liturgical activities.[25]

Because the latifundia were self-sufficient, the commercial class barely managed to survive in the moribund towns of the backlands, and the formation of an industrial class was also preempted; "in summary: no commercial class; no industrial class; no urban corporations. In the vast area of agrarian estates, only great rural manors exist; outside, everything is rudimentary, formless, fragmentary."[26]

The impact of this process on the development of a civil society, namely, on the social and economic organization of the bourgeoisie, was deep and deleterious, and permitted the patriarchal order to take the upper hand. In so far as social organization was strictly patriarchal (though it was not completely so, for certain entrepreneurial capitalistic elements did penetrate it) it was hardly able to become the vehicle for demands on the central state, or to demand the creation of a legal order that would control the use of violence and establish rational norms for orderly contracting. To this same extent, a constitutionally established political authority, accountable to the civil society, could not develop. The patriarchalism of local society corresponded to the patrimonialization of the larger society.

What, then, were the forms of solidarity in fact developing within the Brazilian seigneurie? In terms of the material reproduction of life, the most important group, the barracks slaves, can be discarded for obvious reasons. On the other hand, because the slaves were unaffected by the particularized solidarity of the rural seigneurie, they were capable of achieving on occasion a distinct *esprit de corps* that led to rebellion, collective escapes, and independent polities. On the whole, though, the condition of the slave must have been very anomic.

Among the freemen were two main groups, subordinated to the lord and his land. Neither of them established firm forms of solidarity. They were the free household employees who lived under the influence and moral gravitation of the patriarchal family,[27] and the *colonos*, who were poor land tenants on the *senhor's* domain.

A large system of communal interaction could, therefore, only grow within the circle of the landlord's family. Indeed, this was the only structure able to encompass two essential yet opposed requirements for moral consociation: on the one hand, a habitual orientation toward the satisfaction of its own economic interests, and, on the other hand, the exemplary character which these interests strove to assume in order to facilitate their own institutionalization within a society deeply marked by status orientations. To a very large extent, the agrarian history of Brazil can be examined in terms of the vicissitudes of landlordism's attempts to create such a system.[28]

However unsuccessful this moral project might have been as a generalized undertaking of the colonial propertied classes, they were, nonetheless, the only groups that succeeded in creating an intricate and vast web of moral obligation that simultaneously helped shape the typical orientation of action of the landed classes and their human appendages, namely the so-called clan complexes.

Oliveira Vianna's intuition about the importance of the Brazilian clan complex is sociologically correct but improperly conceptualized. The notion of clan applies in fact to a community whose members share a common line of descent, and any other stratification or stereotyping within the clan is external to its formative principle. As the Brazilian clans were stratified according to the *same* principle as the larger society, that is, by property in land, it would be more appropriate to relate the Brazilian configuration to the concept of tribe, that is, a political association of families with a territorial base and communalized by blood obligations.[29] In Brazil, behind the "clan" lurked the landlord's family. In Brazil, "clan charisma" could only be based on the landlord's family, not on the clan as a whole.

The "clan" in patrimonial Brazil reinforced and increased the landlord's power of discretion over the local peasant.[30] Nor was the peasant shielded against the landlord's abuses of authority by a system of cross-cutting personal ties linking him to a plurality of lords, as was the case in Indonesia.[31] Unencumbered either by the checks of an elaborate kinship structure such as the Chinese or by the normative precipitates of an intricate system of land organization such as the Balinese, the Brazilian landlord was more the petty "oriental despot" than the oriental lord himself.

I will make two general observations on the impact of local landlordism on the process of state-building before I conclude this brief introduction.

First, a "feudal" interpretation of the excessive concentration of power in the propertied classes would be misleading. All forms of prebureaucratic rule, not just the feudal, display a considerable degree of administrative decentralization of government. Local oligarchies are no more indicative of feudalism than of other political arrangements. Furthermore, as both feudal and patrimonial structures are patrimonially administered, the characterization of feudal and patrimonial structures in terms of the degree of administrative centralization is inadequate. Finally, the peculiarities of the feudal and patrimonial models reveal themselves principally through a comparative analysis of the political implications arising from the bonds of solidarity between overlord and lord that prevail in the two types of administration. Perhaps the most synthesized presentation of their differences by Weber, was given in his *The Religion of China* :

> Feudalism rested on [status] *honor* as the cardinal virtue, patrimonialism on [patriarchal] *piety*. The *reliability* of the vassal's allegiance was based upon the former; the *subor-*

dination of the lord's servant and official was based upon the latter. The difference is not a contrast, but a shift of accent.[32]

The institutional consequences of this difference are clear from the perspective of practical reason. The moral obligations of the feudal bond, because they are based on a contract between free men, facilitate political representation and encourage the creation of a politically guaranteed legal order; the moral obligations of the patrimonial bond, because they are based on statute from lord to prebendary, facilitate administrative cooptation and encourage the creation of a corporatively guaranteed legal order.[33] The administrative cooptation of agrarian notables and their corporative association in the form of a *Guarda Nacional* in the nineteenth century will clearly show the path taken by the Brazilian organization.

Second, the negative effects of unrestrained landlordism lay not so much in its abuses or in the delay in creating a national system of institutions, whose objective necessity it could hardly have obstructed. The more important negative effects lay in the obstacles to the conscious acceptance of the prevailing legal order as a normative code orienting everyday social action, in other words, to the validity of such an order. This issue will be discussed later.

To summarize: at the end of the colonial era, the Brazilian state displayed, in a typically patrimonial fashion, a combination of, on the one hand, a highly centralized authority at the head of which stood the Portuguese monarch and the upper bureaucratized layers of the royal administration, and, on the other, a highly decentralized power monopolized by delegatory landlords in their capacities as patrimonial officials. As in Tokugawa Japan, this pattern of patriarchal discretion reached into the basic cell of the community; no kinship mediation stood—as was the case in China—between the peasant and the *daimio* (Japanese feudal lord) and the latifundium. Outside the urban coastal seats of the ceaselessly bureaucratized patrimonial administration, and outside the latifundium, engaged in the formation of a "civil society," the very development of which it thwarted, lay a desolate land, "une solitude profonde," as Saint-Hilaire once described it.

Landlords and the Military: the Colonial Roots

This section will examine the two social groups involved in the organization of power and authority during the colonial and Imperial periods in Brazil, namely, the landlords and the military. This analytical division should not obscure the important fact that more often than not the same individual occupied both statuses. It should be remembered that the prebendalization of the royal administration was, in effect, an important source of militarization, and that access to land prebends was generally limited to *homens de qualidade* (patriciates). I will examine the two categories in the light of the possible development of a status ethic, which at first sight would appear to have been highly probable, but which did not in fact occur.

There is no evidence pointing to the establishment of corporate forms of patrimonial landlordism in Brazil during the colonial period or in the last century. This is surprising, considering the presence of certain factors that would seem to have favored their development, such as a common social origin, a common cultural tradition, endogamic trends in the family, the entailment of rural domains, and a considerable degree of military power and ideology. The inability of the landlords to develop corporate forms of solidarity vis-à-vis the monarch can be explained from different standpoints. Three factors, however, seem to be particularly relevant from our perspective. The first is the divorce between the higher ranks of officialdom at the nucleus of the metropolitan bureaucracy and the outposts of local administration during colonial times. It was only in the nineteenth century, with the appearance of the *bachareis* (law graduates), that local office began to provide a springboard to offices of higher consequence.[34]

The second is to be found in the relatively unstable stratification of Brazilian colonial society, which displayed much social mobility because of the easy access to frontier land. This fluidity largely inhibited the institutionalization of a determinate stratification pattern and a status principle.

The third factor is kinship solidarity. The "clan" factor inhibited the formation of a corporate association of *senhores de terras e escravos,* and consequently of a sentiment of solidarity among them. Lacking in Brazil was the religious ethic that Weber showed was decisive in dissolving taboos before the emergence of a political association of burghers.[35] On the contrary, economic interests guided social action toward utilitarian and individualistic objectives that corroded solidarity.

In addition, there were formidable obstacles to the institutionalization among the propertied classes of a rational, bourgeois, social ethic that might have cut across the diffuse solidarity of blood bonds. Agrarian Brazil did not possess all the essential characteristics of a full-blown market society. It was not, in brief, the possessive market society of Macpherson's characterization,[36] but was in fact closer to the model of a simple market society, in which the process of production is regulated by the market and labor is not yet a market commodity. Under such circumstances, the complete economic articulation of Brazilian society was not possible, and consequently class consciousness could not reach, with Lukacs, "the point where *it could become* conscious."[37] The incomplete economic socialization of the landlords was therefore partly responsible for the characteristic opacity of their own unity and *esprit de corps*.

Is it possible, however, that they might have developed a form of solidarity based on their common identification with genteel forms of life stylization? Researchers who believe this was the case almost always quote the following statements made by foreign observers. The first, by a cleric writing in the eighteenth century:

> Being a *senhor de engenho* is a title to which many aspire because it implies being served, obeyed and respected by many. And when the man is, as he is supposed to be, a man of wealth and authority, it may be judged that in Brazil being a *senhor de engenho* is comparatively as highly esteemed as the title of *fidalgo* in the Realm.[38]

The other, by French naturalist Saint-Hilaire, in the nineteenth century:

> Among the agricultural people of Rio de Janeiro, ownership of a sugar *engenho* grants a noble status of sorts. Lords of *engenhos* are looked upon with respect, and obtaining such an eminent position constitutes a general ambition.

The physical constitution of the *engenho* lord shows his good nutrition and mild exertions. At home he wears drill clothing, sandals, sloppy trousers, and no necktie; his personal care, in a word, shows his love for self-indulgence. When he rides out on a horse, however, his attire must correspond to the occasion, and he consequently puts on a coat, appropriate trousers, shining boots, silver spurs, and he uses a very fine saddle. A black valet, dressed in a sort of uniform, is a matter of course. The lord stands up straight, raises his head, speaks out with the strong voice and the imperious tone of the man used to commanding many slaves.[39]

From these and from similar observations, a number of students have claimed that Brazilian colonial society created a landed aristocracy, with its characteristic gentility and monopolizing of social honor. There are, however, both empirical and theoretical qualifications that invalidate such a claim.

In the first place, such circumstances as those pictured above were neither typical nor generalized. They were at the most confined to the northeastern sugar economy. The coffee planter of São Paulo in the nineteenth century, for instance, did not develop consummatory values of an aristocratic nature, but was personally involved in the economic exploitation of his estate.[40]

Besides, the Brazilian titled nobility did not *as a class* enjoy any privileges; being a noble definitely had advantages for the individual, but no politically guaranteed status structure of nobles existed.[41] The Brazilian landed nobility as a whole in fact resembled the Russian *boyardom:* both strata owed their social prominence to the ownership of large estates; both occupied important positions in military, economic, and political life; neither was organized into a separate political order with special corporate privileges; both acquired their properties not through a contract of feudal obligations, but through patrimonial prebends; and finally both relied on slavery rather than serfdom in the organization of their agrarian economies.[42]

Second, the extravagant aristocratic pretensions of a few powerful landlords should not be considered an indication of a status group. Whatever "status honor" this stratum might eventually have enjoyed was derived exclusively from its class situation, that is, from its monopolistic appropriation of landed property; at no moment was status honor derived from a genteel style of life, nor did it pertain to any specific quality of the group. One essential element was lacking that could have transformed the usurpation of economic opportunity into stereotyped and characteristic life chances, thereby institutionalizing a status order, namely, stability in the distribution of economic powers, the absence of which we have already noted.

The Brazilian landlords' "seigneurial" rights were not based on feudalization (which was the typical European pattern) but on the prebendalization of political authority.[43] Thus, social prerogatives as well as political privileges did not belong to a stratum of *senhores*, but to a group of prebendary officials. Also, the Brazilian *senhor de terras* was far from orienting his conduct ethically, whether by standards of conventional propriety based on literary scholarship, as did the Confucian *literatus*, or by religious asceticism, as did the Buddhist Brahmin, or by the military *virtus* (such as the Japanese samurai or the early Tudor aristocrat). Carvalho Franco has correctly pointed out that "as a rule, freemen cherished a seigneurial project . . . the road to which was founded on hard work."[44]

The Brazilian landlord's conduct was not distinguished by gentility. If anything, "the general trend was toward the diffusion of the cultural patterns, rather than their fragmentation into separate worlds."[45]

The Portuguese values of *fidalguia* (nobility of blood) could readily have provided the form for the development of an aristocratic project, but *fidalguia* was based on a paramount military ethos that, allied to a stable social stratification on the one hand and to a relative land scarcity created by daily warfare with a foreign invader on the other, made it a genuinely active determinant of social action. In the relatively peaceful milieu of Brazilian agrarian society, whose external danger was the market crisis rather than the heathen Moor, these values remained inert and abstract.

The seigneurial stylization of the pattern of life of the Brazilian landlord was not the "cause" of a monopolistic and rent-producing disposition of goods and services. The opposite was in fact the rule; only the rationalization of his *pa-*

trimonium, that is, its transformation into an enterprise, could allow him to "seigneurialize" his rustic life-style. This stylization was not apparently an urgent concern. [46]

The seigneurial aspects of the landlord's position are much more visible within the confines of his patriarchal domain—in his disciplined commensality with his dependents, in his discretionary adjudication of justice, in his absolute monopoly of violence, in the *regime d'exception* of his children's schooling, and in the authoritarianism and paternalism that marked his daily life. [47]

If the seigneurial traits of the Brazilian agrarian classes are more obvious within the patriarchal domain, their weaknesses can be interpreted in the context of Bloch and Homans' explanation that the association between feudal manorialism and open-field agriculture arose because it was easier for the lord to mobilize labor from a preestablished group than to create one for his purpose. This meant that "the manor could be strong only where the village community was strong." Otherwise work services on the demesne were impractical and were replaced by rents in money and kind. [48] On the other hand, this association is particularly close where the elasticity of the supply of land is so near to zero that stratification and privilege take root.

These conditions did not hold true in agrarian Brazil. The low demographic density, the lifelessness of the urban center in the backland (like "the desert within walls", as da Cunha put it[49]), and the persistent presence of an open frontier worked against the institutionalization of manorial domains.

It is interesting to observe in this context the analogies between the Brazilian *senhoriato* and the eastern Prussian *Junkertum*, as presented by Weber in his work on agrarian capitalism in Germany.[50] They shared a host of common structural factors.

Unlike western and southern Prussia, which had a more differentiated urban structure, a denser population, and a peasant economy oriented to the domestic market of intensive trade and the predominance of small farmers, the region east of the Elbe relied on the export of grain cultivated on the vast estates of the eastern plains, which lacked an infrastructure of local communication and trade. As a consequence of these different arrangements, two different types of landlords emerged.

In the west and south, the vigorous development of a peasant economy, linked to a varied network of local markets, was a permanent incentive to production. The landlord was able to live off the peasants' surplus and services; he was able to enjoy, therefore, a style of life based on rents and taxes from the dependent peasantry, and he was spared a personal role in the operation of his estate. These were the Prussian *Grundherren* (landlords), whose economic base was not entrepreneurial and capitalist profit, but rather patrimonial and seigneurial benefits. This was a characteristically aristocratic stratum that differed radically from the *Gutsherren* (lords) of the east, who were agrarian capitalists engaged in the extensive cultivation of their land, employing their expropriated peasants not as taxpayers but as a labor force. Given the very low demographic density and the slack urban and agrarian development of their land, it was out of the question for the *Gutsherren* to establish, as the *Grundherren* did, a system of privileges based on rents, taxes, tithes, and the like, exacted from the peasantry. Under these circumstances, any *Gutsherr* interested in pursuing an aristocratic style of life was compelled to obtain income from his own agricultural entrepreneurship.

The similarities between the *Gutsherren* class of eastern Prussia and the Brazilian *senhoriato* stand out clearly:

1. both economies developed in a sparsely populated land;

2. colonization in both cases took place in a land without a feudal tradition of corporate privileges and obligations for the different orders and, consequently, each lacked the economic advantages of a network of feudal services from a dependent peasantry;

3. both "seigneurial" life-styles were economically dependent on rational enterprise and capitalist profit rather than on political privilege and manorial benefices;[51]

4. both were specialized mono-crop producers for an international market that indirectly helped to stifle the vigorous development of local trade, thereby reproducing the very

conditions that prevented the creation of an economic base for aristocratic differentiation.[52]

This depressing effect must, however, be seen as short-term. In the long run, the multiplying effects of this pattern of export on the local economy are conducive to the development of a monetarized economy. Henri Pirenne has shown this to have been the case for the development of a national market in Europe, and Marx gave a theoretical rationale to this historical pattern.[53]

The landlords were not the only group that could have aspired to, or could have claimed, corporate aristocratic privilege in agrarian Brazil. The military was also in a position to develop a secular ethic of its own, a peculiar style of life, and a characteristic social honor, and to surround its members with the social distance and exclusivity typical of status groups. In what follows I will examine the fate of this group and assess the extent to which it approached an ideal-typical construction.

Colonial landlords in Brazil did not, generally speaking, enjoy corporate privileges as a status group. But this statement becomes problematical when applied to the same individuals in their capacity as military officials. Both landlords and the military participated, of course, in a status *situation* to the extent that they enjoyed the probability of receiving social honor from other groups. Their chances of attaining social honor through the creation of a peculiar style of life and education nevertheless varied. On the whole, it is safe to say that the military approached the ideal-typical characterization of a status group more than the landlords did. In the case of Brazil, the possession of land paved the way for military rank, rather than the other way around, but this is to be understood not strictly in terms of opportunities, but rather in terms of social valuation.

However, to speak of the colonial military in general terms is incorrect, considering the profound functional differentiation of its structure. The Crown's official instruments of physical coercion were concentrated in the navy. The metropolis understood that its military responsibilities were satisfied with the defense of the coast against corsairs and external invasion, and the maintenance of order in the land was in large measure delegated to private groups.[54]

Besides the navy, which was isolated in the coastal area away from the larger community, and its metropolitan membership, there were three military structures in late colonial times: the royal professional army or the *tropas da linha* (first line troops), aided by auxiliary second line troops (the *milicias*), made up of part-time, nonsalaried civilians,[55] and the *corpos de ordenanças,* composed of civilians not enlisted or conscripted by either of the above. The *ordenanças* were not remunerated, and acted only within their own municipalities.

Of these groups, the royal army was the most bureaucratized. This was because, in addition to a hierarchical organization of office staffed by permanent career officers and a salaried and regimented troop, there was a corporative impediment to membership by men of certain conditions. Though formally membership was open to all, in fact officialdom was made up almost exclusively of men from military and landed families, while the rank and file consisted predominantly of colored people and laborers.[56]

Despite its formally open, associative, and bureaucratic characteristics, the professional army tended to be a closed, corporative, and hierarchical status group. In this respect, the royal tradition of military organization was also influential, as was the incumbent's own interest in fully prebendalizing his access to office. The professional military itself was interested in stabilizing and stereotyping the chances of access to the ranks; cadetship, the first step, was limited to the sons of noble and military families.[57]

The royal concession of corporate privileges to the professional military in Brazil arose more from the dead weight of a metropolitan tradition and a hierarchical concept of social order, than from the patrimonial remuneration for services rendered to the royal house by a particular stratum of subjects. Historically, two sets of conditions have been conducive to the formation of an aristocratic corporation of warriors. The first is the warrior's involvement with the administration of hierocratically oriented polities, where the hierocratic ethos is probably the charismatization of political domination brought about by armed conquest, examples of which are the pre-Columbian empires such as the Aztec, Maya, and Chibcha, and Middle-Eastern patrimonial polities. The second is the warrior's involvement with the military defense of territory gained by the political community under conditions of permanent or semipermanent warfare.[58] The latter circumstances were characteristic of Portuguese history for more than eight centuries, but not of Brazilian history.

Furthermore, the professional military was as a group severed from the very area in which it might have developed a community of interests, namely, the royal bureaucracy. On the one hand, fiscal and judiciary functions were basically a monopoly of the *letrados* (men of letters, lawyers); on the other hand, with the notable exception of the governorships, the vast machinery of colonial provincial administration was in the hands of prebendary landlords and *honoratiores*.

But the professional military did not abandon its objectively extravagant claims to social honor. It lived, after all, in a society visibly stamped by hierarchical distinctions in all provinces of life, distinctions that frequently opened or closed the door to patronage, favor, authority, name, etc. and that belonged to an institution fastidiously imbued with ceremonial symbols, pomp, and circumstance. It is therefore understandable that the Crown should have taken measures to buttress corporate privileges for the army in order to encourage membership by the nobility.[59]

Despite the status situations thus enjoyed by the professional military, it failed to develop a peculiar style of life. To do so it would have required—apart from a status ethic that at no time seemed to flourish—a prebendal anchorage in the patrimonial economy, and perhaps a crisper and more clearly defined participation in the administration of government.[60] Without any of these supports, the professional military lived in a marasmic and secondary condition until the second half of the nineteenth century, when an armed conflict with a neighboring country brought its political relevance to the foreground.

It is not surprising that the more bureaucratic sector of the armed forces, the royal army, was also the most ineffectual organ of royal patrimonial organization.[61] The *milicias* and *ordenanças,* commanded by captains and captain-majors from the privileged classes,[62] achieved more coalescence between the armed forces and private groups. Both, especially the *ordenanças,* conformed to the typical pattern of coalesced military and administrative functions discharged by private individuals.[63] The commanders of the *ordenanças* acquired their functions, not through official entrustment, but through a constellation of factors, among which the following were significant: the colonial tradition of military participation in the administration; the unclear division of administrative functions—fiscal, judiciary, executive, and legislative—among the different structures of government; the insufficient degree of bureaucratization of the local levels of public administration; and, finally, the relative incapacity of the local patrimonial and bureaucratic officials to cope with the needs of daily government. These and other factors less relevant from our standpoint encouraged the involvement of the *ordenanças* in the organization of the political and administrative order of colonial society.

In the latter part of the eighteenth century the cooperation of the *ordenanças* for the administration of local government began to be enlisted, when a centralization effort under the Marques de Lavradio brought the *ordenanças,* which previously had performed informally a variety of functions,[64] inside the official fold to help secure the institutionalization of royal authority.[65] Typically, access to officialdom was through the governor's appointment of members chosen from three lists, presented by the legislative body of the country.[66]

It would seem admissible to characterize the enlistment of local notables to participate in the management of government as *ordenança* officers as a typical instance of cooptation. A closer examination of the services rendered by these notables shows, however, the liturgical nature of their services. (Liturgical services are negative privileges exacted from privileged groups for the satisfaction of the administrative wants of the political community.[67]) Whereas the notion of co-optation accentuates the strength and control of the central apparatus that co-opts, the notion of liturgy stresses the fact that the administrative services represent a collective and corporative undertaking of a stereotyped nature, and that these services are practically *claimed* as a monopoly by the notables.

In trying to characterize the patrimonial nature of colonial Brazil, it is, moreover, important to note that the *ordenança* officer was not a royal prebendary. There was not, in fact, a private appropriation of office, a "fixed right to office," nor did this go together with remuneration of any kind. The nonprebendalization of *ordenança* posts should not be interpreted as indicating a ceaseless bureaucratization of local administration, although it removed an obstacle to its later progress; it is perhaps more correct to view it as the manifestation of a relatively advanced degree of economic differentiation and stratification, with more or less stereotyped life chances for entire collectivities, making dispensable and at the same time difficult attempts to patrimonialize economic resources for the remuneration of services.

For exactly the same reason, that is, the institutionalization of an economic order with a fixed distribution of economic opportunities among the different strata of the population, it was possible for the royal patrimonial bureaucracy to entrust a considerable area of the local administration to a class of *honoratiores*. This group was part of the heritage left by the distribution of land prebends during centuries of colonial rule. Thanks to their privileged situation, the members of this group gradually gained the superordinate position they enjoyed in the local community, on the one hand, and, on the other, the free time that their superior economic status allowed, to fulfill nonremunerated administrative functions. The *ordenança* officialdom as a rule was a part of this pool of local notables, and it was from this group of economically independent and socially respected individuals that an administration by *honoratiores*, a local "bureaucracy of aficionados," arose.

It would be a mistake to represent this stratum of *honoratiores* as a patrimonial organ of the metropolitan kingship. We have to remember that their character as *Gutsherren* precluded any attempt to disregard the care of their economic interests for the sake of public service and that they could not depend on remuneration. The liturgical services of these notables for public administration was a complement to the official activity entrusted to such local representatives of the bureaucratic apparatus as magistrates and chiefs of police. It was the squalid and rudimentary state of this apparatus on the local scene—not its absence from it—that made the liturgical contributions of the landed notables necessary.

The local landlord, without the prebendal anchorage in office and being materially unable fully to become an administrator, naturally lacked the conditions to develop an administrative ethic for his daily conduct or to appropriate the means of administration. As a member of the local ruling class, he defined the objectives for their application as well.[68]

A modern student may be tempted to underrate the functions of low justice, police, and the like, as rather insignificant expressions of social power. But in a more historical context— particularly with regard to the restricted scope of effective centralization, the characteristically diffuse definition of office jurisdiction, and the reduced degree of structural differentiation in the administration—it is clear that the holders of such offices exerted a considerable degree of social power and political authority. This power was increased by the economic and patriarchal power they enjoyed as landlords. A measure of their ultimately weak and dependent position, however, was their inability to claim hereditary possession of office. Despite their privileged life *chances* for the monopolistic appropriation of land, royal office and favor, and social honor and political authority, the striking legacy of the colonial landlords was—for reasons we have already discussed—their unwillingness to antagonize royal patrimonial authority in the process of political centralization.

It now remains to be seen what particular vicissitudes befell this stratum during the Empire, with particular reference to the military organization it assumed in the form of a peoples' militia. Before that, however, let us first examine the process of bureaucratic state-building during the nineteenth century, in order to be able to appraise the need for the patrimonialization of local government.

2

The Expansion and Differentiation of the Bureaucratic State

In the previous chapter, I outlined some of the major elements of the structural organization of the Brazilian political community during the colonial period. The objective of this chapter is to sketch, against the colonial background, the process of administrative expansion and bureaucratic differentiation of the state apparatus during the nineteenth century in Brazil's Imperial era. I will first assess the relevance of the liberal ideology and the status orientation of the time for the organization of a patrimonial experiment in local government. Then I will analyze the process of bureaucratic expansion and the political problems that the central state had to confront vis-à-vis local society.

The Liberal Contrast: Brazil and Hispanic America

The flight of the Portuguese Court to South America in 1808, provoked by Portugal's involvement in the Napoleonic Wars, immediately set the future pattern of Brazil's political evolution apart from that of the Hispanic-American countries. Some of these differences are reflected in the social and political organization of the country immediately after it gained its political autonomy from Portugal in 1822.

In contrast to the French model of liberalism adopted by the Hispanic-American colonies, which stressed democratic and republican values, the brand of liberalism adopted by Brazil helped preserve the hierarchical and authoritarian representation of the political community inherited from colonial times.

During the eighteenth century, colonial Brazil was not uninfluenced by liberal political ideologies. Indeed, the two political rebellions that took place at that time, the *Inconfidencia Mineira* of 1789 and the Pernambuco movement of 1817, were inspired by liberal principles. However, the liberal principles absorbed by the Brazilians were Lockean, or predemocratic, and not democratic, as was the case in North America. As Vicente Barretto put it in a recent study:

> Liberalism was not so much associated with emancipation as with the institutionalization of power [a ordenaçao do poder]....Democratic values were not part of the concern of Brazilian liberals during the first two decades of the nineteenth century.[1]

After Brazil's independence from Portugal, the hierarchical and organic character of its society remained intact, since the new order grew very easily out of the old colonial one. This "organic" representation of the community, in its turn, further weakened the validity of a status structure made up of independent groups. This is in striking contrast to the rest of Latin America, where the new order was born only when the old one was abolished. In the Hispanic-American countries, to account for change one would have to understand the new foundation for the legitimacy of the new political order, but in Brazil, this would mean understanding the continuity of the old legitimacy within the new political order.[2]

In direct consequence and in sharp contrast to its neighbors, the political aspects of Brazil's process of reform did not gain ascendancy in public issues. Serious systematic attention to the administrative organization of the state apparatus was delayed in the rest of Latin America until the 1840s, because of the political agitations of the previous decades, while Brazil, unimpaired by war, was able to begin as early as the 1820s.

This relative "depoliticalization" of public life, together with the organic continuity of the *ancien régime*, favored the public prominence of the landed military corporations in the institutional life of the country during the early nineteenth century.

Again, in contrast to the rather swift transition that made the formation of an autonomous Brazilian state a singular case, the other Latin American countries faced a protracted and disaggregating revolutionary process—from approximately 1810 to 1825—for the conquest of their political autonomy. The effects on the respective military institutions cannot be ignored. Indeed, José Murilo has suggested that the absence of wars of independence prevented the democratization of the Brazilian army.[3] In other countries, as is to be expected, the reverse held true. Halperin Donghi's detailed scrutiny of revolutionary Argentina has shown that the americanization of the militias and the regular troops went hand in hand with their democratization.[4] A similar pattern appears in the revolutionary armies of the Gran Colombia, where many officers—Paez, Cordoba, and Mata, for example—came from very modest social origins. Thus, it is likely that the low level of democratization of the Brazilian army also favored the structural continuity outlined above.

There is, moreover, another important change in the Hispanic-American revolutionary armies that contrasts with the Brazilian pattern, namely, their early professionalization. The conduct of a long but successful war against a well-organized and powerful enemy necessarily demanded the rationalization of the revolutionary war apparatus. Discipline, training, centralized command, and full-time professionalism were prerequisites for the process of liberation. As the revolutionary leadership concluded, "the new order calls for armies, not militias."[5]

Paradoxically, this professionalization of the army in Latin America was accompanied by an acute degree of politicalization of the military, because of the political void left by the expulsion of the metropolitan cadres. Politics became an extension of the military art, and vice-versa; only an analytical distinction could be entertained between the two domains. Halperin Donghi's eloquent remark on the Argentinian experience also holds good for the rest of the hemisphere:

> The career of arms culminated, in the context of the River Plate Revolution, in a political career in which the military leader did not act exclusively as the representative of the points of view and the corporate interests of the Army, but as a politician whose military status might at times give him means of action lacked by his other colleagues, but who owed simultaneous loyalties to family alliances, the solidarity of a secret lodge, or agreements between factions.[6]

This stands out in sharp contrast to the Brazilian experience. Not only did little professionalization of the militias occur in Brazil—it was not called for—but also the professional military remained relatively distant from political life. Systematic professionalization of the armed forces only proceeded as a consequence of the war against Paraguay in the second half of the nineteenth century. The dearth of military representatives in the national political arena—with outstanding exceptions, such as the Duke of Caxias and a few others—was a typical trait of Imperial Brazil.

Brazil's tardy military professionalization should not be mistaken for a lack of early militarization. Professionalization was certainly delayed until the armed conflict with Paraguay, but society as a whole had been exposed to an intense process of militarization since the colonial period. In contrast to Brazil's pattern—early militarization of society but delayed professionalization of the military—the Latin American pattern was one of early professionalization and late militarization.

Brazil's pattern favored a prominent role for the militias, in so far as early militarization represented a rapid growth of military corporations, and also in so far as the late professionalization of the army left ample room for the militias' prominence. As a result, in contrast to the Latin American pattern, in which politics gained early institutional identification with the army, politics in Brazil were more related to the militias.[7]

The Growth of the State

Although outwardly similar to colonial society, the society of early nineteenth-century Imperial Brazil was a more developed organism. In contrast to colonial society, it acquired the two Durkheim-flavored forces that Bergson identified as the fundamental sources of all morality and solidarity, the attraction of a past and the attraction of a project.[8] Part of the project was the creation of a Brazilian state apparatus adequate to meet the institutional needs of a new society just emerging from colonial status.

The unique circumstances that allowed Brazil to enter into the process of state-building considerably earlier than her neighbors have been noted. From an administrative standpoint, the most immediate effect of the transfer of the Court and of the royal bureaucracy to Brazil was the fantastic swelling of the state apparatus and the central governmental machine in Rio de Janeiro. It has been stated, perhaps without exaggeration, that the benefices awarded in the first years of royal administration on Brazilian soil were more numerous than those distributed throughout the entire dynastic period,[9] as the transfer caused an acute accentuation of the patrimonial dispensation of benefices to an immense group of royal favorites and personal dependents who had no means of livelihood on the American shore.[10]

This sudden and intense process of prebendalization temporarily arrested any significant process of the rationalization of office. The typically patrimonial blurring of the distinctions between public administration and the management of the royal househould continued under Pedro I. The characteristic royal use of discretion, free from bureaucratically defined boundaries, was equally evident.[11] For example, Dom Pedro's drastic reduction of the royal stable from 1,200 horses to just over 150 at the beginning of his reign by no means reflected an awareness of the distinction between household and *res publica;* it was simply forced on him by the poverty in which the royal coffers were left after his father's return to Portugal.

As budgets were ordinarily incomplete and limited to the Court and the Province of Rio de Janeiro, the lack of data series for the period from 1822 to 1831 makes it impossible to reconstruct the trends and changes suffered by the state apparatus, as reflected in the fiscal behavior of the different branches of government. A regular budget appeared for the first time in 1831–1832. Characteristically, its apparatus was schematically simplified. The Imperial administration rested in the hands of four ministerial departments—Interior and Foreign Affairs (*Ministerio do Reino e Negocios Estrangeiros*), Exchequer (*Ministerio da Fazenda*), and Defense, assumed by two ministries, War (*Guerra*) and Navy (*Marinha*).* The needs of defense were by far the largest, a fact in perfect accord with the militarization of the political community since colonial times. Military expenditure generally covered salaries, ammunitions, equipment, transportation, and the like. The fiscal resources devoted to defense were staggering; for the fiscal year 1822–1823, forty-six percent of the public budget of Minas Gerais, sixty-eight percent of that of São Paulo, seventy-one percent of that of Rio Grande do Sul, and eighty percent of that of Bahia was allotted to defense.[12]

Two other major needs were covered by public finances, the civil administration (*folha civil*) and the ecclesiastical administration (*folha ecclesiastica*). The former paid salaries and pensions for bureaucrats, political representatives, and magistrates, and financed public works; the latter covered the prebends for vicars and bishops, as well as salaries for their domestic employees and servants. Typically for the patrimonial structure of the state, civil administration did not represent a very heavy demand on public finances. In 1822–1823, the provinces of Bahia and São Paulo, for example, assigned less than twenty percent of their respective budgets to civil administration, Rio Grande do Sul about twenty-five percent, and Minas Gerais about forty-five percent. This peculiar fact is partly a result of the legacy of the feverish bureaucratic

*Ron Seckinger drew my attention to the fact that I had not included Foreign Affairs as an independent department, despite its separation from Interior in 1823. The reason was simple: Foreign Affairs did not have a regular provincial budget. For the fiscal year 1833–1834, for instance, only the Province of Rio de Janeiro had an allotted budget. Ten years later, during the fiscal year 1842–1843, Foreign Affairs expenditures existed only in the Court, the Province of Pará, and London. Finally, in the fiscal year 1875–1876, ependitures were budgeted in the Court, Bahia, Alagoas, Pernambuco, Pará, Rio Grande do Sul, Mato Grosso, and London.

fiscalism imposed by the metropolitan power during Minas Gerais' golden and not too distant past.[13] (See Table 1.)

This pattern of expenditure dispels any simple association between the militarization of Imperial society and the objective needs of defense. There is no question that the respective strategic positions of Bahia—facing the sea—and Rio Grande do Sul—facing the Hispanic settlers—were a factor in the relative primacy of defense allocation, but these allocations were also high for the other provinces. Militarization, as expressed in public expenditure, did not have the character of a frontier phenomenon, as it did characteristically in other societies. Its causes were not only geopolitical, but also largely historical.

Thus office prebendalism, simplified administrative schematism, and a disproportionate military expenditure were traits that typified the administration of Imperial government during the First Empire (1815–1831). Now, what were the changes that took place in the successive periods, the Regency (1831–1840) and the Second Empire (1840–1889)? This question is particularly relevant in the light of the aversion of bureaucratic patrimonialism to change. In fact, left to itself, a patrimonial bureaucracy is a most static kind of organization. It is essentially a "pragmatic" bureaucracy, in that its system of action is not oriented by a formal and universalistic canon. Such pragmatism, also characteristic of the legal empiricism to be found before the emergence of a formal, bourgeois legality, is seen in the fact that administrative decisions are guided by "experience," not by formal principles, as is the case with full-grown bureaucracies. The lack of a constitutive principle of organization makes it difficult to institutionalize technical rationality as a guiding pattern. Pragmatism thus leads to an understanding of the key to patrimonial bureaucracy, namely, its irrationality (in the sense of a lack of a systematic and technically efficient use of the resources at its disposal).

The consequences of such pragmatism and irrationality are formidable: patrimonial bureaucracy stifles structural differentiation and restricts the process of growth to an extensive modality. The monotonous, secular, and typically elementary schematism of the administrative division of work

TABLE 1.

Public Expenditures by Province and Item: 1822–1823 (in mil-reis)

	Defense (Folha Militar)	*Civil Administration* (Folha Civil)	*Ecclesiastical Administration* (Folha Eclesiastica)	TOTAL (%)
Bahia[a]	525:715 (80.3)	110:647 (16.9)	18:586 (2.8)	654:948 (100)
Minas	144:529 (46.0)	142:978 (45.6)	26:341 (8.4)	313:848 (100)
Rio Grande do Sul	206:802 (71.3)	78:022 (26.9)	5:196 (1.8)	290:020 (100)
São Paulo[b]	163:193 (68.3)	45:228 (18.9)	30:465 (12.8)	238:886 (100)

[a]Bahia: 1819
[b]São Paulo: 1819

SOURCE: *Exposição do estado da Fazenda Publica,* Rio de Janeiro, 1823.

during the colonial era and later during the First Empire becomes more intelligible when seen from this perspective. The prebendalization that accompanied the expansion of government throughout the period, moreover, would have made any process of rationalization of office more difficult. Monstrosity may be defined as a mode of being, the essential changes of which are contingent and accidental. If we accept this definition, we can readily apply it to patrimonial bureaucracy; on its own, it may be noted, patrimonial bureaucracy continues but does not grow; it expands without developing. In practical terms, its essential metamorphosis comes from the political arena—from without. Indeed, an external pressure must exist to make it adopt a rational principle that will transform it. We saw in the previous chapter, for instance, how the material interests of the Portuguese Crown were responsible for the bureaucratization of the fiscal administration; another case where the beginning of administrative rationalization coincided with the material interests of a pressure group was supplied by the professional *letrados*.

Both instances define, in effect, the bureaucratic boundaries of the patrimonial bureaucracy during centuries of colonization. The line of demarcation between a bureaucracy and a patrimonial administration coexisting in the same empire was subject to constant redefinitions during the nineteenth century. Two sources were decisive in establishing it: one was the presence and the activity of the central bureaucratic agencies, ceaselessly pushing for the rationalization of the patrimonial periphery of the *sertão* and the hinterland. The second source may be subdivided into two. On the one hand, there was the rationalizing joint effect of the bourgeois and capitalistic organization of the economy and society, both of which had been reinvigorated since the end of the first quarter of the 1800s by the coffee industry. On the other hand, there was the drama of war with Paraguay some decades later. In order to be able to stage this war, the central administration had to put some rationalizing order into its finances.

All of these factors gradually restricted the area of competence of the patrimonial forms of administration. An illustration of these changes is the renewed emphasis on secrecy as an official procedure for the discharge of business. Conventionally, sociological tradition has accentuated secrecy as an important element of bureaucracy. In Brazil, the policy of official secrecy dates back to the initial period of conquest.[14] The same policy recurs as an ordinary practice in the conduct of public affairs during the reign of Pedro I, the first emperor of Brazil.[15] After 1830, however, the rationale on which official secrecy was grounded changed significantly. Thus far, secrecy had been justified as an expedient in attaining the practical goals of the patrimonial agency. The new justification was characteristically normative and bureaucratic, based on the idea that the correct procedure for decision making was handicapped when it operated under undue influences. This radical shift appeared in a directive distributed to all branches of government. It started by regretting the public disclosure of official correspondence, but was quick to add that publicizing administrative acts was a constitutional duty. There had to exist, however, a

> distinction between acts and preparatory dispositions for the discharge of the offices of the Public Administration, and definitive decisions handed down to the public at large. Prior publication is not regular, it being therefore contradictory for an official or an agency to make public or permit publication of the contents of their official letters or requests—ordinarily bearing the seal of the Imperial arms— which have been entrusted to the mail with the warranty of inviolable secrecy.[16]

A new, more technical and bureaucratic conception of administrative secrecy was not the only indication of the new times. Equally important was the extent to which the symbol of the emperor gradually faded from public documents, to be replaced by more impersonal notions like "this government," "the country," or, simply, Brazil, *tout court*. This trend, beginning in the 1850s, unquestionably denoted a subtle and profound shift from the particularism of patrimonial rule to the universalism of a more bureaucratic authority. The Empire had ceased to be the personal domain of the emperor; the government was no longer exclusively His Majesty's.[17]

The official data on expenditure shown in Table 2 illustrate some prominent points; on the whole, the expansion of the central bureaucracy during the 1830s was excessively timid. There were, in fact, impressive decreases in public expenditure in the Ministry of the Interior for the provinces of Rio Grande do Sul, Minas Gerais, and Bahia, as well as for the ministries of War and Economy for Bahia and Rio de Janeiro. With the exception of Minas Gerais, the only item which in general expanded during that decade was the Ministry of Justice. As for overall public expenditure incurred by the provinces, this dropped considerably for Bahia and Rio de Janeiro, and remained low for Minas Gerais and the Court. A protracted rebellion in Rio Grande do Sul accounts for the significant public expenditure there. Though moderate, expansion was the prevailing process at the Court during the 1830s. In fact, during the period following the abdication of Pedro I,* the refurbishing of the government apparatus as a new Brazilian institution accounts for the impressive rate of growth of the Ministry of the Interior. During no other decade was it to grow so rapidly.

The next decade witnessed a drastic accentuation of the bureaucratic principle of government. However, the administration remained excessively schematic and undifferentiated in its functional division of labor. The four ministries mentioned above, plus the Foreign Office, lasted out the decade.

Despite the persistence of patrimonial features, the Brazilian state apparatus advanced toward a more centralized and voluminous condition in the 1840s. The effort toward centralization and expansion is dramatically reflected in the rates of growth of public expenditure. In the previous decade, the Ministry of the Interior had attained a rate of growth at the Court that was to remain unsurpassed throughout the Empire. In the 1840s, however, the Court bureaucracy was unmatched in the rate of growth of its total expenditure (6.19 percent). The provinces of Bahia and Rio de Janeiro, which had shown a decrease in the 1830s, now joined Rio Grande

*This occurred in 1831. His successor was his son, Pedro II, who, because he was five years old at the time, started his reign under a regency.

TABLE 2.

Public Expenditure by Ministries and Provinces: Early Nineteenth Century (annual rates of growth)

	Court	Rio de Janeiro	Rio Grande do Sul	Bahia	Minas Gerais	São Paulo
1830/1 to 1842/3						
Interior	12.29	11.16	−15.60	−5.70	−13.87	6.70
War	2.05	−10.21	12.69	−4.53	6.62	8.05
Economy	−2.71	−15.56	4.18	−10.23	1.86	−5.69
Justice	8.89	31.85	7.99	4.38	−8.96	8.85
Combined annual rate	1.23	−12.14	10.92	−6.53	1.68	4.17
1830/31 to 1851/52						
Interior	8.44	6.00	−6.03	−0.45	−6.11	7.70
War	4.78	−4.05	13.24	−1.63	−3.91	1.13
Economy	0.01	−5.50	10.25	−4.22	0.46	4.92
Justice	6.93	23.46	9.46	5.06	5.64	13.93
Combined annual rate	3.33	−3.30	12.31	−0.02	−1.36	4.46
1842/43 to 1851/52						
Interior	3.51	−0.01	8.45	7.03	6.04	8.71
War	8.53	4.82	13.97	2.37	−16.15	−5.34
Economy	5.17	9.80	18.89	4.42	3.60	16.72
Justice	4.36	13.10	11.45	5.98	28.81	19.23
Combined annual rate	6.19	9.88	14.18	2.73	−5.28	4.75

SOURCES: *Balanço da Receita e Despesa do Imperio*, pertinent volumes. São Paulo year-base: 1833–1834.

do Sul, still seething in armed rebellion, in its rapid bureaucratization. In fact, practically all ministerial branches of all
provinces grew at annual rates that were sometimes fantastic
(28.81 percent, 19.23 percent, 18.89 percent, etc.). The only
significant reduction of public expenditure was the war item
in Minas Gerais and São Paulo. The most spectacular increase
during the decade was in the administration of justice. It is
indeed remarkable that all the provinces—with the exception
of the more modest rate of Bahia—grew at annual rates of
over 10 percent.

Obviously, this dramatic increase reflects the attempt to
create an adequate institutional apparatus for the operation
and organization of the new legal order. This order began to
establish a firmer footing in Brazilian society, particularly in
the second quarter of the century, when the economic cycle
initiated by the coffee industry helped capitalism and new
relations of production to penetrate into the countryside.

A look at the overall process of state-building during the
1830s and 1840s further dramatizes the singular growth of the
legal apparatus. This was, in fact, the only area of government with continually higher rates of annual expansion during the entire period. Finally, throughout this period of over
twenty years the relative expansion of the state apparatus
was primarily concentrated at the Court itself, the growth of
the *Riograndense* apparatus being almost exclusively accounted for by the need for defense, as we have seen above.

This outline of the state-building process of the first part
of the nineteenth century casts serious doubt on the conventional interpretation, which places the real beginning of the
centralization of the state in the second half of the century.
According to some Brazilian analysts, the relative decline of
agricultural export during the fourth decade of the century
delayed the process of centralization.[18] Our findings so far
do not support this view. What they show, rather, is a resil-
ient state apparatus simultaneously able to wage a protracted
war on its own soil against southern *fazendeiros* (landowners)
for ten consecutive years (1835–1845) in Rio Grande do Sul,
to suffocate half a dozen provincial rebellions, to lay the foundations of the legal apparatus of the new political order, and
to refurbish and bureaucratize the government's administra-

tive cadres without compromising either its integrity or its ability to grow. All this attests to the formidable extractive capacities that the young Brazilian state possessed, and to its invigorating presence in the social organization of the nation.

The state-building that began in the earlier part of the century gained momentum during the second half. This period actually started with a central administration already in an overt process of growth, and with a nucleus based at the Court progressively radiating its influence over the periphery. This process of bureaucratization of the administration of the peripheral areas is characteristic of the latter half of the century. The Court was to continue its expansion as a matter of course, but the rhythm of that expansion did not differ substantially from that of the earlier period. The expansion rate of the earlier period was 3.33 percent, as opposed to a new rate of 3.51 percent.

The peculiarity of this period lies rather in the massive bureaucratization of the state instruments at the provincial level. During the 1830s and 1840s, the peripheral areas had in fact lagged behind; the growth rate of total state expenditure for Minas Gerais, Bahia, and Rio de Janeiro had been negative, whereas that of Rio Grande do Sul had increased thanks only to the massive war costs. Public expenditure during the second half of the century began to accelerate to such an extent that one province, São Paulo, exceeded the Court's annual rate, while another province, Minas Gerais, barely differed from the Court. On the whole, though the above differences are not great, they permit the generalization that the rhythm of state centralization proceeded at a more or less uniform pace both at the center and at the periphery of the country, during the second part of the century.[19] This statement holds true both at the aggregate level and by provinces.

A glance at Table 3 shows a remarkable degree of uniformity of growth rates for all branches of government in all provinces. The inter-provincial and inter-ministerial disparities of the earlier period are lacking. Most probably this indicates that the basic organizational foundations of all the major organs of government had by that time been completely laid down in all provinces, thereby dispensing with the need for the galvanization of this or that agency so that

TABLE 3.

Public Expenditure by Ministries and Provinces: Late Nineteenth Century (annual rates of growth)

	Court	Rio de Janeiro	Rio Grande do Sul	Bahia	Minas Gerais	São Paulo
1852/53 to 1888						
Interior	2.06	1.84	1.39	3.46	4.66	2.48
War	2.73	2.08	0.63	1.31	0.70	2.94
Economy	4.71	3.03	2.90	3.78	3.66	4.36
Justice	2.57	−0.86	4.85	2.21	2.90	3.83
Combined annual rate	3.51	1.98	1.20	2.70	3.12	3.66
1830/31 to 1888						
Interior	4.71	4.16	0.08	2.81	1.60	4.80
War	2.80	−0.06	3.12	0.24	−0.83	2.27
Economy	3.18	−0.55	5.27	1.02	2.78	4.47
Justice	4.37	7.47	6.74	3.51	4.38	7.15
Combined annual rate	3.25	−0.16	3.38	1.02	1.85	3.98

SOURCES: *Balanço da Receita e Despesa do Imperio*, Rio de Janeiro, Typographia Nacional, various years.

it could catch up with the rest. The growth of the state then, for the first time, approached an incrementalist model. Moreover, this patterned behavior unquestionably shows that the bureaucratic principle of administration was finally able to set the tone and tempo for the organization of the state apparatus. Sudden improvisations and audacious experiments, had no place within this cosmos.

At the same time, the only major change in the functional organization of bureaucratic work occurred in 1860 with the creation of an independent ministry to deal with agriculture, trade, and public works. This measure was taken in apparent response to the growing importance of the coffee industry, in particular, and to the increasing impact of capitalism in the rural society and economy of the Empire in general.

On the whole, however, Brazilian bureaucratic administration was cautious and rather unwilling to try out less schematic and more differentiated forms of administration, forms that became increasingly necessary to meet the growing demands of a more differentiated social structure. This resistance to differentiation can be viewed as another expression of the preponderance of, and preference for, centralized government. However, other conditions being equal, this view would in fact be to some extent mistaken. When such a trait is nonetheless framed in terms of the patrimonial heritage of the Brazilian state, it becomes less problematic. This immediately refers us back to the central question of the antagonism between public and private authority.

State and Local Power: the Art of Accommodation

> Handle a large kingdom with as gentle a touch as if you were cooking small fish.
>
> Lao-Tzu, *The Way of Life*

No serious discussion of the process of state-building in nineteenth-century Brazil can omit the problem of the relations between state and local power. This issue insinuates itself into the discussion because of the continental size of the political community of Brazil, and the resulting difficulty of establishing and continuing a politically guaranteed legal order, which is indispensable to the exercise of legitimate coercion. The objective evaluation of these relations has nonetheless frequently been impaired by an inadequate evaluation of the role of administration in the organization of the state and in its interaction with society. There are those who, along with Weber and Machiavelli, assume a basic continuity between administration and power and consequently try to locate the center of power, influence, and authority in the administrative formula,"He who administers, rules." Oliveira Vianna, for example, translated the process of state centralization during the Empire into the formula, "The king reigns, governs, and administers."[20] The integrity of the state appears to be irreconcilable with the wielding of power by local groups.[21] Raymundo Faoro is perhaps the most evident champion of this transitivity between administration and power. To him, the alleged existence of a corporate officialdom automatically implies that it controls not only the reins of administration but power as well.[22] The argument, suggestive of zero sum models, is that the centralization of administration implies not only a centralized authority, but also the elimination of local power; in brief, the two cannot possibly coexist.

At the other extreme of analysis are to be found those students, Marxist and non-Marxist, who approach the state administration as an instrument of power. The growth and expansion of the state apparatus is seen, not as a potential threat to localism and agrarian power, but rather as an indication of its vigor. There is again an equation between power and administration, the former being in this case the source of the latter.[23]

One variant of this position is represented by those studies that deemphasize administrative centralization on the assumption that the existence of an economically powerful landed class is sufficient reason for the decentralization and feudalization of the political community. This has probably been one of the most widespread representations of the historical organization of Brazil.[24]

The most satisfactory scheme for the interpretation of the relations of state and local power during the Empire is one which conceives of the interaction between central authority and local power as a complex process made up of relative antagonisms, relative identities, and relative autonomies. The state had a relative autonomy that eventually led it to antagonize private groups, and vice-versa. At the same time it shared a certain degree of identity with private groups, which enabled it to antagonize other factions, and so forth. Neither an administrative monism nor an agrarian one would have been able to comprehend the dialectical aspects of the process. A particular brand of dualism, manifest on the one hand in a relatively centralized government and on the other in a powerful landed oligarchy, was at the heart of this process, for the efficiency of the government—given the patrimonial and avocational nature of local government—was dependent on the enlisted and liturgical cooperation of the landed oligarchy. Each was weak without the other. If the role of either is independently stressed above that of the other, we do violence to the real development of the process, and at best mistakenly transform what is essentially a dialectical antagonism into a chain of evolutionary stages, or at worst fail to acknowledge the opposite moment of the process, thereby falling into a one-sided monism.

A similar perspective has been developed by other contemporary scholars. José Murilo, in his valuable study of Imperial elites and state-building, documented several of the compromises with social groups on which the power of the state was built.[25] Similarly, Roderick Barman amply documented that "the necessity for cultivating local interests and the impossibility of disregarding local demands complicated any design for the establishment of firm government control over the countryside."[26]

Out of this interplay of reciprocal influences emerged a dialectic with more or less centralized moments that was characteristic of the organization of power during the seventy years of monarchical rule. The first half of the century—when the foundations of a more bureaucratic state began to be laid—partook of one of those cycles. The third decade of the century saw the most radical experiment in decentralized government after the initial centralization created by the constitutional pact of 1824. Thanks to the Additional Act of 1831 and the Code of Procedures of 1832, the central organs were dismembered, to be reconstituted at the municipal level. The degree of political decentralization is impressive; provincial legislatures gained the power to define the most essential policies (budget, recruitment of police force, etc.); and elected judges of the peace took over the administration of justice and with it an amalgam of administrative, judiciary, and police prerogatives. The political apparatus of government became the property of the landlord. Because a parallel administrative decentralization did not take place, however, the move toward decentralization remained incomplete. Side by side with the provincial legislatures of unquestionable local character, arose the provincial president appointed by the central authority and responsible solely to the Crown. As Francisco Iglesias has correctly remarked, "It was inconsistent to aim at the decentralization of provincial legislative organs, while keeping the presidency dependent upon [Imperial] appointment."[27]

The role of the provincial president as an instrument of the political center can hardly be minimized. Following a typically patrimonial practice (found also in China), the president was usually appointed to a province other than his native one and for an alarmingly short tenure.[28] The effect was that the provincial presidents "never identified themselves with the regional spirit of the jurisdictions they administered."[29] The interests of the political center rather than those of the province were served. (See Table 4.)

TABLE 4.

Provincial Presidents: 1822–1889, Selected Provinces

Province of Birth	Province of Office		
	Bahia	São Paulo	Mato Grosso
Bahia	17	7	1
São Paulo	1	14	3
Mato Grosso	—	—	2
Other places	29	29	27

SOURCE: Adapted from Eul-Soo Pang and Ron L. Seckinger, "The Mandarins of Imperial Brazil," *Comparative Studies in Society and History* 9:2, Winter 1971, p. 232.

The 1840s began with a systematic effort to curtail the political weapons of the local landlords and their instruments of government. Not only was the nomination of the vice-president wrested from the hands of the provincial legislature, but, far more seriously, the provincial control of the local monopoly of justice and police came to an end. The municipal legislatures, the *camaras*, were deprived of their right to elect local judges. In 1841, after the so-called Law of Interpretation (of the reforms of 1831), municipal judges were appointed by the central administration and combined both judiciary and police duties.[30] The justice of the peace, that bulwark of local discretion, was divested of his police and criminal jurisdiction; the court judge (*juiz de direito*) and the chief of police, also no longer locally elected, became the undisputed center of the local administration of their respective fields. These were the last strokes of the new bureaucratic and centralized apparatus of monarchical rule, which was to remain reasonably intact for the next thirty-five years. The last wave of decentralization was to gain momentum at the beginning of the 1870s. Additional changes also helped the formal organization of government accommodate the birth pangs of a liberal bourgeois society, in which "all facts point to the ceaseless decay of the monarchical principle."[31]

Nevertheless, whatever the degree of governmental centralization during these periods, the central state was unable to rule effectively without striking bargains with, and gaining the cooperation of, private groups. It was keenly conscious of the fragile limits of its authority and the legal order it had instituted. Although the patrimonial bases of local administration provided the opportunity for the state to organize a system of government with some continuity, that is, an administrative order, the same bases also handicapped the expedient and rational execution of the state's decisions. Viable government was based on the state's recognition of local demands and interests, which it could ignore only at its own peril.[32]

The state and its branches were desperately conscious of the impossibility of ruling in isolation. It is instructive to partially reconstruct some aspects of the situation by briefly examining relations at the height of the monarchical reaction during the 1840's and 1850's, as reflected in the exchange of letters between the provincial president (an agent of Imperial power) and the local oligarchies. The state apparatus, supposedly impervious to compromise because of its immense amassed authority, appears, in the official correspondence between its higher officials, gingerly conscious of the need to coopt and to curry favors and liturgies from the local lords. These official letters show that the first obstacle to a fully bureaucratized and depatrimonialized authority was the lack of qualified personnel to whom the local administration of government could be entrusted. This lack was particularly severe in the judiciary; the immediate consequence was that functions that should have been discharged by professional lawyers designated by the central bureaucracy were actually executed by the avocational services of local *honoratiores*.[33] The state, willing or not, needed the services of local individuals for this administration.

A second obstacle was closely associated with the scarcity of a properly bureaucratic officialdom, namely, the frequency with which the conflicts of jurisdiction arrested the rationalization of functions. This lack of functional specificity, obviously linked to the avocational and *aficionado* orientation of administrative action, indicated the precarious institutionalization of the new administrative order. In the late 1840s the President of the Province of Rio de Janeiro forwarded a monthly official report on public order to the Ministry of Justice. It is significant that two basic problems were regularly reported, actual disturbances on the one hand, and conflicts of jurisdiction on the other.[34]

By exacerbating local antagonisms, this lack of definition of administrative competence helped bring local factions of *honoratiores* into the politico-administrative arena. These ambiguities projected antagonisms originating in other areas of interest, and in the absence of structurally differentiated mechanisms of conflict resolution that might have been capable of managing them, they became frequent.

Thus the paucity of bureaucratic officialdom and the functional diffuseness of administrative roles helped determine a central policy of tacit pacts and tactical alliances with the privatized power of the local notables. Favors and privileges were suggested as moves to gain the sympathy and cooperation of local families and prominent landlords. At times these favors were persistently solicited:

> Having suggested some names to your Excellency—the report of which, I have been told, was lost—as worthy of being considered in the distribution of graces, I will not forward it anew in order not to exacerbate new jealousies at the present time; I nonetheless think it is most convenient not to forget the name of José Lourenço de Castro e Silva in order to further settle the relationships of the Castro e Silva family with the Government.[35]

The baron of Maroim in the rather distant province of Sergipe was, during the early 1850's (a period teeming with centralizing fervor), a very wealthy landlord with a fabulous yearly income of about thirty contos, a numerous and equally wealthy kinship, which was influential and loyal to him, and a peaceful temperament. He was also, as the provincial president reports to the center of the Empire, without a criminal record. This provincial Croesus owed his influence and authority principally to his large fortune, we are told, since his intelligence, being rather modest, diminished his authority. However, he was sufficiently clever to realize that to protect his authority he should be ready, as he had been in the past, to "sacrifice" his partisan and ideological leanings in order to maintain his good standing vis-à-vis the Imperial government. In the president's words: "What the Baron prefers over any other thing is to see his kinship and friends in the official positions; what he by no means wishes is *to lose the town of Maroim.*" Though rather inept as a party leader, he was indispensable because of his partisan prodigality, and not to be disregarded as an ally: "The present Government may count on his services and even sacrifices provided he be appointed Higher Commander of Maroim. His kin, who as I said are numerous and rich, are loyal to him, and possess some influence. As an ally, he is not therefore to be disregarded."[36]

Mutual awareness that the state and the landlord each needed the other in equal measure gave rise to a tacit pact resulting in a pattern of exchanges and reciprocities, the state granting authority and status in exchange for the landlord's cooperation and service. This pattern was apparent not only in those provinces with an economically expansive landowning class; it was a general trait equally valid for the stagnant or depressed agrarian economies. From north to south, from periphery to center, the pact was a constant. When needed, it could also enlist the economic support of the local bourgeoisies. Why not a little beribboning of local businessmen by the Imperial Government?—proposes the president of tiny Parahyba do Norte. "Your Excellency knows that those ribbons have many times led businessmen to make large offerings from their pockets for the general welfare."[37]

These pacts and negotiations were not sealed with the local clan, the local lord, and the local bourgeoisie only. With the progressive institutionalization of party politics gaining momentum around the middle of the century, the provincial governments began to request resources from the central state in exchange for electoral support. Provincial authorities reporting favorable electoral outcomes were hasty to add, in the next paragraph, urgent requests to meet the varied needs of the locality.[38] The political system thus organized itself through a series of pacts of ever expanding radius. Increasingly, party patronage became an important mechanism for filling local bureaucratic posts. With each passing day, kinship structures became less efficient vehicles of the affirmation of local power, and, consequently, of political authority. A pattern of political organization—remarkably similar to that found in eighteenth-century England after the gradual dissolution of the great territorial baronies—was introduced, by which the local notable's influence was now dependent on his connections in the capital.[39]

This discussion indicates how the process of political organization developed in the form of varying "blends" of kinship and partisanship as the basic structures for the stereotyping of patrimonial and bureaucratic opportunities for public office. A schematic and simplified pattern reveals itself; the closer we move toward the periphery and the early periods of the Empire, the more kinship defines and stereotypes the chances for the appropriation of office on a traditional, patrimonial basis; conversely, the closer we move to the center and the later periods, the more partisanship defines those same chances for the appropriation of office in a rational, bureaucratic way. Of course neither of these ever operated in its pure form, but they do serve to accentuate typical aspects that never appeared alone. For example, partisan institutions were immensely relevant for the institutionalization of a politically valid administrative bureaucratic order, in so far as they contributed to the decline of previously established claims by kin groups to the exercise of administration.[40]

The primacy of party as a structural mediator and as an integrative link between the political center and local landlords should not be neglected. In sharp contrast to the political development of eighteenth-century England, where party politics represented the aggregation of new interests coming from the gentry, party politics during the Brazilian Empire did not reflect new political interests different from those of the first half of the century.

A key figure in this connection was the *bacharel*, the law school graduate, in whom kinship and party were blended together at the national level. In a general sense, the *bacharel* completed the process of the articulation and accommodation of interests between the private and public orders. He was generally the complement, at the national level, of the local *coronel* (a military title, honorific or real, denoting local power and authority).[41] The relative professionalization of politics created new conditions that "forced the old type of municipal boss to a strategic retreat: the *coronel* went backstage. However, for the political management of his fief, he cautiously left in the foreground the son-in-law lawyer, the modern facade of *coronelismo* as a political force."[42]

In order to realize the particularistic interests of the family clan, nothing was more convenient than technical rationality; in fact: "[The] flower of the [landlord's] family was picked for the law school—the law school being the training-ground, not for the magistracy only, but for the parliament and the cabinet also, and for diplomacy."[43]

The Brazilian *bacharel* can be compared with the Chinese *literatus* as described by Weber.[44] Both acted under similar conditions, namely a centralized bureaucratic Empire with local nuclei of power, including a patrimonial administration under the strong influence of kin groups. In both instances, kinship groups produced the future *literatus* and *bacharel*. For both, admission to the court and to the central organs of government took place through those groups. However, in Brazil, the typical chances for career promotion were appropriated by those *bachareis* appointed by the Emperor as *juizes de direito* (court judges) and provincial presidents. Provincial deputyships did not lead to a career.[45] In both cases again, *bacharel* and *literatus* established a link that mediated between the center and the periphery; though rotation and rapid turnover in regional offices were introduced to avoid ties and allegiances between bureaucratic official and local interests, these mechanisms proved unsuccessful in both cases, since *literatus* and *bacharel* generally stood as advocates for, and staunch defenders of, kin particularism; so much so that, in general, their efficient advocacy depended on their having a relative in the Imperial bureaucracy.

Two major contrasts deserve special consideration. First, Chinese politics were essentially court politicking; party politics, strictly speaking, did not exist because only administrative and kin factionalisms were allowed by the ruler. Brazil, on the other hand, developed a parliamentary system hand in hand with the "ministerialization" of administration, in other words, the creation of bureaus with substantive areas of jurisdiction. This contrast worked for the *bacharel* and against the *literatus*, as far as the exercise of political influence was concerned. Second, the Brazilian *bachareis* did not develop a corporate organization with a monopoly on office, the right to control corporate membership, a distinctive group solidarity, a peculiar status honor, and a characteristic work ethic, as the Chinese *literati* did. This contrast worked for the *literatus* and against the *bacharel*, as far as the exercise of administrative influence was concerned.

One other institution tried to establish a link, a mediation of sorts between the center and the periphery, namely, the National Guard. The *Guarda Nacional* was, throughout its sixty years of operation in the Imperial system, possibly the most elaborate and vast experiment in the politics of reciprocal accommodation and compromise so characteristic of the political pact between landlords and prince.

We have examined the process of the bureaucratic organization of the Imperial state during the nineteenth century and a series of factors associated with it, with special emphasis on the organic continuity between the new post-Independence Brazilian liberalism and the *ancien régime*, the relative acceptance of status criteria as a principle of political association, and the politics of accommodation between landlord and prince. These processes developed along with the differentiation of the state apparatus and the consolidation of bureaucratic power. Their combined effect, however, was to permit the parallel organization of a patrimonial structure of government, which officially materialized in the *Guarda Nacional*. We will now turn to examine in detail the vicissitudes of the Brazilian patrimonial saga during the nineteenth century, with the conviction that, in so doing, we will also learn about the bureaucratic order that grew alongside it.

3

The Organization of the Patrimonial Militias

This chapter will discuss the structure and the organization of the National Guard, the military corporation of freemen under the direct administration of *honoratiores* that was introduced to the Brazilian scene in 1831.

The Militarization of Local Society

Well into the nineteenth century, an important incident took place in the unobtrusive town of Paranaguá, in the province of São Paulo. The local parson died, and his place was sought by a priest who was considered morally unacceptable by a large portion of the local patriciate and notables because, as they stated in a public document, "in detriment of public morals and the religious dignity of which he is invested, and oblivious to social conventions, he entertains illicit relationships that inveigh against the maxims of morality and religion."[1] Attempts to bar the priest's candidacy triggered off a series of spiraling petitions from the local patriciate to the city legislature, to the diocesan bishop, to the president of the province, to the Minister of Justice, and finally to the emperor himself.

The remarkable fact to be noted in these petitions, and in this movement, is the social status of the protagonists. In the first petition, addressed to the municipal *camara*, nineteen out of twenty-six individuals of identified social status held military titles; in the second petition, twenty-seven out of thirty-nine did so. In both cases about seventy percent of the prominent members of the community enjoyed positions as officers. This high percentage should not be interpreted as typical of this particular region or as indicating a particular phase in the organization of Brazilian society in the last century; a quarter of a century after the Paranaguá affair and in another region of the country, of the eighteen electors with specified social status who received the largest number of votes in a parish in Minas Gerais, twelve held military rank.[2]

This surprisingly large degree of militarization was not just an agrarian phenomenon; the urban society of the time was similarly affected. In another new region farther north, the top twenty candidates for the offices of alderman and justice of the peace of the capital city of Pernambuco included twelve with military rank.[3] It was not only in the political arena or in the more general and diffuse leadership of local interests that the military presence was strongly felt. A glance at the records of the sale of slaves and land in the booming areas of coffee production such as Valença bears out the vigorous presence of the military as busy landlords and slaveholders.[4]

This pervasive influence of military institutions was not, moreover, restricted to the local elites of aldermen and *honoratiores*. It in fact reached, as we will discuss more thoroughly later, deep into most if not all groups of freemen of the Empire, regardless of station and status. These institutions shaped not only the lives and careers of powerful patrician landlords, but also those of the little citizens without family tradition. The biography of a Francisco Henrique de Mattos, typical in many ways, depicts how deeply the Imperial patrimonial structure could reach into the personal biographies of its subjects.

Mattos was born in 1831 in the distant province of Ceará, of unknown parentage. *Negociante* (trader, merchant) by profession, he first enlisted in the National Guard at the age of twenty; he was called to service in September 1852, becoming a second lieutenant standard-bearer on that same date. In May 1855, we see him as an agent of the Administrative Council of the National Guard, and two months later he was appointed first lieutenant. In 1857, he was sent out in detachment to the regular army for fifteen days. He was promoted to the rank of captain the next year and sent out in October to the regular army. From September 30 to October 24, 1859, he acted as provisional fiscal of his battalion, which he commanded for a week; thereafter he returned to his service as fiscal until the first week in November. He was sent out again in detachment for two weeks in September 1860. From December 29, 1860 to February 10, 1861, he acted as commander of his battalion. From February 22 to April 13, 1861, from September 10 to November 30, 1861, and again from May 21 to July 10, 1862, he served as police delegate. He was provincial deputy from August 28, 1862 to December 31, 1863. The next year he obtained a transfer to the reserve battalion of the provincial capital. He also presented his battalion with an expensive standard of a cost equivalent to the yearly income of a well-to-do person; he contributed to the uniforms and instruments of the musicians of his corps as well as to other expenses. He received in different periods short leaves of six months for the benefit of his health and his business. Finally, in 1875, he asked for and obtained his retirement.[5]

What is most striking in the above case is the consideration that Mattos's involvement with institutions of the body politic was entirely unexceptional. Probably he was more of an achiever than other ordinary subjects; he was, after all, from a province usually considered rich in achievers. But the smooth organization of the state was based on the liturgical cooperation of thousands and thousands of Mattoses throughout the land. This huge collective enterprise was made possible by the virtual militarization of local society. I have already discussed the penetration of the military into all corners and institutional sectors of the land. But this militarization should not be interpreted in the contemporary sense of a process whereby military institutions control the reins of the state apparatus and, more generally, appropriate social roles and status on a corporative basis.[6] In fact the royal army was, and remained throughout the Empire, a numerically insignificant corporation; in 1850, for instance, it had a total effective force of 15,000 men; and at the end of the Empire the force numbered only 13,500 men.[7] It must also be born in mind that the constitutional role of the professional army was exclusively restricted to the control of the frontier, and for that purpose it was required to remain stationed close to the border.[8]

The professional army, therefore, was not capable, given the reduced scale of its organization, of forcing its presence on the large territories of the young nation. Thus the idea conveyed here by the term "militarization" is rather the opposite of the "civilianization" of the military suggested by the contemporary meaning. What the Brazilian Empire experienced was a process of *literal* militarization of that part of the status system associated with the discharge of state functions and the political organization of civil society.

The distinction may be expressed as follows: contemporary bureaucratic polities militarize the state, whereas the patrimonial Brazilian state militarized civil society. In the former case the military is "civilianized"; in the latter case the citizen is "militarized," and this latter case must be emphasized as one of the most fundamental aspects of the organization of Brazilian state and society in the Imperial epoch.

We will now turn to the historical agent responsible for this militarized social formation, namely, the National Guard, a status corporation that was able to mobilize in the first years of its creation about 200,000 freemen, at a time when the professional army had an effective force of about 5,000 men.[9]

The *Guarda Nacional:* Its Structure and Functions

The *Guarda Nacional* was a private militia made up of freemen. It was bureaucratically controlled and supervised by administrative agencies of the central state, but it remained a patrimonially administered corporation. It was, moreover, an heteronomous corporation; its organization was externally determined by the state, its members being unable either individually or collectively to change any part of its formal structure and functions.

The law that gave it birth was issued on August 18, 1831. Jeanne Berrance de Castro, to whom we owe the only monograph on the *Guarda Nacional*, shows that it was based on a similar law issued in France five months earlier.[10] But the similarity ends there. The process of bureaucratization of the French state began in earnest in the eighteenth century and was well advanced in the third decade of the nineteenth century. The role of its National Guard was in all likelihood much less relevant as a patrimonial instrument of government than was the case in Brazil, where the bureaucratization of the state began to expand after the creation of the *Guarda Nacional*, as discussed in the previous chapter.

The law that created the *Guarda Nacional* was somewhat altered in successive years. In addition, the provincial governments created their own organic versions of the formal organization of the new militia, although this small degree of provincial autonomy was of very short duration. It existed only in the initial years of the creation of the militia, and in the 1840s a uniform legal organization was introduced for the militias in all provinces. Moreover, notwithstanding these provincial variations, the basic legal format was provided by the political center. At no time, not even during the period of extreme decentralization, did the bureaucratic authorities at the Court waive the right to appoint men of their own choosing to the higher ranks and posts of the provincial militias.

Therefore the following sketch is descriptive of the organization as a whole, regardless of local variations. The peculiar form that the *Guarda Nacional* took in Rio Grande do Sul will be discussed in a later chapter.

First, for what purpose was the *Guarda Nacional* created? The manifest goal set down in the opening article of the law that created it was "in order to defend the Constitution, Freedom, Independence and Integrity of the Empire; to maintain the obedience to laws, preserve or restore order and public peace; and to assist the regular Army in the defense of frontiers and coastline."[11] The immediate political circumstances were marked by two events. First, the authoritarian rule of Pedro I had just been replaced by a national Regency. This was the beginning of a new administrative experiment open to structural innovations (which was, incidentally, badly needed, given the lack of adequate instruments of government). Second, the political atmosphere was fraught with a general sentiment of malaise and apprehension arising from the ominous possibility of restorationist countermovements. The municipal *camara* of São Paulo had in the preceding year taken the initiative to suggest to the Assembly the creation of a national guard. In March 1831, São Paulo had sent its senator at the Court a request to submit such a measure, with the intention of "preserving the Constitution against the insidious plots or coups of any liberticide faction that might perchance still show forth."[12] The land was by no means pacified after the political upheavals; the state was not completely confident in its own authority; provincialism and separatism were still vigorous sentiments; and the royal army was made up of Portuguese officers loyal to the king and the idea of restoration. Mrs. de Castro has stated the situation clearly:

> It was the distrust of an army still identified with Pedro I, of an officialdom still Portuguese born, the loyalty of which was cause for apprehension. Perturbances and insubordination of the troops, together with the strengthening of an absolutist faction, made the measure justifiable.[13]

From the very start, then, the mission of the *Guarda Nacional* was understood to be the institutionalization of the new legal order; it was supposed to lend a powerful hand to the annihilation of any group contesting the new Imperial authorities and their monopoly of legitimate coercion. The state, moreover, showed no reluctance, remission, or timidity in translating these expectations into practice with regard to political aid of the new militias. With astonishing speed the vast land of the Empire was covered with local contingents of the National Guard. Two or three years after its creation, the majority of local districts, no matter how distant, had organized their own local corps.

The law set down with misleading simplicity the kinds of liturgical services it expected from the *Guarda Nacional*— "ordinary service within the country," "detachments outside of the country," and "in-service-corps or companies assigned to lend assistance to the regular Army."[14] In fact, however, the execution of these services represents, without exaggeration, the history of local patrimonial administration in nine-teenth-century Brazil, as will be shown. There is no question that the local administration of police and justice was based on the liturgical services of the militiamen. Their legal sub-ordination to the Imperial magistrates and the legal appara-tus, rather than to the organs of defense, is a clear indication that the intention of the lawmakers was to enlist the corpo-ration of freemen in the process of judicial administration. As the law said, "The *Guardas Nacionaes* will be subordinate to the Justices of the Peace, the Criminal Judges, the Provincial Presidents, and the Minister of Justice."[15]

It is important to note that these liturgies were not simply accidental contributions by certain occupational groups and social classes to the political organization of the land; they were, on the contrary, a planned and regular part of the pro-cess of state-building, on which the state counted for the es-tablishment of an administrative routine. On one occasion in the mining province, some guards of the legion of Ouro Preto requested dispensation from dominical service. The reply of the president of the province did not take long:

> I must inform you . . . that as soon as the Government has available enough force it will stop this onus, which must, in any case, be mitigated by the consideration that in serv-icing the *Guarda Nacional* we protect ourselves and our fam-ilies from the aggression of criminals who will continue to threaten us as long as public order is not regularly main-tained. It is additionally true that a society that offers con-veniences and guarantees is entirely entitled to request rea-sonable sacrifices. That is the reason why in civilized countries nobody complains about being in the National Guard; on the contrary, everybody cooperates willingly."[16]

It is clear that these liturgies were not simply contingent on the availability of governmental forces; the official ideol-ogy expressed above demonstrates that they were expected as a matter of course by the state. They may even have been validly expected from the entire community of freemen through the corporative mediation of the militia. A couple of years later the same province experienced a series of public disturbances and crimes allegedly committed by runaway slaves and military deserters. The local commander of the battalion of the *Guarda Nacional* of the village of Ayuruoca asked to be relieved of his post in a gesture of spite, inspired by the government's delay in satisfying an urgent request for armaments to cope with the disturbances. The government's reply indicates its views on the political role of civil groups:

> I do not deem it sufficient reason to grant you the discharge asked for because of the lack of armament for your Battalion inasmuch as, in situations of danger, every citizen is required to fight for the benefit of society. Now, if slave insurrections are dreadful, with no less fearful and cruel consequences, it is also true that they cannot be disciplined forces, and to put them down and reduce them to obedience, all kinds of arms are appropriate. We are therefore convinced that the local Authorities, invested with the moral force that the laws give them, will find powerful assistance from all Citizens, who in such circumstances will not shun to ready themselves with their own arms for service which concerns us all.[17]

Brazilian historians and social scientists in general have disregarded these liturgies, probably because the *Guarda Nacional* they have in mind is the *Guarda Nacional* of the Old Republic and the last years of the Empire, which in fact did not perform any liturgical services for the state. This organization was a spiritless and emaciated copy of the original, made up, to all intents and purposes, of a set of officers with no sense of mission. But a lack of attention to the administrative contributions of the original organization leads to an incomplete understanding of the patrimonial structure of the modern bureaucratic Brazilian state.

Practical demands and the inability of bureaucratic officials to meet them came to define the major areas of liturgical cooperation of the militiamen. Apart from their important involvement in the war front in the south (to be examined later), these municipal corporations rendered a variety of services to the bureaucratic administration, the most pervasive and constant of which were the daily supply of militiamen, on the requisition of the local judge or police delegate, for the capture of criminals; the transfer of defendants from one town to another or their removal under custody of the judge;

the transportation of public coffers and valuables; and the patrolling and policing of cities as well as the garrisoning of towns and jails. In addition to these routine functions, the services of the *Guarda Nacional* were enlisted for the periodical destruction of *quilombos*, runaway slave settlements, and for the repression of the slave traffic, as well as for more hieratic and pompous circumstances of the Court calendar—religious parades, military reviews, and all sorts of symbolic consumerism. The exact extent to which the history of this corporation is organically and institutionally linked to the administration of local government and the establishment of a legal order now becomes apparent.

The entire liturgical edifice collapsed, however, forty years after its creation. The life blood of the *Guarda Nacional*, as we have just shown, lay chiefly in its patrimonial contribution of services; once these ceased to be exacted from its members, its institutional vigor and presence immediately lessened. Indeed, in 1873, a new law was issued whereby the *Guarda Nacional's* services were restricted to extraordinary cases of external war or domestic rebellion. This law also established that corporate meetings would take place only once a year. As if to make sure that the patient would not recover from its moribund condition, the law drastically reduced the upper age limit for membership from sixty to forty and suspended— horror of horrors—honorific distinctions for members of its officialdom. All its functions were assumed by the police forces. The state was now experienced enough; it had matured sufficiently in the previous decades to entrust all these public duties to a duly bureaucratized structure. Local administration by *honoratiores* was no longer called for. It was too irrational, too unpredictable, too discontinuous, and deceptively cheap for the growing needs of an increasingly complex and bureaucratic state and an increasingly differentiated bourgeois society. The successor to the *Guarda Nacional*, an emaciated structure of officers, then gained acceptance in the collective memory of Brazilian history. The expressive character of the *Ersatz* has regretfully obstructed interest in the nature of the original corporation.

The continuously impoverished patrimonial state could not allow its subjects any exercise of discretion concerning corporate membership. Thus administrative liturgies were obligations imposed on all citizens who had the actual or virtual status of electors. All freemen over eighteen and under sixty, with an income greater than 200 mil-reis in the cities of Rio de Janeiro, Bahia, Recife, and Maranhão, and greater than 100 mil-reis in the rest of the Empire, were eligible for service. The only exceptions were members of the armed forces, justice and police officials entitled to requisition militiamen, personnel of the penitentiary institutions, and religious ministers. Each year a local qualifying council, made up of the winning electors and presided over by the local justice of the peace, drew up a record of enlistment (*lista de matrícula*) of all qualified members of the parish or district. All those who belonged to the reserve force by nature of their exceptional circumstances or occupation were dispensed from service. This affected invalids, and those bureaucrats, students, royal dependents, lawyers, physicians, and pharmacists who so desired. Also freed from active service were people over fifty, representatives of political bodies, magistrates, mailmen, and administrators of rural estates with a slave force of over fifty head or a yearly cattle production of a similar amount. The new law extinguished the old *militias* and *ordenanças*. Its officers could also opt for the reserve.[18]

The regimental organization of the new *Guarda Nacional* was not based simply on the militaristic tradition that the colonial society had bequeathed to the new. Such regimentation could certainly have been facilitated and suggested by Brazil's historical tradition, but the most important factor was the need for collective services that arose in a patrimonial prebureaucratic environment. In the absence of bureaucratic structures, the discipline, motivation, and other requirements necessary for the organization of collective services could not possibly be achieved, except through the establishment of functional equivalents capable of channeling the collective energies into an ordered routine. Thanks to this device, the liturgical mobilization of hundreds of thousands of subjects was routinely organized throughout the Empire for about half a century.

The militiamen were organized into three different branches—infantry, cavalry, and artillery. The artillery played an insignificant role and was concentrated in a few areas on the coast. The basic organizational unit for the infantry and cavalry was the company, which consisted of up to 140 men in the infantry and 100 in the cavalry, under the command of a captain. Districts with less than 60 or 70 militiamen, respectively, had only sections of a company. Four to eight infantry companies (between 240 and 1,120 men) formed an infantry battalion commanded by a lieutenant colonel. Two cavalry companies (between 140 and 200 horsemen) formed a cavalry squadron. A cavalry corps was composed of a minimum of two and a maximum of four squadrons. The largest unit was the legion, for those counties with more than 1,000 militiamen, under the command of a colonel. The different municipal legions belonging to a province were subject to the command of a provincial *comandante superior*, one of the most important figures in the hierarchy.

Local administration by *honoratiores* cannot operate without a profound degree of stratification of life chances and privileges. Without a stratum of notables who can claim monopoly of office thanks to the leisure afforded them by their peculiar style of life, two avenues are open: the creation of a salaried officialdom or the prebendalization of office. The first option, as we have seen elsewhere, began to materialize only toward the middle of the century with the expansion of the bureaucratic apparatus. The second was excluded in so far as the posts of the *Guarda Nacional* were honorary and without remuneration. To become military prebends, the posts would have had to turn into rent-producing functions for the livelihood of the officer. Prebendalization of office was, in consequence, also ruled out. The only solution was avocational administration by local notables.

Originally, however, the democratic principle of election was legally instituted for the selection of the officialdom of the companies, battalions, and cavalry corps. The officialdom of the companies was elected by the troops in assembly, whereas that of the higher formations (battalions and corps) was elected by the officers and subofficers of the lower units. Provincial variations created slight changes in the pattern, but one element was uniform throughout: the top chains of command (legion commanders and provincial commanders) were appointed by the central state.

This elective character did not last long. First the province took this privilege away from the municipalities; then the central state spread its nominating faculties to progressively lower groups of officers. The first steps in this direction were taken five years after the establishment of the law, in a move led by the Province of São Paulo, and followed by Pernambuco, Rio de Janeiro, and Ceará. In five more years the elective principle has practically died out in all the provinces, Minas Gerais being one of the last to keep it. The reorganization of the *Guarda Nacional* in the second organic law of 1850 no longer contained a single instance of elective procedure. With the exception of the company subofficers (who were appointed by the commander of the *corpo*) and the officialdom of the company (which was appointed by the president of the province based on the recommendation of the commander of a higher formation), all officers were appointed by the central state based on recommendations from the appropriate commanders.[19] The elective principle usually runs counter to the selection of military *honoratiores*, in so far as it fosters the selection of individuals by corporate criteria that do not necessarily correspond to the ascribed properties of local notables or to the demands of an avocational leadership. This, rather than an abstract *raison d'état*, was a factor in the spiraling centralization of appointments, as was the incompatibility between the status character of the corporation and the avocational nature of its organization, on the one hand, and the elective principle on the other.

The members of the *Guarda Nacional* had certain additional obligations toward the corporation, other than their obvious services either as officers or as simple militiamen. As a regimented association, the militias wore uniforms as a matter of course. One of the duties of members was to secure these uniforms by their own means. This was only one instance of a general pattern that characterized the behavior of the state with regard to the material needs of the corporation; the tendency was to reduce as far as possible any expenditure of resources. Official policy with regard to the rest of the equipment was indicative of the same attitude; thus, militiamen belonging to cavalry formations were supposed to obtain their horses by their own means—there was no question of provision by the state. Similarly, a policy of self-armament was established, which was waived only when individuals were unable to come by their own equipment and armament, in which case they became responsible for the care and eventual repair of the pieces provided by the corporation. Other factors, to be discussed later, also attest to the considerable success of the bureaucratic-patrimonial state in developing a national system of public institutions, with the active and liturgical cooperation of status groups.

The orderly satisfaction of these liturgies, part of the daily routine of the majority of Brazilian freemen, necessarily led the central state to set down measures for the control of the geographical mobility of its subjects. Two measures were designed to achieve this end. The first was a temporary dispensation from ordinary service, the so-called *licenças de serviço* (service leaves). Requests for such leaves, ordinarily for a period of from three months to a year, were directed to the company commander. The processing of these applications showed excessive centralization of decisions. Once in the commander's hands, he would send an application, along with a favorable or unfavorable opinion, to the *comandante superior*, who would in turn relay it, again with his opinion, to the Ministry of Justice at the Court. The ministerial mandarins would then study the question. On receiving three official reviews from different sections of the Ministry, a dispatch was written with the decision taken by the central bureaucracy. On the basis of this decision, an Imperial decree was then issued granting or rejecting the application. Ordinarily, the request was approved or rejected according to the original opinions forwarded by the corporative authorities, and ordinarily the *comandante superior* would take the opinion of the lower commander. The whole process was, incidentally, surprisingly quick, the granting of leaves taking not more than two weeks.[20]

The second mechanism created to forestall an uncontrolled dislocation of officers from their residences was the legal permit, *guia de mudança* (permission to move), issued by governmental authorities. Such a document was necessary for officers who wished to move from one county to another or to a different province. During the first years the mobility of officers was very limited. Society in general was not exposed to strong currents of interprovincial mobility, probably because of the rather weak degree of modernization of the agrarian economy. Under these circumstances, it was easy to obtain a *guia de mudança*, since the justice of the peace was qualified to issue them. The large degree of decentralization in the approval of such decisions is probably a good indication of the rather infrequent occurrence of this process.[21]

The 1840s, however, brought about profound changes in Brazilian agrarian life, caused by the capitalist development of rural society, the effects of which had significant repercussions in the rates of personal mobility over the following two decades. The flow of requests began to grow steadily, until the state was forced to introduce tighter control over the entire process. This was of course reflected in the promulgation of new laws and decrees designed to establish institutional procedures to protect the liturgical capabilities of the mobile groups. To obtain a *guia de mudança*, the officer of the *Guarda Nacional* had to be in possession of his *patente* (title), which qualified him as an officer who had properly met the formal requirements of his post, namely an oath of fidelity to the state authorities, possession of the corporation uniform, payment of the fee for the expedition of the *patente*, and the like. He had furthermore to possess a *guia de passagem* (permission of transfer), a *guia* which was issued by a provincial dispatch on the request of the commander of his corps. This commander, finally, would have the commander of the official's new place of residence informed of the move.[22]

These *guias* were required throughout the period when the local classes contributed more actively to the process of patrimonial administration, that is, until the middle of the 1870s. Curiously enough, they still appear as a requirement for physical change of residence for officers in the 1880s, although less often than in the previous decades. It is still more surprising, in view of the apparent extinction of any instrumental function on the part of the officialdom of the corporation, to find that even after the end of the Empire (1889) in the Old Republic, there appeared requests for these *guias*.[23]

There is no practical reason to account for the survival of this pattern in a liberal society predicated on the free movement of individuals and politically administered by bureaucratic agencies with no room for dilettante officials. However, the persistence of such a vestige is probably a sign of the formidable degree of institutionalization of a specific pattern of relations between the bureaucratic-patrimonial state and civil groups in the larger society.

We will now examine the actual organization assumed by the *Guarda Nacional* as the major corporative and institutional mediation between the state and social classes, as opposed to its formal organization discussed above. The gap between the ideal pattern and the actual organization is not merely one more illustration of the allegedly inexorable, yet conclusively tormenting pathos that leads from professed values and manifest ends to actual patterns of behavior and unintended consequences. There is more to it than that. In what follows, I will examine the tensions that derived from objective and concrete circumstances. The vicissitudes of the *Guarda Nacional* stemmed not only from the daily struggles of its members to give life to a status association in the midst of a society which, as we have seen, never succeeded in developing a status order, but also from the irrationalities arising from the liturgical enlistment of dilettantes and *honoratiores* to serve the increasingly rational demands of an administrative order.

The history of the *Guarda Nacional* thus unfolded along with the decline of an old order and the consolidation of a new, and with the transition from patrimonial to bureaucratic power. In the meantime, in organic connection with this metamorphosis, a national system of public institutions with a separate set of rules, norms, and values, entirely distinct from those of the household and the private sphere, appeared for the first time. The *Guarda Nacional* was blood and bone of that splendid metamorphosis.

4

The Militias and the Administrative Routine

The Public Funding of the Administration

Enough is too much.

Ascetic Samurai maxim

There is a significant contrast between the scant and simple official directives on the administration of the *Guarda Nacional*, and the variety of administrative practices created by the patrimonial officers in response to actual exigencies, which arose from the creation of a routine for the satisfaction of their liturgical obligations.

The paucity of directives is not of course an indication that the *Guarda Nacional* played a secondary role. This interpretation would be inconsistent with our findings so far, namely, that there was a central state actively involved in the control of its patrimonial officers and also in the mobilization of different branches of the royal bureaucracy for the supervision of such military bodies. The paucity of directives is, rather, an expression of the extent to which the central state entrusted the leadership of the administration of the militarized association to notable members of the dominant strata. This was to be expected in a state thoroughly steeped in a patrimonial tradition. Equally influential in deciding the institutional patterns of behavior of the *Guarda Nacional* was the bureaucratic thrust of the new state and its impact on this corporation.

Out of these antagonistic principles—the status principle behind the patrimonial satisfaction of administrative needs in the form of liturgical services, and the bureaucratic principle behind the state's control of such services—emerged the organizational routine of the *Guarda Nacional*. Consistently with the patrimonial traits we have discussed so far, the *Guarda Nacional* represented a minimal fiscal burden on the state's coffers. Characteristically, the organic laws devoted little attention to the codification of the state's financial responsibility to provide for the needs and the management of the corporation. In law but not necessarily in fact, the central state took on the payment of a few basic items. The list was quite short; it included armament for the militiamen and the appropriate ammunition; harness material for the cavalry corps; and musical instruments for the *corpos* bands (drums, trumpets, and bugles). Additionally, the *corpos* would be supplied with the items necessary for the ordinary discharge of duties—paper for correspondence as well as ledgers for the recording of official acts. Short as this list was, it was nevertheless almost always reduced by private contributions made by the officers, necessitated by the deficiencies of the state's supplies.

The officers' service was honorific; no remuneration was made in compensation for it. Corporate duties were rigorously assumed to be liturgical obligations imposed on freemen. The officers of the royal army, temporarily ascribed to *corpos* of the militia as commanders, chiefs of the general staff, or instructors, were exempt from unpaid service. Occasionally the members of the band were provided with a salary with the obvious proviso for those cases "in which their service cannot be gratuitous."[1] The law of 1831, moreover, did not set any rules with regard to the physical location of the headquarters. It simply assumed, typically by the way, that the private household of the lord would also suffice as the public headquarters of the officer.

As the above facts suggest, the whole *Guarda Nacional* enterprise was viewed as an entirely nonbureaucratic yet collective duty. The essential bureaucratic link between ruler and official, that of a salary representing a means of livelihood for the official and an instrument of subordination for the ruler, was entirely lacking. The administration of the corporation, in consequence, assumed not only the typical avocational form characteristic of patrimonial polities, but also the regimentation necessary to permit the expeditious discharge of obligations on the part of the lower strata of freemen.

All things considered, then, it is not surprising that the place occupied by the *Guarda Nacional* in the system of public expenditure was a permanently minor one, as is indicated in Table 5.

Table 5 gives a clear picture of the insignificant position of the *Guarda Nacional* in the budgetary structure of the central state. An indication of the real value of the above sums

TABLE 5.

Ministry of Justice: Service Expenditure by Fiscal Year, Minas Gerais (1853–1854) and Rio de Janeiro (1856–1857)

Items	Minas Gerais (in mil-reis)	Rio de Janeiro (in mil-reis)
	%	%
Lower-court Judges	7:906 $ (26.39)	44:600 $ (45.20)
Police and Public Peace	2:577 $ (8.61)	1:000 $ (1.01)
Police Personnel	—	8:870 $ (8.99)
Guarda Nacional	945 $ (3.15)	6:000 $ (6.08)
Bishops and Parsons	18:531 $ (61.85)	38:200 $ (38.72)

SOURCES: For Minas Gerais, AN, IJ¹ 620, ms. *Exercicio de 1853 a 1854: Balancete da despesa feita pela Thesouraria da Fasenda da Provincia de Minas Gerais por conta do Ministerio da Justiça em o 3me, de Abril a Junho de 1854.* For Rio de Janeiro, BPER [*Guarda Nacional: avisos diversos:* 1856], ms., *Quantias distribuidas a Provincia do Rio de Janeiro para o serviço do Ministerio da Justiča no Exercicio de 1856–57,* Secretaria de Estado dos Negocios da Justiça, 3.03.1856.

For a similar budgetary structure for the province of Bahia in 1833, see AN, IJ¹ 620; and for 1842, IJ¹ 400.

may be obtained when we consider that the six *contos* (one thousand mil-reis) spent in the Province of Rio de Janeiro for the *Guarda Nacional* were the equivalent of the purchase cost of half a dozen slaves. Officially, such general expenditure as there was was met by the Ministry of Justice, while the Ministry of War supplied equipment and ammunition. Thus, military supplies and the budget allotted by the Ministry of Justice were the only sources from which corporate material wants could be satisfied. In fact, as we shall see, the material wants of the *Guarda Nacional* were largely satisfied by military *honoratiores*.

The gradual bureaucratization of the state should have increased state expenditure on the *Guarda Nacional*. But in fact the reverse was true. In 1861, less spending on the *Guarda Nacional* was urged on the provincial presidents, who were exhorted to "reduce as much as possible the annual costs incurred by the offices of the different higher commands and corps of the *Guarda Nacional*."[2] Although in the 1850s commanders in the provincial capitals, at the Court, and at the frontiers received remuneration, in the 1870s only the *comandantes superiores* of the Rio Grande and Pernambuco areas and at the Court were paid at all! Thus, items formerly included in the budget were struck out, accompanying a general shrinkage of expenses. The salary received by the secretary of the *Guarda Nacional* at the Court was reduced by half between 1874 and 1875. Other measures were taken along these lines. Moreover, the mandarins of the central bureaucracy were of the official opinion that the remunerations discussed above should be abolished, arguing that they could no longer be justified.[3]

There is no doubt that the central state considered the defrayal of the administrative cost of the *Guarda Nacional* a liturgical collective liability to be imposed on freemen and independent members of the community. Under these circumstances, only an economically dominant stratum of notables was in a position to cope with the material and administrative needs of the militia. Only in a society marked by the vigorous presence, if not the institutionalization, of what may succinctly be called the "status principle," could such liabilities be met with a maximum of spontaneity and voluntary cooperation. In their absence, some form of regimentation was needed.

The Private Basis of the Administration

Whereas the political development of liberal democracies in Europe meant the continuous disaggregation of old solidarities,[4] nineteenth-century Brazil developed the other way around—through the aggregation of ever-expanding solidarities, until a national level was reached. Thus, the process of state-building did not eliminate local power, but stripped it of its legitimate use of coercion. The dominant agrarian strata, in this context, played a decisive role in the composition of the new bureaucratic state and its new administrative order.

Patrimonial forms of local government were resorted to largely because of the immense obstacles confronting the establishment of a state bureaucracy, resulting from the dire pecuniary conditions at the Court. The complaint is frequently heard that the state simply could not pay its officials and public servants. Although monotonous, persistent requests arrived at the court from all corners of the land asking for duly instituted officials to replace the avocational administrators, whose lack of legal training and ignorance of the law made difficult the institutionalization of orderly procedures, and who occasionally lived at distances beyond the immediate locality, and although there were also complaints about the total absence of magistrates, about the lack of, or the insecure condition of, jails, and about the absence of public peace and personal security,[5] there was little hope of the state being able to meet these demands for *more* salaried officials, considering that it could barely pay the ones it had.

At times, the salaries were so meager it is not at all surprising that "there is nobody willing to accept the offices of prosecutors in those counties, the upshot being a great inconvenience for the administration of justice, namely, the latter's [the county] remaining without those officials, as is the case in Chique-Chique."[6]

The calamitous state of the Royal Exchequer led to pathetic situations that dramatized the weak foundations of the state's bureaucratic apparatus and the obstacles to the creation of a political order. In 1843, the court judge of Barbacena in Minas Gerais reported to the president of the province on the need to withdraw a police detachment from the locality. It so happened that, not having been paid their wages, "many privates were degraded to the point of roaming to beg for alms, which fact, together with the state of drunkenness in which they usually find themselves, has led the authorities and the people at large to withdraw all their support from the detachment."[7] The state's habitual inability to meet its fiscal responsibility toward troops and detachments was, after all, no novelty.

It would be inadequate, however, to believe that this inability to pay salaries was restricted to police and military officials or agents. In fact, the entire notion of a salaried officialdom was at stake, in so far as the other branches of government also could not escape the pauperism of the state. As a result, objective conditions were created that fostered the existing patrimonialization of local government. The daily reenactment of such a pattern was a matter of course, as was the irrational particularism, the frequency of *ad hoc* decisions, the terse pragmatism, and the typical lack of distinction between household and office revealed in the official request submitted by the President of Bahia to the Ministry of Justice, for a reimbursement of 800 mil-reis to be paid to the chief of police of the province,

> on account of the excessive work performed by the Chief of Police of this Province in the exercise of his job, the high price of food, and the expenses he will have to defray at his own risk in his eventual but necessary visits to some districts or major counties . . . and due to the inexistence, in this city [the capital], of an unoccupied house that may be exclusively devoted to the official work of the Police, as laid down in article number ten of the Regulation, the above said Chief of Police established his office in the first floor of the house in which he dwells.[8]

Thus a precariously salaried officialdom, conspicuous structural forces conducive to the continuity of patrimonialism, and a diffuse and pervasive but nonetheless active and penetrating official ideology of communal mobilization for the erection of a political order were the basic aspects of the institutional structure of Brazilian society in the last century. It is against this background that the liturgical liabilities of the military *honoratiores* of the *Guarda Nacional* stand out clearly. The private bases of the administration were so vast, indeed, that the only way to save the public nature of the administration was to allow it to be cast in a patrimonial mold.[9]

The militiamen provided the state with two general classes of private cooperation. The first was material assistance in kind, including arms and equipment, band instruments, uniforms, horses, cattle, clerical office material, locational facilities, and monetary resources (money gifts, remissions of salary, etc.). This type of cooperation was provided mostly by the officer stratum. The second was time, used in the implementation of institutional functions such as those of police, justice, and war, as well as in the daily management of the companies, *corpos*, batallions, squadrons, and legions.

The provincial archives abound in documentation revealing the numerous and generalized private contributions of the militiamen to the *Guarda Nacional*. The most common form of this type of private cooperation was the officers'—particularly the company commanders'—provision of uniforms, and occasionally of military equipment such as swords, to those militiamen without sufficient means to equip themselves. A particular practice that gained wide popularity was the officers' or commanders' collective defrayal of the cost of the uniforms and musical instruments for the members of the band. Originally they contributed monthly quotas for the maintenance of the band. After the relative democratization of the officialdom brought about by the election of officers by the rank and file, together with the increasing cost of these items, the officers frequently did not possess the means to pay for them and so stopped doing so. A new practice was then inaugurated in the mid-1830s; those guards willing to be excused from weekly or monthly service—and they were many—paid a small monthly contribution (ten mil-reis) for the maintenance of the band of their *corpos*. This practice took firm root in the corporate routine, and became popular in all provinces throughout the Imperial period. It proved so successful that the state took the opportunity to put an end to its official commitment to remunerate members of the band. When the appointment of officials began in the 1840s, officers once again started making their own contributions. The rank and file who wished for exemption from service were able to continue making their personal contributions. [10]

There were other, more irregular, forms of private contribution. Thus, it was not infrequent for the militiamen to assume the repair costs of equipment delivered by the royal magazine in poor condition. [11] Even groups of guards on detachment missions were occasionally paid by private financing, although it is true that this extreme privatization of financial responsibilities took place chiefly in critical circumstances. In one case, the residents of Parahiba do Sul in the Province of Rio de Janeiro financed, through public subscriptions, a contingent of guards to be sent out to stem the approach of rebels coming from the neighboring province of Minas Gerais. [12] Whenever danger was more permanently at hand, as was the case on the southern frontier, the private association of neighbors would assume a more lasting existence. After aggression suffered by some Brazilians on the border with Paraguay, a group of notables of the frontier city of Uruguayana formally asked permission from the local commander to create

> a defense corps . . . which will not represent a burden to the public coffers because it is merely preventive, and because it will consist of men who are all locally established. . . . Moreover, as the necessary armament is not at hand, permission is also asked for each one to have it brought from Buenos Aires. [13]

The local commanders' satisfaction of some of the *Guarda Nacional's* material wants was, on the other hand, the *Leitmotiv* of daily administration throughout the Imperial era. Typical routine arrangements were the encampment of each company on the *fazenda* or in the *cercado* (yard of the house) of its commander, [14] the official use of the private residence of the commander, and his supplying of office material.

It is indicative of the state's patrimonial definition of these services that there was no budgetary program to cover satisfactorily expenses arising from the daily management of the corporation. It is even more striking to see this pattern operating at the very center of the Empire; given the overwhelming amount of office work involved in the command of twelve *corpos*, and given that the position of the general secretary of the *Guarda Nacional* at the Court was unpaid, the higher commander suggested to the central bureaucracy the *ad hoc* solution that he should be assigned the salary of a general instructor, a remunerated position.[15] Needless to say, within this context any administrative initiative had to be liturgically financed. The higher commander of the *Guarda Nacional* of the provincial capital of Rio Grande do Sul was well aware, for instance, that the most effective way for an order to reach officers scattered throughout the province was through a notice in the local press, to be paid, however, "at the expense of the remuneration of this Higher Command."[16]

Finally, private cooperation of these military *honoratiores* was also indispensable from a financial perspective, particularly during the first half of the century, when the state had not yet institutionalized the practice of anticipating the budgeted money to be spent subsequently by its agencies. This procedure was not widespread until the end of the 1850s; before that the Imperial authorities would advance the money provided that the commander presented a cosigner who would be responsible for its proper expenditure. But during the previous generation, the commanders had personally defrayed contingent costs—harness, provisions, etc.—which were then acknowledged later by the fiscal authorities on the presentation of duly constituted validations and receipts. The state's payment of these bills often became a matter of mortification for the commander, in so far as the authorities called for a degree of accountability hardly considered necessary in a local culture incipiently dominated by market rationality, and suffused with the status notion of personal honor as a basis for impersonal credit.[17]

By such means as these the military *honoratiores* coped with the material needs of organization, not only in those areas where the Imperial state fell short of its own officially assumed responsibilities, but also in other areas that proved, in the practical and daily routine of the corporation, equally indispensable to its functional continuity. It is hard to ignore the magnitude of such an enterprise, particularly when one considers that, besides the materials and money liturgically provided, large amounts of time also had to be donated for the corporation to operate as a going concern. We have already seen that the *honoratiores* belonged to the only group that had enough spare time to fulfill unremunerated functions.

We have seen that the intense regimentation of the Brazilian free people secured the performance of collective duties by the laboring classes of freemen. From this point of view, their inadequate performance of these duties was a judgement on the inadequacy of the regimentation and of the patrimonial structure designed to attain regimentation. Liturgical duties were extracted from the stratum of notables who made up the officers' groups essentially by the establishment of a status project to entice the landlord to cooperate with the corporate mission. There were chronic imcompatibilities between the military *honoratior's* own material needs and the avocational needs of the corporation, which reveal the growing contradictions between such a status project and the market principle determining the level of material success of an officer.

We must now address our attention to those social factors that had some bearing on the fate of such a "seigneurial" project. As I have suggested, the success of the *Guarda Nacional* as an instrumental agency was to a very large extent based on the existence of a stratum of *senhores* able to devote their energies to avocational duties.

The "Seigneurial" Project

> I am a wise fellow; and, which is more, an officer; and, which is more, a householder; and, which is more, as pretty a piece of flesh as any is in Messina: and one that knows the law, go to; and a rich fellow enough, go to; and a fellow that hath had losses; and one that hath two gowns, and everything handsome about him.
>
> Shakespeare, *Much Ado About Nothing*, Act iv, scene ii

In Chapter 1, I examined some historical and structural factors that obstructed the path to a Brazilian "seigneurial" project. Until the birth of the *Guarda Nacional*, no such project had been possible; the appearance of this body introduced for the first time the conditions that *could have* made such a project viable, although in fact, for reasons I will examine, this possibility was not fulfilled.

There is a tendency to associate organically patrimonial or, more generally, traditional social formations with the presence of a status group of lords in Brazil. Thus, Fernando Henrique Cardoso, in a brilliant piece of historical analysis of the agrarian society of southern Brazil, presents the agrarian foundations of patrimonialism and observes:

> The military, the *gaúchos*, in short, obtained grants of land as a benefice distributed by the commanders, governors and captain-generals on behalf of the Crown to explore them and use them for their own benefit and in the royal interest, availing themselves of the only means to keep the latifundium: the exploitation of the available labor force, that is, that of the dispossessed and of the enslaved. Since the eighteenth century, *therefore*, it was established with the assistance of the great estates what was inevitable in terms of the conditions of the organization of power and work then possible: *a society organized in status groups*.[18]

Later he remarks that the meaning he attributes to the term "lord" does not include, as in the specialized literature, the existence of manorial rights. He prefers to apply the term to a more general "social type of head of household and slaveowner who exerted decisive influence in the Brazilian society."[19]

It is apparent that this approach leads to a blurring of the analytically useful distinction between a status group of lords and a stratum of lords. A status group of lords is, strictly speaking, a communal association of notables with a peculiar social honor and a transparent consciousness of genteel and culturally privileged forms of action that sets the group apart from the surrounding community, which in its turn has some kind of traditionally defined service obligations toward the status group. A stratum of lords, on the other hand, is simply an abstract aggregate of lords; this notion does not imply any obligations that have been materialized with the help of tradition into a constellation of collective rights and obligations and, more generally, into a status order. In Brazil a stratum of lords, but not a status group of lords, developed.

It would be incorrect to suggest the presence of such a status order in nineteenth-century Brazil, but this does not of course mean that some social forces were not striving to build such an order. The state for one took measures that, however incipient, represented a first step toward the materialization of a status structure, in that it legally ascribed some differential privileges and obligations to certain classes of Brazilian society. The *Guarda Nacional*, moreover, represented a military attempt to order civil obligations on the basis of status. Finally, there is no question that individual landlords occasionally contemplated personal projects of seigneurial stylization, as Maria Sylvia Carvalho Franco has observed. However, a status order in which the political, economic, and other social obligations and rights were defined by the individual's corporate status did not materialize in Brazilian agrarian society.

Consequently, I will use here the abstract notion of a stratum of lords that does not predicate the presence of a status order. This distinction is not superficial or scholastic; the existence of such an order was the precondition for the smooth running of a local administration by militarized *honoratiores*. Without it, a genuinely avocational and liturgical corporation of dilettantes was not possible under prebureaucratic circumstances.

The state made some attempts to bring the *Guarda Nacional* as close as possible to a status corporation. First, it restricted membership to those who enjoyed the political status of freemen. Slaves were excluded. Second, the state limited membership to an approximate equivalent of the category of freemen traditionally known as "the people" in Anglo-Saxon liberalism, that is, those freemen who enjoyed some degree of economic independence and who had obtained the franchise for the autonomous exercise of political rights. Thus a potentially open and universal association of freemen was transformed into a closed and selective corporation of electors and would-be electors. Third, official steps were taken to stereotype and stratify access to the higher ranks of the corporation, so that the corporate hierarchy could reproduce the social hierarchy of the groups and classes of society as a whole. As noted previously, the income required to become an officer was double that required to become a simple militiaman.

The compound effect of these decisions was to have an inevitable consequence in the development of a hierarchical status orientation within the corporation. To strengthen it further the state devised additional measures, the spirit of which was to invest the corporation with social honor. Some measures were merely decorative, such as the precedence of the *Guarda Nacional* over the professional army in public parades and ceremonies, while other measures had the same results, like the *aviso* of December 16, 1854, which granted officers of the *Guarda Nacional* the same honors enjoyed by those of the first generation with regard to cadetship privileges for their sons. The state, moreover, was rather generous with the granting of honorific distinctions to officers for services rendered, particularly with respect to military commendations and titles of nobility. Finally, other measures were intended to establish legal privileges for some groups of notables, such as the exemption from ordinary service of landlords who were owners of a predetermined number of cattle.

In short, not only was the working of the *Guarda Nacional* dependent on the stable distribution of social opportunities; the state also tried to foster it and endow it with appropriate symbols and collective images, on the correct assumption that the "idealization" of performance and the emphasis on ceremony was a significant force for *Vergemeinschaftung* and the institutionalization of expressive values. The state, in fact, was very alert to any attempt at professionalization of the corporation, not only because of the professional limitations inherent in it, but also because of the state's own fiscal restrictions. It tried systematically to set the militia apart from the professional army through restrictions against the induction of its own men as militia officers and other measures.[20]

In summary, it is possible to see an official initiative pushing for the relative aristocratization of the patrimonial corporation. Besides the external forces discussed above working in that direction, there were other internal factors that favored such a seigneurialization. It could be suggested that the *Guarda Nacional* in some way made up for the deleterious effects that slavery had had on the development of an aristocratic culture among landlords and *honoratiores*. Slavery indeed deprived the Brazilian lords of a manorial context of domination, in that it preempted the organization of a division of labor wherein *work* would have become the means of daily affirmation and institutionalization of a system of subordination to a lord. In *The Phenomenology of Mind*, Hegel shows the crucial importance of work for the development and maintenance of the self-consciousness of lordship and bondage; the subordinate develops his mode of consciousness vis-à-vis his superior by means of his service experience. Both get their respective identity and recognition through the mediation of service.[21] If the notion of validity or legitimacy is brought into this phenomenological canvas, it is possible to turn it into a sociological one. It is possible, in brief, to distinguish between master and lord. The slave has a master; he never spontaneously accepts his enslaved condition as part of his humanity; he only accepts his condition by physical force and repression. A different order of things occurs when work is organized and divided on the basis of tradition or habituation, not force; then the oppressive master may become the benevolent lord. Habitual service daily reenacts the validity of the structure of authority. These favorable conditions did not, generally speaking, materialize in agrarian Brazil. The landlord no doubt had service from dependents who were not slaves, but freemen, as discussed in Chapter 1. But these were rather marginal in terms of the labor cosmos of the rural estate, which was essentially operated by slaves.

The appearance of the *Guarda Nacional* created the possibility of modifying these conditions on a large scale. For the first time, the possibility existed that vast numbers of freemen would be subjected to a service discipline that could allow the relationship of subordination and authority between the landlords and the people to develop, in an area that could not possibly be filled with slaves and that had not yet been preempted by royal officials and bureaucrats. Yet, such a development did not take place. The *Guarda Nacional* could not build the necessary discipline because, among other things, it lacked any genuinely effective means to carry it through. It is possible, all the same, to reconstruct the history of this militia in terms of a series of frustrated attempts at aristocratization.

The *Guarda Nacional* possessed such a sense of status and corporate spirit that from the start it demanded a privilege reminiscent of the Iberian *foro* (the right of being judged by one's peers), to which it considered itself entitled.[22] Also— more significantly—privilege was thought to be the exclusive prerogative of the avocational public servants.[23] The officers also tried to extend their immunity and preferential treatment as much as possible, which was only to be expected. For example, one local commander asked the chief of police to release an ensign imprisoned for the falsification of commercial documents. The commander complained that, in the first place, the defendant had not been removed from his corporate status, in the second, that the sentence had not been proffered, and in the third, that his place of detention ought to be in a military garrison.[24]

Such practices as these strengthened the image of the corporation as a status community of notables, and this image was bolstered by the growing tradition of civic morality and honorability expected of its members. Thus, though immunities were reserved for the officers, civic virtues were expected of all ranks. Perhaps Antonio Jose's "bad character and depraved habits" would have been less irritating, and he might not have caused an "unprecedented scandal" by living with the wife of another man, had he not been a militiaman. In any case, because he was a militiaman, he could not get away with such conduct, and he received a stern "exemplary" punishment and was expelled from the corporation, to which he was now nothing more than a source of "dishonor and opprobrium."[25]

In certain respects, however, the standards of good conduct and decorum were higher for officers. The resulting stylization of conduct reflected the values of a hierarchical agrarian culture. But there were also functional exigencies that fostered this orientation: for example, avocational leadership depended on status to be effective. Thus, authority rested on private rank, given the lack of an institutionalized status order. The bases of authoritative leadership were social:

> Just for the good of the service, I must frankly tell Your Excellency that all my efforts will prove useless, and that the Battalion will never obtain the degree of order and discipline which is now wanting for the attainment of its legal purposes, unless the appointment of Officers proceed with the keeping very much in mind of the fact that, they deserve, by virtue of their private status, the same consideration and respect within the service as without.[26]

There is here a transparent awareness of the social bases of authoritative leadership.

Besides, in general terms, the state did not have the capacity to establish an extensive network of repressive agencies, which it needed to make good its legal threats of punishment against recalcitrant members who were unwilling to cooperate liturgically, or who did not show adequate discipline within the association.[27] This led some commanders not only to realize—correctly—that efficient leadership was very much linked to authority and status, but also to propose even more stringent and elitist criteria for corporate membership. Behind these measures lay the hope that "status conventions" could make operative what "legal injunctions" could not, although in fact these "status conventions" did not come to pass.

The cavalry units presented a good opportunity to act out the idea of the genteel officer. Given the need for self-armament, membership in cavalry units was obviously predicated on the aspirant's possession of a personal income large enough to pay for a horse, its harness and its upkeep. Although not in itself a very costly matter, it was sufficiently so to discourage the less privileged militiamen from this course of action. Thus this restriction sometimes led to a marked degree of stratification according to branches, a phenomenon that strengthened status orientations. As a result, stratification, which tended on the whole to be created by the economic differences among the militiamen, was further reinforced by the status qualifications allowed by that very stratification.

Occupation was a crucial element in defining the applicant's chances of acceptance as an officer, regardless of his pecuniary conditions. As a rule, artisans and petty merchants were excluded. A local fisherman who had managed to become a company lieutenant, even though he had a reasonable means of livelihood and a shop in the market place, was considered for demotion on account of his selling fish; he was not considered to behave with the honor appropriate to an officer. Not even a good service record, complemented by talent and camaraderie, would do; notwithstanding a certain lieutenant tailor's honesty and probity, his intelligence and zeal in service—commented the commander on the man's request for reincorporation—his request had to be rejected because of the "lack of an establishment appropriate to an officer of the *Guarda Nacional.*"[28]

The line dividing honor and opprobrium was sometimes flexible, at certain moments stressing the wealth of the individual rather than the stigma of his occupation, as is exemplified in the case of the coachman who in his first unsuccessful application tactlessly made the mistake of emphasizing his occupation rather than his "abundant fortune." This he prudently rectified in his second request, upon which his business was no longer considered "indecorous."[29] As one commander put it, trustworthiness alone was not sufficient; "it is necessary that together with it [the militiamen] have the means to defray the indispensable expenditures of a cavalry man."[30]

This stratifying practice had unforeseen but rather obvious consequences. It became characteristic, for instance, that although the cavalry units displayed an acceptable degree of self-sufficiency and its members wore uniform, the infantry and artillery units tended to have slipshod discipline, had no instructors, and only their officers wore uniform. Occasionally, the consequences were more serious for the functional purposes of the corporation; the entire stratum of notables, "all the individuals notable for their talent and wealth," of the district of Macaé enrolled in the cavalry, "which made it impossible to proceed with the election of infantry officers, as the Guards could not find citizens of trust who were enrolled in that branch and for whom they could have voted."[31]

These attempts at aristocratization and status formation were not exclusive to the cavalry officers, nor were they limited to the first generation of officers. There were, of course, regional differences that will be introduced in another section but, on the whole this pattern tended to reach the other two branches of the *Guarda*, as well as the subsequent generation toward the mid-century, even in cases where the criterion for promotion to officership was officially declared to be seniority. Thus the officer corps of the artillery battalion at the Court in 1858 was outraged by the appointment to the rank of lieutenant of a militiaman and a sergeant who did not have the appropriate status qualifications. Five years later, an artillery lieutenant was recommended for transfer to the reserve, or for discharge, "in view of his unquestioned inability to remain in the milieu adequate to his status, and his absolute lack of means, which even deprives him of the satisfaction of his [corporate] pecuniary commitments."[32]

The last area that indicates a basic drive toward the formation of a status corporation was that of promotion to the officer level—as opposed to admission thereinto. Promotion was, as a rule, based on a variety of factors and conditioned by varying criteria, according to place and time. Political patronage, for instance, was decisive at some moments, and so were, as we have stressed, personal status, economic position, and local authority. Other determining factors were based on the material organization of life as well as on historical accidents that influenced certain provincial cultures. Some of these factors will be discussed in a later chapter. Here we will simply stress that behind the complex and particular variations by branch, by province, by epoch, by local economic organization, and so on, it is possible to detect a few occasions on which the status principle was revealed in the policies of promotion.

One such occasion, characteristically, attended the organization or reorganization of the militia units. At such times the corporate ideology was more concerned with preserving status qualifications for admission and promotion. This was the case during the first generation of officers, and again just after the reorganization of the corporation at mid-century. As a rule, the corporation qualified the process of promotion by status criteria on two occasions: when militiamen passed from the rank and file to the officer level, and when officers were promoted to a post of command. Particularly in instances such as these, the trend toward a status orientation of the militarized *honoratiores* became acute.

Traditional standards and stereotypes came, as might be expected, to reinforce such a trend. A personal record of command was an evident source of legitimate claim to the continuity of authority, not because daily practice had provided a familiar and thorough knowledge of the corporation and the experience of leadership, but simply because of the ingrained expectations held by the associated members. Thus a commander of a cavalry corps who had served for many years, but actively only *pro forma*,

> is in the position to be appointed Lieutenant Colonel; he was the founder of the Corps and always has commanded, and it will be a great handicap and even [a reason for] demoralization for the very Corps as well as [a reason for] dislike among the officership, should the appointment fall perchance upon any other citizen.[33]

Inchoate forms of prebendalization of military office emerged when the objective factors leading to admission and promotion were sufficiently stereotyped. Thus, in the second half of the century, the sons of the first generation of militarized *honoratiores* acquired a *de facto* opportunity of access to the officer level. This trend toward prebendalization, incidentally, helps make sense of an otherwise extemporaneous and surprising corporate decision of the 1860s to take the parental status of the candidate into consideration.[34] Thus, being the son of an officer was a relevant piece of information for matters of access; significantly, those who could not qualify by virtue of the militarized status of their parents had, alternatively, to include the parental status. There were also significant differences in necessary qualifications based on parental status, so that these criteria were restricted in large measure to the rank and file, the officer level being screened with the help of other social properties. (See Table 6.)

Table 6 shows that, in the absence of a family tradition of military service, genteel birth tended to be instituted as a qualification for corporate status. Genteel birth was not, of itself, sufficient qualification, nor was it even a necessary one. Neither was genteel status restricted to civil candidates. The above tendencies were simply established trends that did not form part of a normative set of procedures. There is one further aspect that deserves mention: the indication of genteel birth and economic status, as one might expect, occurred with much more frequency in proposals for promotion from militiaman to ensign, than in proposals for promotion to other higher ranks. It is nonetheless valid that, other conditions being equal, genteel status was more necessary for civil candidates than for militiamen, and more necessary for militiamen than for officers. This pattern reveals and makes plausible the proposition that genteel birth was not merely an indicative attribute such as height and weight, but a classificatory mark of virtual social honor.[35]

With the affirmation of these trends and a relative secularization forced on the corporation by the larger changes taking place in society, status qualifications based on wealth tended to be required as exceptions in those short-circuiting

TABLE 6.

Parental Status as a Function of Corporate Status: Province of Rio de Janeiro, 1870

		Corporate Status	
		Officer	*Rank and file*
Parental Status	Supplied	0	11
	Not supplied	20	0

SOURCE: BPER, [*Guarda Nacional:* Magé e Estrela: 1870], Official proposal for corporate appointment from cs to pp on February 11, 1870, and official proposal from the same to the same on March 28, 1870, the former being for the reserve and the latter for ordinary service.

cases of promotion from the rank and file to posts of command. Moreover, at times there appeared to be a tension between the ascriptive principles of admission and the performance principle for promotion. On the whole, as we have suggested above, neither worked by itself. Their varying combination, however, was not haphazard, but obeyed patterns that I have summarily reconstructed. In a very general and schematic way, it could be stated that the *Guarda Nacional* worked much in the same way as systems of education do, with one principle of admission heavily based on social rank and status, and a parallel one for promotion dependent on other factors—zeal, performance, seniority, talent, and the like.

It would nonetheless be wrong to assume that the *Guarda Nacional*, once constituted, was so encapsulated within itself that it could have ever managed to develop to the full such a parallel system of role allocation. We have sufficiently stressed the strength of those forces pushing the militias toward a status group association despite the nonexistence of a comprehensive status order; such a constellation of forces was obviously an obstacle to their rational bureaucratic organization. It now becomes necessary to identify those forces that kept the militias from achieving their ideal of a genteel stylization of social life, embodied in the culture of a militarized group of landlords. This constellation of forces stood in the way of a genuine liturgical organization of the patrimonial state. In order to identify them, it is necessary to examine the demise of the seigneurial project.

5

Corporate Routine
and Corporate Project

The Obduracy of Actuality

> One criticizes a person, a book, most sharply when one pictures
> their ideal.
>
> Nietzsche, *Mixed Opinions and Maxims*, 157

I now propose to examine in the light of the breaking-up
of the patrimonial corporation of *honoratiores*, the solvent effects of the forces we have discussed so far, and certain other
forces, on aristocratic values and ideals.

Of course, various factors adversely affected the satisfactory organization of the militias as an instrument of patrimonial administration. Some of these factors were "external"
to the corporation, and were to be found in the larger society,
such as the lack of a valid tradition, limited resources, provincial historical differences, and the like. Others were "internal," and arose from unresolved tensions and antagonisms between the amount of available resources and the
scope of institutional objectives, between the material needs
and interests of the militiamen and the organizational interests of the corporation, and between the immanent pressures
for corporate professionalization and the transcendental values of militarized dilettantism. Analysis artificially separates
these factors, although they belong organically together; inevitably, the discussion that follows will reduce to an abstract

and analytically manageable opposition a problem that was in fact Medusa-like in its complexity.

One of the chronic difficulties faced by the militias was how to find a way to carry out their liturgical services in spite of severe deficiencies of essential supplies and equipment. At times the insufficiency was so great that one wonders whether the role of the corporation, rather than to manifestly assist the magistracy and the police, was not to latently socialize the citizenry into public institutions and institutional patterns, the dearth of which was so notorious in the agrarian society of the time. This problem was common to all the provinces, with the relative exception of the frontier province of Rio Grande do Sul, which for obvious reasons of defence received periodical supplies of adequate armaments from the state arsenals. This inadequacy of supplies plagued the organization of the militia units during both halves of the century.

Officially supplied armaments—such as there were—did not necessarily imply adequate levels of equipment. In the first place, whenever such supplies were available, they were almost always insufficient for the number of militiamen needing to be equipped. At times they hardly satisfied the requirements of the central areas. At the end of the 1840s, to give an example, the higher authority of the Province of Bahia requested permission from the central bureaucracy at the Court "to buy more armaments [he had just bought five hundred pieces of artillery] with which I may at least equip the *corpos* of the Capital." In the second place, the quality of the armaments was also inadequate. For several decades, the units of the *Guarda Nacional* were supplied with old equipment that had belonged to the extinct *corpos de milicias* and *ordenanças*. This equipment, retrieved from veterans of the old militias and stored in the royal magazines, was distributed among the *corpos* with a spirit of economy totally inappropriate to the ruined condition of the arms. The militiaman was as likely to obtain a damaged piece as he was a working one. Repair and maintenance, as I have observed elsewhere, were his responsibility.

In these circumstances, then, it is not surprising that whenever there was no landlord commander in the vicinity to cater to the proper equipping of his subordinates, they simply had to do their patrolling and other official duties armed with rustic sticks and clubs, "which besides being useless, is indecorous." Not infrequently, the sight of these uniformed but grotesquely armed patrimonial servants was a source of public ridicule that had a negative effect on their willingness to continue in service. The following official letter, sent to the Ministry of Justice by a colonel who was chief of a legion in the Province of Rio de Janeiro, is typical of thousands of letters of the same kind:

> I request Your Excellency to grant me the Grace and authority to send the Armament and Horse Equipment received from the defunct second line to the War Arsenal for repair. These arms are not functional, and the Guards do not want to accept them in such condition. This has been the cause of noncompliance with requisitions made by the Justices of the Peace for troops. The Iguassu Battalion has not one single weapon that will do for service; the same has occurred with the Companies of Mirity and Pilar; the Magé Battalion and the Itaguahy *Corpo* have very few serviceable weapons. Though I have to supply Guards for the Jails of the Counties of the Legion, Detachments for the Fiscal Posts, and Contingents for the errands of the Justices of the Peace, it is not possible to perform these services with damaged Armament.[1]

Along with this problem appeared another, the effects of which were equally disturbing to satisfactory organization, namely, the insufficiency of military training for the militiamen. Two reasons contributed to make this problem a chronic one. In the first place, the vast distances between the different companies assigned to a single instructor were frequently a severe obstacle to regular and effective training of an agrarian population that had little familiarity with swords and firearms, and little knowledge of military discipline and organization. In the second place, there was a tremendous lack of qualified instructors. The problem proved more or less endemic, with local variations. It was particularly acute during the early years of the organization, but it persisted up to the time of global reorganization in the 1840s. Avocational instruction by "landlords little experienced in military service, living in more or less outlying areas, busy with their agriculture and business" was hardly adequate or efficient. Commanders often clearly perceived that only majors from the professional army had the necessary knowledge and ability to transform the unarmed and uninstructed *corpos*—those "illusory" units, as one of them put it—into organized structures. For these reasons, it became customary for army majors to occupy posts as instructors.[2]

These two problems, lack of armaments and lack of training, had repercussions on the question of military discipline. Without adequate training, even armed units faced problems of organization and, equally, in the absence of sufficient equipment, training was of little avail. Under these conditions the satisfaction of both needs was extremely difficult. But one other factor affected the satisfactory performance of the liturgy by the militia, namely, the stratification of liturgical service, which, generally speaking, was structured along two lines, as I have indicated elsewhere. The branch of service was one line of stratification. As a rule, the cavalry tended to be composed of the local *honoratiores* and, with the exception of the *gaúcho* formations, it was generally more conspicuous than instrumental. The second line of stratification was leadership; again in broad terms, the posts of command— from captains of local companies upward—were also appropriated by landlords and notables. The presence of a considerable number of state authorities in the cavalry attests to the rather desultory character of this branch of service outside the *gaúcho* context. In fact, not only were there no units of reserve for the cavalry (as though in tacit acknowledgement that its ordinary service was a *de facto* reserve), but there were also proposals that underlined its *aficionado* orientation. Commenting upon the reorganization of the local militias in Minas Gerais, the Ministry of Justice said,

> [The cavalry] is more appropriate to a central province, where there is no threat of external aggression, and no coastline to defend. Moreover, the *Guarda Nacional* is less fit for service which, to be useful, calls for officers with theoretical studies and experienced guards which the *Guarda Nacional* cannot obtain.[3]

The practical effect of this stratification was that the burden of liturgical services fell to the infantry. The cavalry was to a large extent excused from toil and from wear and tear. Needless to say, service liabilities fell primarily on workers, artisans, and petty employees, while the royal bureaucratic rank and file was generally excused from service by a variety of mechanisms. Militia commanders, particularly those of the larger urban centers (the Court and the provincial capitals), were usually sensitive to the inequities brought about by this pattern of service, and often addressed official letters to the state authorities bitterly complaining of such practices. The similarity of reasoning in their expositions is noteworthy; the rich militiaman always managed in one way or another to avoid active duty, so that this fell entirely on the laboring classes. Bureaucratic officials were also excused from service. This, in the militiamen's eyes, was an undesirable practice, as it left actual service entirely in the hands of the working classes, who depended so much on their own labor.

Such liturgical responsibilities were a serious problem for the already meager economies of members of the laboring classes. Some commanders proposed the mobilization of privates from the professional army to replace artisans, small traders, and merchants in militia service. This would have allowed the artisans and traders to maintain their personal incomes without reduction by gratuitous service, and the professional army privates, permanently salaried by the state, could have turned to some account their abundant free time. The state paid no heed to such complaints or suggestions; accustomed as it was to the ideology of the collective mobilization of private resources as a normal expedient to satisfy its public obligations, it continued to place this burden on the shoulders of the poor freemen. Even in the mid-1860s, it was still possible to find official letters essentially similar to those written almost forty years earlier:

> Artisans, laborers, and peasants are among those who have served most often, because it is precisely this class which constitutes the qualified [for ordinary service] *Guarda Nacional*; the majority of the bureaucratic officialdom has been exempted from service by competent authorities. The number of wealthy men who are National Guards [i.e., not officers] is very small.[4]

This inequality in the allocation of service duties soon became a notorious source of disorganization and lack of discipline among both the ranks and the officers. A variety of subterfuges was instituted that called into question the entire notion of liturgical service and that in exceptional cases led to an outright refusal to cooperate. A favorite device was to request a transfer from the infantry to the cavalry. The multitude of requests for transfer to the cavalry cannot be interpreted as attempts to act out personal projects of mobility or as searches for status affirmation. Behind many of these requests there lurked the utilitarian motivation of avoiding bothersome duties. These are the more notorious, as requests for transfer from cavalry to infantry were very unusual.

Not even the lack of a horse stopped a determined militiaman; if need be, he would surreptitiously rent one in the hope of deceiving the commander as to his real economic status. Or he would simply present a *fait accompli* and appear dressed in cavalry uniform, thus making it extremely unreasonable to reject him in view of the expenses already incurred. Another habitual form of evading service, a typical practice particularly among the bureaucracy, was to register for a vocational course in commerce, and thereby qualify for exemption. "It will be no surprise," ironically observed one commander, "if in a little while the registration of students for the different courses at the Lyceum exceeds that of the Battalions of the *Guarda Nacional* of this country." Others would pretend a change in residential district, in which case the enrollment process would have to start anew. Still others, with the connivance of the local justice of the peace, would have themselves appointed as magistrates' assistants, a practice that was a permanent source of conflict between local authorities and patrimonial commanders for many years.

When none of these subterfuges were practiced, there still remained those that were ordinarily available, such as the request for transfer to the reserve service because of illness or other pressing necessity, or the favorite mentioned above, the simple transfer from infantry to cavalry. Both the state and the commanders were trapped in these cases by their own ideology of communal spontaneous service and consensual cooperation as being the best foundation for liturgical liabilities. Conscious, indeed, of the fragile limits of their authority to exact these services from all freemen legitimately, the state and the commanders had no choice but to accept the branch of service expressly preferred by the militiamen. There were very few occasions on which the militiaman's preference was not satisfied, since there was an uneasy awareness that only voluntary service really worked. Euphemistic, yet correct, was one commander's remark that "the best profit is drawn from voluntary service." Another statement synthesized the militiamen's attitudes in the following terms:

> they are persuaded that the law grants them the option [to choose their branch of service], and I think it is convenient to make the best of the services these Citizens are willing to give, as Your Excellency well knows all the means to which they may resort in order to elude orders and legal dispositions, should they perchance be forced against their will.

When and if these subterfuges did not work, outright refusal to cooperate probably followed. Such an opposition could assume individual as well as collective forms. It could apply to both clerical and administrative work inside the militarized unit, as well as to service in the bureaucratic agencies of police and justice. At times the problem was compounded, for example when militiamen refused to accept clerical or administrative work in exchange for dispensation from police or justice service. This could occur among members of the rank and file or at the officer level. Poor discipline was not, in fact, qualified by hierarchical divisions, but one feature was significantly uniform: very rarely was liturgical obligation contested by the patrimonial servant on rational legal grounds. Subjectively, the Brazilian freeman evaded this obligation with the consciousness that in so doing he was violating a traditional and legitimate norm, and that objectively he would only get away with it because of the repressive inefficiency of the state's agencies. This was painfully discovered on more than one occasion by commanders who saw that "the National Guards would rather subject themselves to confinement, the only penalty Your Excellency may impose, than take duty for three consecutive days without salary."

The great variety of subterfuges attests, it could plausibly be argued, to the fact that the means of circumventing the norm signified implicit acceptance of its validity. The few who contested the legitimacy of service itself were the forerunners of a modern conception of political legitimacy and obligation that could only flourish side by side with the development of the modern state. It is suggestive that the freemen who did claim a rational legal norm for their liturgical obedience only did so in response to occasional demands for their cooperation from bureaucratic agencies, never from their patrimonial niche. Thus, a captain felt entirely justified in refusing a request that he should raise troops for the local justice of the peace, because of the absence of legal norms that compelled him: "It is a legal principle, which everybody knows, that an authority can exact only what is explicit in the law, and not demand from others that which the law does not command." Again, had this same commander refused a justice of the peace's order to sit on a qualification council of the corporation, he would have considered himself to be neglecting his corporate duties. The dual normativity of the bureaucratic patrimonial state is here transparently revealed; although the commander performed his daily patrimonial duties as a matter of course, he questioned, on the basis of a legality that he had failed to apply to his liturgical duties in the first place, the attempt made by bureaucrats to extend his personal obligations with regard to bureaucratic duties.[5]

Thus the conditions of disorganization and lack of discipline were quite severe, and they obstructed the smooth discharge of liturgical liabilities by the Brazilian freeman. The impact of this on the establishment of a rational legal order is hard to ignore; the daily satisfaction of the administrative functions of local government was, after all, predicated upon the existence of a readily available mass of patrimonial servants. Any difficulty in the enlistment of these servants affected the ordinary expectations associated with bureaucratic obligations attached to state agencies and officials. This was dramatically indicated, for instance, by the local legislature of the Villa das Dores do Indaiá, which three times begged the President of Minas Gerais for the reorganization of the *Guarda Nacional*, which had been "neglected for so many years, [and] the absence of which has encouraged the flight of convicts. . . . The escape of criminals and murderers is made possible by the incompetence of local sentries; this would not be the case were there competent and trustworthy National Guards."[6]

Magistrates were without human resources to implement orders of imprisonment; local penitentiaries were unable to keep inmates under control for lack of guards; town and villages could not be adequately patrolled. These factors, as well as dozens of other minor chores entrusted to the militias but inadequately carried out, had to have detrimental effects on the institutionalization of a public order politically guaranteed by the state representatives.

Regional Counterpoints

The perversion of the purpose of the corporation was neither permanent nor uniform. Periods of an intense lack of discipline can be detected against a background of more or less satisfactory—or at least quiet—discharge of corporate duties, and there were significant provincial variations.

The creation of local commands had been a very swift process, considering the conditions of communication in the second quarter of the century. Generally speaking, in a matter of three to five years, the effective political area of each province was covered by militia corps.[7]

The *Guarda Nacional* was occasionally an instrument of settlement and territorial colonization of the vast hinterland. This function did not escape the notice of local authorities, who would ask the provincial presidency to designate some specific area as headquarters for the *corpos*, so as to enhance its demographic and economic growth.[8] As a rule, however, militarization of the territory took place immediately after the territory had been economically settled. A rapid interpretation of the electoral pattern of Minas Gerais during this period bears this out. An analysis of local electoral rolls (which ordinarily gave the name of those elected, together with their economic or military status) shows, for instance, the reduced participation of militarized freemen in the electoral processes in the peripheral areas of recent settlement, such as Alto São Francisco, the Triangulo Mineiro, and Jequitinhonha, in contrast to the considerable participation of militarized *honoratiores* in the areas of old settlement, such as the Zona da Mata and the south of the province. Such a pattern seems to indicate a historical process that had its origins in the colonization of the land by settlers who gradually created a local economy serving as the foundation of civil society. This was the predicament characteristic of the peripheral zones. Later, the civil society would also be exposed to a process of militarization characterized by the establishment of political institutions. Needless to say, it was thanks to the *Guarda Nacional* that this process took place.[9]

Leaving for later analysis the *gaúcho* militias, it is quite evident that the whole notion of a genteel militarized stratum of *honoratiores*, stylized in the form of equestrian virtuosity, was unsuccessful. The vicissitudes of cavalry organization are relevant, as I have suggested, not only because of the objective possibilities the cavalry might have offered for a status project, but also because of the probability of it becoming a major factor in the patrimonial satisfaction of the material needs of the members of the corporation, with regard to uniforms, arms, and all the resources that the Imperial state could not afford to satisfy. Not, of course, that the officerdom of the other two branches—infantry and artillery—were in principle unable to satisfy those corporate needs that the state would not or could not meet. The fact empirically observed is, however, that in Brazil, as elsewhere, the patriciate and the wealthy members of agrarian communities generally opted for the cavalry branch, because of the cultural representations that have historically established a connection between status honor and cavalry.

As a consequence, the scanty presence of cavalry formations may be taken as a general indication of the perversion of the status project of the corporation. Except for the southern province of Rio Grande do Sul, the cavalry represented not more than fifteen to twenty percent of the total contingents of militias.

Characteristically, it was at the center of the Empire—at the Court and in the Province of Rio de Janeiro—that the preference for the cavalry materialized to the greatest extent. In no other place did the status orientation develop with such a distinct character as at the Court. As I have discussed in other sections, because of the status qualifications for corporate membership in general and for cavalry corps at the Court in particular, it is perfectly understandable that Court life, with its apparatus and symbolism, contributed significantly to the cultivation of a status orientation. The surrounding provincial area was equally affected. It would be a mistake to link genetically the rise of such status orientation to the rise of an agrarian patriciate, which emerged, along with the flourishing of Rio de Janeiro's coffee economy, in the second quarter of the century. The fact is that even before such a development took place, the province had shown a sharp and widespread affinity for the cavalry. Thus, between the middle and late 1830s, practically the entire Province of Rio de Janeiro was pervaded by *honoratiores* on horseback. From Niteroi to Campos, passing by Saquarema, Maricá, Itaborahy, Cabo Frio, and Macaé, as well as in the direction of São João do Principe, Vassouras, Valença, Paraiba do Sul, and Iguassu, the traveler would have found cavalry formations. A different situation arose in Minas Gerais, where during the same period only Ouro Preto, Rio Preto, Campanha, and Curral (today Barbacena) had units of cavalry. And in Bahia, surprisingly, their development was even more limited.

There were, in effect, practically no requests for transfer from one branch of the corporation to another in the documents examined from the third decade in Bahia. The legion with headquarters in the capital of the province had only one cavalry company, that is, 100 horsemen, as opposed to 900 infantrymen. The situation was, however, far from static. The inchoate organization of the late 1830s gave way in the 1840s to a greater development of cavalry units. To take the case of Minas, the list of places with cavalry units in the latter period of the middle years also included Uberaba, Piranga, Pouso Alegre, Sabará, and Curvello.

In general terms, it may be said that with the passing of the years this trend toward the relative growth of cavalry units gained some strength. A constellation of forces pushed in that direction—personal status projects; the wish to avoid liturgical service; the attempts at seigneurial stylization of the landlords, and the relative agrarian expansion begun in the 1840s. Combinations of these and probably other factors encouraged such a trend in the provinces examined. With the general reorganization of the militias in the early 1850s, the trend was reinaugurated with singular vehemence. Bahia, for instance, suddenly revealed a previously nonexistent taste for cavalry, which was no longer limited to the capital but extended to other areas of the province.

Nevertheless, neither the militias of Bahia nor those of Minas Gerais received requests for transfer to the cavalry with the same frequency and regularity as did the militias of the Court and Rio de Janeiro, whose daily administrative routine was distinguished by the need to deal with this problem. The contingents of the Bahia branch were smaller and fewer, and, furthermore, their militiamen do not seem to have cultivated a seigneurial project that could have encouraged such requests as intensely as did the militiamen in the center of the Empire.[10] This agrees with my general findings based on the analysis of archival documentation, namely, that the dominant strata in Minas Gerais and Bahia contributed financially to the administrative apparatus of their corps much less than did their counterparts in the Province of Rio de Janeiro.[11]

Indeed, the trend was toward the growth of cavalry. And this trend cannot be divorced from the question of the lack of discipline, which periodically plagued the militias. The disciplinary problem was a serious one from the start. In the urban centers and capitals, particularly at the Court, as we have noted, this disorder manifested itself in attempts to evade service, principally because of the neat stratification of liturgical services, which essentially caused them to fall on the shoulders of poor freemen. This was the source of continuous discontent. In other areas the problem was more severe. It would be futile to offer detailed evidence with regard to its intensity in, say, Bahia or Minas. The official correspondence between commanders and bureaucratic authorities is full of complaints about the absence of guards on training maneuvers, the lack of uniforms and armaments, the refusals to obey orders of imprisonment issued by the disciplinary councils, the variety of pretexts used to evade service, the officers' unwillingness to serve, and so on.[12] In the mid-1840s, problems of discipline and organization again became acute. The militias in the vast *sertão*, that *terra ignota* so beautifully described by Euclides da Cunha, became skeletal structures made up only of officials. "This province cannot count on the *Guarda Nacional*," observes the President of Bahia, "which only exists badly organized and above all badly qualified. . . . Throughout the *sertão* there are only officers."[13] Even the militias of the central Province of Rio de Janeiro were afflicted by the virus of poor discipline. In a report on four of the seventeen provincial legions, a top commander remarks, "they are in a miserable state: no training, no discipline, no arms; they are groups of men who only gather together every now and again, and then only those who wish to do so."[14] The state, moreover, was unable to stem the tide; from the mid-1840s to the end of the decade, it ignored the number and the organized state of most provincial militias, and the official statistical reports of that time, issued yearly by the Ministry of Justice, were forced to accept the status quo. Exasperated with the general disarray, the state promulgated a new organic law in 1850 in order to instill new blood into the infirm corporation.

The patient recovered, but slowly. Only at the end of the mid-1850s was its general organization satisfactorily restored; offices of command were filled, enlistment was again effective, and discipline was reinstated. Along with this, the status orientation reappeared with vigor. Yet this time it spread to all the provinces on an unprecedented scale. It is perhaps not an exaggeration to suggest that it was in the period from the mid-1850s to the mid-1860s that the militias of *honoratiores* and landlords developed their keen sense of status identity. Elsewhere we have noted the attempts at office prebendalization that appeared at this time, as well as new forms of status qualification that aimed to restrict corporate membership to the wealthy classes of freemen. Nevertheless, the institutionalization of this pattern of office appropriation, as well as the pattern of status stratification, would have re-

quired a more stable society than Brazilian society of the mid-
century, which was subject to the convulsions and transformations brought about by agrarian capitalist development.
In addition, a major accident occurred that added to the cor-
rosive influence of economic development; the war against
Paraguay, which lasted from 1865 to 1870, put to a severe test
the military efficiency of the stratum of militarized *honoratiores*.

The corporation and the society it embraced were not to
remain unchanged by the war enterprise and the embattled
capitalism that went along with it. Gone were the persistence
and continuity of tradition and the attachment to values that
justified patrimonial obligation toward the body politic. The
prince's charisma emerged wounded from the battlefield—
death-stricken, to be precise. For the first time, the liberal
movement that questioned the principle of monarchical legitimacy gained a degree of articulation and a momentum
that had no precedent, and that resulted in the Popular Manifesto of 1869. In a moment of political wisdom, the state
realized that it was no longer possible to enlist liturgical
cooperation without further ado. In 1873, a new organic law
robbed the militias of their police functions. From that time
on, these functions were filled by police institutions bureaucratically administered and controlled by the state itself. Also,
from 1873, the *Guarda Nacional*'s activities were limited to the
exceptional contingencies of "external war, rebellion, sedi-
tion, or insurrection." As if to stress even further its dispensable character, the law drastically reduced the age limit to
forty, allowed only one troop meeting per year, and, agony
of agonies, abrogated the concession of honorific posts. Sen-
sibly enough, and correctly judging where the functional
value of the militia in fact lay, the law ruled that only the
units of frontier command would continue to be subject to
the legal *status quo ante*.[15]

The militias were in the throes of death. Actually, the
prewar recovery—the apparent reinvigoration that occurred
before the war with Paraguay—resembled the lucid state of
mind so typical of moribund humans. The 1873 law was tan-
tamount to a death certificate. However, the crisis in the corporation did not begin with the war effort. It had already
appeared in the 1860s, with the virulent increase in requests
for *guias de mudança* (permissions to move), submitted by

those members of the corporation who planned to change their residence from one county or province to another. The number of these requests in the first half of the century was quite negligible; they began to increase, and torrentially at that, at mid-century with the expansion of capitalism and the pressure for greater mobility of factors. As the efficient organization of the liturgies required a relatively stable society with a low level of physical mobility, such massive movement was destined to have a pernicious effect on the discipline and organization of the militias.

These factors, together with the redefinition of the corporation's role in 1873, gave it a drastically different physiognomy. The official correspondence between the patrimonial commanders and the Imperial authorities, so voluminous, frequent, and detailed before 1873, was now exiguous, and in the majority of cases was restricted to questions concerning requests for permission to move, transfer, and retire. For the first time, the student of these documents receives the clear impression that the corporation was turning, at an accelerated speed, into nothing more than an association of officers. This trend became even stronger in the 1880s. There were, of course, individual instances of officers who still took the trouble to comply with the formalities of their office or, at least, to justify their accidental lack of compliance. On the whole, however, these cases make the profound disarray of the moribund corporation even more pathetic. One brief laconic sentence sufficed for the Provincial President of Rio de Janeiro—at the center of the Empire—to inform the central bureaucracy about the activities of the corporation in the year that had just passed (1879): "the *Guarda Nacional* of this Province was not called upon for service."[16]

Commands remained acephalous for years, and this ceased to be an exceptional occurrence. A review of the documentation of these final years provokes the uneasy sentiment that the corporation had lost its sense of mission. There is nothing to indicate the existence of purpose to be fulfilled, or the employment of rational means, or the presence of an organizational routine embodying both.

Characteristic of the process of decay is the perversion of the status qualifications for corporate association. The care taken in earlier decades to substantiate a candidacy for appointment on the basis of wealth, local prestige, military rank, etc. no longer exists. The new trend is, rather, to justify the entire list of candidates *en bloc* with a *pro forma* qualification that all deserve promotion. There is no question that we are faced here with a different corporate climate in which the very idea of status association is fading; and in which the corporate penchant for office prebendalization is withering away. Such a phenomenon is neither unexpected nor extraordinary, when viewed in the larger context of the institutional transformation taking place both in the organization of the Brazilian state of the period—progressively bureaucratic and regressively patrimonial—and in the new value system emphasizing individualism and market, that is, *Gesellschaft*.

Some Sources of Perversion

We have already examined the vicissitudes of the militias in different areas and epochs, as well as the disciplinary problems that they faced. But the erosion of the patrimonial corporation and the concomitant perversion of its project deserves a closer look. In this respect, the obstacles to stable and authoritative leadership, the ambiguity and duality of institutional principles, and the tensions arising from the incompatibilities between the corporate and the material needs of the members were decisive.

Political factionalism was a permanent cause of instability of command. Given the early stage of institutional development in Brazil and the structural differentiation of the polity, the *Guarda Nacional* was destined to play a significant role as a political instrument, and it could, indeed, hardly avoid being involved in politics. In a very general sense, then, the status principle and the electoral principle of the first decades, as well as the political patronage affecting appointment in the following decades, ran counter to one another. Frequently, elections for the rank of officer favored militiamen without sufficient social rank. In such cases, the commanders would often ask the Ministry of Justice to revoke the elections. Faced with the dilemma of either maintaining acephalous posts or filling them with undesirable candidates,

the higher commander at the Court opted for the former
course of action. It was better, he remarked,

> that for the time being the vacant offices in the *Guarda Na-*
> *cional* continue as such until new measures [a suggestion
> for the abrogation of popular elections] for improving the
> lot of the *Guarda Nacional* be introduced, since some of the
> elections carried out lately are very disagreeable because
> through them inadequate persons have been selected.

At other times, commanders suggested the dismissal of officers on the grounds that they lacked appropriate funds. It
is interesting that this lack was more likely to prove cumber-
some when there was an election in the background; in fact,
all the eight officers suggested for discharge by a commander
at the Court were elected. Extreme and very exceptional measures would include, if necessary, the dissolution of the
unit.[17]

The instability of office thus produced was a factor that
eroded the basis of spontaneous social cooperation on which
the liturgical organization was built. Furthermore, this instability created conditions of uncertainty with regard to the
continuity of leadership and command. The command of a
provincial legion, it is reported, "is entrusted to a Major, due
to the fact that almost all the officerdom was discharged by
His Excellency Aureliano [the previous provincial president]
and the Chief of the Legion. . . also, the three Lieutenant
Colonels who were to substitute those discharged have not
thus far taken office, despite having been ordered several
times to do so."

The report goes on to express a typical complaint of that
period, particularly in the Province of Rio de Janeiro:

> The uncertainty in which the officers live, and the strange
> way in which they are at times dismissed—without having,
> through any neglect of duty, given cause for discharge—
> has brought them to a precarious and vacillating state. [It
> is expensive for an officer to get his uniform and] there are
> many who, after having incurred this expense, and having
> presented themselves on their first day in their lavish uni-
> forms, are deprived of them the day after.

The upshot of all this was an anomic climate that led to further disorganization. The lieutenant colonel of a battalion pointedly communicated his reason for refusing office:

> Your Excellency is not unaware of the serious expenses that I must incur to acquire the necessary uniform, and I would do this with much pleasure, had I not knowledge regarding the short tenure of officers at the *Guarda Nacional*, discharged at will and on any excuse by the Government: a fact that contributes and has always done so, to the lack of discipline and insubordination . . . The public service, in which I have been employed since 1828, and only for patriotism, without self-interest has, Your Highness knows, deteriorated my fortune almost to the point of ruin. In view of these circumstances, an office involving so much and which offers no guarantees cannot benefit me: I mean, one without a *Patente* [official document confirming rank], with which I would consider myself safe.

A perplexed commander observed that this disorganization, transforming corporate command into a "contrived vehicle of the Government with no moral force in the *Guarda Nacional*," was "the predicament to which we were reduced by the bloody elections and the factional spirit, the utility of which in favor of the public cause I have yet to discover."[18] It was also observed that vacancies were deliberately kept open so that they could be offered at opportune moments, that is, in preelection periods, to interested individuals in exchange for their votes.[19]

But politics could only partially account for the perversion of authority and command. Less sinister, yet equally consequential, was the effect of the lack of qualified individuals on the relaxation of status requirements and indirectly on stable leadership. The connection between status and authority within the context of the corporation was by no means a fabrication. It was, on the contrary, a frequent issue of concern for officers. This awareness, allied to the critical scarcity of qualified notables, was at the root of the commanders' antipathy and opposition to any nominee's refusal to accept his official post. Commanders would argue that it was a bad precedent, in view of the higher needs of the corporation, to let notable citizens nominated to corporate status decide for themselves whether to accept or not. Acceptance should be, when necessary, legally compulsory.

In search of a legal remedy, a legion commander remarked: "There are few people in the Province who are able and also available for officer posts, because all those who can get a dispensation do so . . . avoid [service] on any pretext: there is a diminution of individuals and of the richer and more influential people of the country." Another commander complained to the government about its acceptance of a newly-elected candidate's excuse for not assuming his office; it was, he added, a bad precedent, "because in subsequent elections, rare have been the citizens, among whom are those most fit to uphold the credit, brilliance, and discipline of the *Guarda Nacional*, who, elected for office, have neglected to take advantage of such precedents to refuse, thus exposing the *Guarda* [*Nacional*] to the possibility of one day finding at its head men without fortune and lacking the qualities necessary for good leadership."[20]

I have suggested elsewhere that this adscriptive emphasis on rank was a rational aspect, given the absence of a fully bureaucratic form of domination. This is born out by those instances in which the traditional or typical command by *honoratiores* was suspended. In fact, the bases of corporate obedience were resented and weakened whenever a landlord handed over his command provisionally to a subaltern official lacking in the authority necessary for avocational leadership in the community. Discipline, already fragile, fell on these occasions to a low point.[21]

Intimately connected with this pattern was the negative effect of economic misfortune on the officer's chances to continue in command. I have previously mentioned the effect of wealth on corporate membership. Any sudden change of economic status, either upward or downward, was likely to have an effect on rank and command. It would be absurd, all the same, to claim that the degree of economic mobility was so high—and so drastic—as to impair the structure of command of the militias. Some mobility existed anyway, and its repercussions were felt within the structure. This mobility was, moreover, particularly important for the stability of corporate leadership, given its immediate impact on the probability of command, an impact that would have been lessened had the status principle become dominant as the major regulative value of that culture.[22]

There was another general source of institutional erosion arising from the tension between the organizational needs of the corporation and the material needs of its members. Avocational administration is predicated, *inter alia,* on the *otium cum dignitate* that only a stable and institutionalized status order can offer. But leisure alone is not a sufficient cause for the establishment of a system dominated by *honoratiores.* Equally necessary is some kind of stratification by status, to permit the existence of an economically privileged status group as well as its cultivation of leisure. Antipathetic to the life-style of the *honoratior* are the notions of profession, vocation, and market. Dilettantism—the uncommitted, disinterested, and graceful dedication to work or contemplation— is the hallmark of his life stylization.

In agrarian Brazil slavery favored the development of a leisure class, but at the same time, together with the growth of agrarian capitalism, it prevented the emergence of a status group of landlords because of its obstruction to the expansion of tradition-bound and nonrepressive forms of subordination of freemen to a stratum of *senhores.*

From the beginning, then, the patrimonial administration of local government by agrarian dilettantes was bound to develop incompletely, as did the bureaucratic form that stimulated it. Both were, incidentally, incomplete for the same reason: the one because the indigent state could not adequately rely on its own resources to bureaucratize its apparatus; the other because impecunious landlords would not, for the same economic reasons, satisfactorily play the role of dilettante patrimonial officers without risk of jeopardizing their means of livelihood. For this reason, the history of the nineteenth-century Brazilian bureaucratic-patrimonial state was very arduous.

These tensions were felt in acute form by the rank and file. The state did not truly manage to enlist for liturgical service the lower echelons of its bureaucracy; it had a wavering attitude, at times issuing stern measures restricting the classes of bureaucrats who could be exempted from the liturgies, at other times increasing that number. In the end, it was this latter policy that generally prevailed. The burden of service thus fell primarily on the craftsmen, the "mechanical" class, small businessmen and merchants, and the small agricultural producers of the countryside. Service interfered in three distinct ways with the occupational activities of the militiaman. Night watches and patrolling, usually beginning in the early evening and lasting until dawn, obviously clashed with the freeman's need for rest. To the extent that this obligation was required of each individual just once a week, it was not incompatible with personal work. But the lenient demands of the state on its own officials were a cause of permanent disaffection for the militiamen and irritation for the commanders. As the workday of bureaucrats ended at two o'clock in the afternoon, commanders saw no justifiable reason to exempt them from night duty. This, together with the fact that bureaucrats enjoyed a stable income, made their exemption from duty, as was put in exceptional legal-rational terms by a *gaúcho* commander, "a privilege, . . . an odious distinction that does not square with the dogma of equality guaranteed by the fundamental law of the Empire, or with the principles of justice upon which our Authorities would always base their decisions."[23]

A second, more severe form of interference was daytime duty, which clashed as a matter of course with the militiamen's daily earnings. It would be futile to document the frequency of requests for dispensation from active service for alleged reasons of health, economic calamities, or other sorts of excuses likely to be considered reasonable. In cases of tension the chain would break at its weakest point, which was, under the circumstances, the public point; lack of discipline and cooperation could hardly be dealt with effectively.

The third way in which tension materialized was in the services of interdistrict detachments, which ordinarily involved journeys of two days or more to the coast for the repression of the slave traffic. Outside the urban centers and the capitals, this was a regular source of liturgy. Its most dreadful expression took the form of long detachments of between six months and a year to other provinces, chiefly Rio Grande do Sul, in times of military conflicts. Guards were, in these cases, subject to the regime of the professional army and received meager pay. It is superfluous, perhaps, to add that this pay did not make up for the damage to their personal finances. The local economies were also affected, as evidenced by the connivance of landlords with the evasions practiced by small farmers and tenants. For example, three months after the promulgation of a decree extending the period of detachment to a year (December 9, 1841), the Court sent a commissioner to the prosperous area of the Parahiba Valley to plan the enlistment of troops sorely needed to stem the waves of internal rebellion. It is instructive to note that the commissioner

> had to suffer the greatest opposition imaginable from all the property owners and landlords who protect their resident laborers or the nonrentpaying tenants on their *fazendas,* and do everything possible in their favor, and suggest that they hide themselves.
> [The commissioner] adds that because this Legion is located on the border of the Province of Minas [Gerais] and because the majority of its men are natives [of Minas], they cross the border with extraordinary ease.[24]

At about the same time, the commanders and officers of the *Guarda Nacional* of a neighboring legion in the equally prosperous area of Rezende submitted a request to the Emperor, asking for a reduction of the duration of detachment, from twelve to two months. They claimed that the local people were by tradition and temperament averse to bearing arms and had not the least military training or skill. They went on to show the ruinous effects of such long detachments on domestic economies.

It is apparent that behind these moves there existed a tacit but nonetheless active joint effort by the dominant agrarian groups and their dependent tenants and small farmers to obstruct the latter's liturgical obligations. To the landlords, the needs of *homo oeconomicus* took definite precedence over those of *homo hierarchicus.* A legion commander replied to the Court's request for the remittance of ninety militiamen as follows:

> The town of Vassouras has to export over 150 thousand *arrobas* [1 arroba = about 15kg.] of coffee this year, [and]

the majority of the bachelors [as well as the childless wid-
owers and married men] who are to be detached are busy
as administrators, supervising the working force in the har-
vest process or the herders of numerous mule trains that
travel all the roads leading to the general market of our fertile Province; there are still many others busy in the sugar
mills and other activities which account for the main income of the Exchequer. I have just made a journey of about
30 *legoas* [1 legoa = about 2.5 miles] and I was a personal
witness to the general unrest amidst this class which is extremely useful to the Nation. The laborious life of its members leaves them no time for even cultivating their own
maize which mainly feeds the slave force as well as the
beasts that transport their produce to the market.[25]

Such obstacles to civilian mobilization were not limited
to the areas of expansion of agrarian capitalism; they were
also present in areas devoted to other economic activities.
Fishermen, for instance, displayed an exceptional degree of
solidarity, which desperately disconcerted the patrimonial
commanders. To speak of discipline among people "who
have gone so far as to receive recruitment for service with
jeers and boos" was an obvious joke. These were, moreover,
the same kind of people as those who collectively refused to
render any service whatsoever for a period of eight months,
with the aggravating circumstance that orders for arrest could
not be executed by guards "who, because of ties of kinship
or friendship, have never carried out orders on the permanent excuse that the culprits could not be found because they
were fishermen and spent more time at sea than on land."
Characteristically, impunity reigned, and this obviously reinforced the difficulty of enlistment.[26] It is important to remark
that these events took place in the coastal area of Macaé, a
very short distance from the center of the Empire. One might
well imagine the conditions of enlistment in the distant *sertão*,
at its political periphery.

And in fact, a similar pattern emerged there. In the areas
of economic prosperity, where the need for labor was great,
the landlord's protection of his tenant-farmers and patriarchal dependents appeared again. A typical instance was that
prevailing on the southern economic frontier of Bahia, a
flourishing cacao area, toward the third quarter of the cen-

tury. According to corporate reports, this protection was under the auspices of high provincial authorities: "I want to communicate to Your Excellency that at the present time it is not possible to recruit volunteers in this city of Ilheus; not because there are many who are ineligible, but because they are protected by precisely those who should admonish them to take part in a cause [the war against Paraguay] which belongs to us all."[27]

Conditions were, if anything, worse in the heart of the backlands where "time had stood still." The central state's presence there was a dim shadow, more of a future project than an actual reality. Provincial institutions had, at best, a provincial and parochial character, hardly a national one. In 1870, the commander of a backland town sent the provincial president his congratulations on the successful termination of the conflict with Paraguay; the provincial authority was both the center and the periphery of the political representation of this rustic; no prince or national state had a place in his world. To read his message only as a self-promoting and petty scheme is to waste a rare opportunity to assess the genuine limits of the political world of the landlord of the backlands, as he saw it. The same idea led one authority to account for the extreme difficulties he encountered: "unfortunately, the *sertão* is still lacking in the requisite civilization, and the majority of its inhabitants do not understand the sacred obligation which binds every Brazilian to the defense of his Country [together with] the antipathy they display toward military uniform."

There was little chance in these backlands, then, for the growth of a patrimonial sense of political obligation that could have facilitated the assumption of liturgies. This chance was further reduced by the strong bonds of solidarity between the landlord and his dependents. The intimate connection between that solidarity and the vicissitudes of the liturgical project are revealed in the following document:

It is indispensable to settle, so to speak, those *sertões* with new people; to practice there a strong yet prudent recruitment of those vagrants and criminals who choose as their only means of livelihood that of serving as bodyguards or, as they are named here, *peitos largos* [broad chests] to the local bosses, who provide them with meat and manioc [basic dietary item] and protect them whenever Justice wants to prosecute them for their criminal behavior.[28]

The incompatibility between the exigencies of liturgical obligations and the material needs of the militiamen, which led to faulty service, materialized not only in the case of the rural freemen of the middle and lower strata; they also operated in the economically dominant groups. Nevertheless, in general terms, such incompatibilities were most apparent among the freemen of the middle and lower strata in areas of agrarian expansion such as the Parahiba Valley, whereas in these same areas the members of economically dominant groups were much less remiss in their patrimonial obligations.

A different pattern may be discovered in areas under a pastoral regime. In contrast to the coffee regions, these areas were more problematic, not so much regarding the services of the rank and file, but regarding those of the officerdom. In fact, while the coffee baronage showed no noticeable tension in coping with both its members' patrimonial liturgies and their personal economic enterprise, this was not true, for example, of the ranch owners and the declining sugar economy of the plains of Campos de Goitacazes in the northern area of the Province of Rio de Janeiro. The contrast is a dual one; a declining sugar economy, together with non-labor-intensive pastoral activity, contributed to a relaxation in the demand for labor, thus making the alternative liturgical employment less problematic. The opposite happened in the Parahiba Valley. The prosperous landlord class of this valley stood in contrast to the decadent *senhores* of the plains, who were under stress to keep up their previous levels of income.

The incompatibility between rational economic activity and avocational administrative service was aggravated by a series of regulations issued by the central state in the 1840s and 1850s, whereby the richer landlords were exempted from active service. In effect, *estanceiros* (ranch owners) raising more than fifty calves per year and coffee or sugar-planters employing more than twenty workers could be transferred to the reserve service. In these circumstances, the burden of the corporate administration tended to fall on the shoulders of the poorer landlord class. This obviously further reduced the likelihood of an efficient patrimonial administration.

In the late 1850s, for instance, the legion commander of Campos reported to the provincial authority his difficulty in finding candidates to fill the posts under his command: "I have not submitted proposals . . . because of the difficulty in finding in some districts individuals who qualify by virtue of their fortune and other qualities required by law, and are in a position to occupy posts in the *Guarda Nacional* as the large majority [of those who are eligible, are exempted by law]."[29]

A telling illustration of the difficulty of overcoming the opposition between the two classes of needs may be seen in the Imperial authorities' difficulty in finding a local notable willing to accept command of the legion in Campos. For over three years they searched in vain for a candidate. Early in 1836, a few weeks after having been appointed by the president of the province, a local landlord, with the firm style of an educated man, declined in a temperate manner: "I am the Father of a very large family, dwelling in the *roça* [land cleared for cultivation], and lord of three sugar mills, not even for the administration of which do I have the necessary time." He goes on to say that he would sacrifice his private and family interests for the public cause, were he not afflicted by illness. And he adds, as though to make sure that he will manage to avoid annoying insistence: "In the second place, I am convinced that the military profession is absolutely alien to me, and that I have not the slightest knowledge thereof, for I never was even a militia or *ordenança* officer."

Six months later, an acting commander reported that no willing candidate had appeared. The search continued with the same results. Almost three years after this communication, the echo of the first landlord's letter appeared in another refusal; the command was declined because, so the new nominee alleged, he lived at some *legoas* distance from the city and had to run two sugar mills, "the administration of which demands all my time. [I am] subject to onerous obligations that I must satisfy punctually at a specified deadline, and above all, [I have] no military background." He concluded with the practical speculation that the local *Guarda*

Nacional was in such a state of disarray and insubordination, that he wondered whether, "I will [not] sacrifice my interests and my tranquillity [in vain]."[30] At long last, two months later, the command was accepted by the justice of the peace, being most probably a "yeoman."

Other notables, less prudent, realized the nature and extent of the incongruity only after accepting the office; thus, the secretary of the command in Campanha, Minas Gerais, asked, in baroque phrasing, for release on the grounds that he could not meet both his personal and corporate obligations: "As this office demands tireless activity, due not only to the laborious monthly reports, but to the continuous other dispatches, the Supplicant, whose occupation is commercial, is forced to shirk an infinite number of business and private tasks, placing his own interests in serious jeopardy in order to adequately perform the duties inherent to this office."[31]

This factor, allied to others and varying from case to case, led to situations of virtual corporate paralysis, which raised the question of the viability of patrimonial structures in a progressively bourgeois social order; thus there was a time in the 1830s when this dismal situation arose at the political center of the Empire; in the mid-1830s *all* the legion commanders of the province of Rio de Janeiro were excused from service. The same source added that most of the higher officers obtained leave on the pretext of illness, but were seen during the day busy with their private occupations.[32]

The consequences of this tension between two types of orientation went beyond the officer's decision of whether to accept or to renounce after having accepted. Administrative acts and the creation of a corporate routine were similarly affected; how far could, and did, the militarized *honoratior* in office want to go in committing his private *patrimonium* to the discharge of his liturgical duties? A satisfactory answer was based on several conditions: the wealth of the officer, the kind of enterprise he lived off, his economic orientation, his corporate commitment, his sense of patrimonial obligation, his status orientation, and so forth. The following case illustrates the rich embroidery of contingencies that formed the background for routine stereotyping.

The acting commander of Ilha Grande de Fora on the coast of the Province of Rio de Janeiro reported on the problems he faced in punishing the constant disobedience of his subordinates—disobedience exacerbated by their knowledge that the steps for its elimination would somehow run counter to the private interests of their superior officer:

> Your Excellency well knows that the Ilha Grande is three nautical *legoas* from the town of Angra, so that whenever I am compelled to imprison militiamen, I have to take my slaves away from their tilling (as I have done) to have them transport the culprits in canoes to the town, for the purpose of locking them up in the Fortress.
>
> Now, not only is this transportation dangerous due to storms that may occur at any moment, causing the death of the travelers, but it also causes me considerable losses, and as I must provide it frequently, I repeatedly lose my slaves' day's work; to do which I do not appear to be obliged, to such great sacrifice; not even for the sake of public service to which I dedicate myself so devotedly, should it be required of me.
>
> Therefore, I see myself constrained to request Your Excellency to submit the above to the knowledge of his Lordship the President of the Province, as I will have to put an end to this means of maintaining discipline because the law, and therefore Your Excellency, will not permit that this service be the cause of my ruin.[33]

The tension between the corporate principle and the market principle, as revealed and discussed above, that is, the opposition between *homo hierarchicus* and *homo oeconomicus*, developed along with the pressure for the rationalization of the administration of the militias, and the counterpressure for its prebendalization—in other words, there were structural pressures for the professionalization of service along with the *honoratiores'* attempt to control the appropriation of officer status on the basis of other than professional criteria.

This materialized in various ways. For instance, not only was there a trend toward one set of norms for admission and another for promotion, but this trend reappeared within each level; that is, admission and promotion were both subject to the effects of these conflicting norms. The adscriptive status orientation, for example, was very noticeable in the process of selection, and it did not take into consideration merely economic aspects. Moral qualifications entered very much into the ideal notion of the militarized *honoratior*. There were, of course, regional variations, which I will examine in the next chapter. Relatively speaking the landlords of Bahia, for example, were much less concerned with the qualifications of honesty, probity, and good conduct than those of Rio de Janeiro and Minas Gerais. But performance orientation appeared with a regularity that leaves no doubt as to its corporate importance. In fact, it is striking to find in such an adscriptively oriented association the presence of criteria such as intelligence, capacity (*aptidão*), experience, and zeal, as institutional standards for membership. Moreover, these qualities exerted their presence in the subsequent organization of a routine. There were, in fact, frequent cases where promotion was proposed on the basis of seniority, performance, or merit, rather than, say, of social status.

At times these universalistic bureaucratic standards insinuated themselves with an assertiveness that was a veiled indication of their position into the hierarchy of the functional exigencies of the corporation. In such cases, corporative rank—in so far as it was progressively predicated on such standards—could help erode socially established hierarchies; officers of rather humble origin vindicated their corporate authority against the wayward claims of subordinate officers and guards of higher social status.[34]

These rationalizing forces made their appearance in the life of the corporation, turning it into a positive instrument for the socialization of its citizen officers in the secular idea of an institutional order transcending private discretions and subject to a normative code. This pattern was likely to appear whenever the need for an administrative order and a delimited area of jurisdiction—which the execution of patrimonial duties required—was trammeled by the abusive and perturbing authority of a superior officer. After an incident in which one commander interfered in the jurisdiction of another, the commander-in-chief insisted on having "norms fixing his attributions, without which everything will be arbitrary and the course of the service will fluctuate according to the opinions of each individual who happens to momentarily exercise this authority. To preserve discipline, a fixed and invariable system is indispensable."[35]

Nevertheless, the avocational nature of office necessarily set a brutal limit on the development of rational organization; the state could not but accept patrimonial cooperation without many reservations concerning the rational qualifications of the servant. More often than not, the limited value of such qualifications was traceable to a state that had abused the liturgical capabilities of the officer in other sectors of the administration. Very occasionally, it was the officer himself who dramatically and inadvertently brought to the state knowledge of its responsibility for his own human limitations. One incident will illustrate the point.

At one period, a justice of the peace in the Province of Rio de Janeiro addressed to the Minister of Justice a complaint against the section commander of Saquarema, who allegedly had not executed promptly a requisition for troops, made by the magistrate, in order to apprehend some criminals. Probably to buttress the veracity of his allegation, the justice of the peace reported that the commander was an illiterate. Ordered to explain his conduct to the Minister, the commander alleged that he did indeed give the necessary orders to his subalterns for the prompt satisfaction of the magistrate's requests. He added with disarming candor, if not with outstanding astuteness in attempting to excuse himself for his alleged inability to check written commands that he had given orally, that his illiteracy, which was a fact, was not the result of his own indifference but of many years spent in the service of a defunct regiment as a simple soldier at the service of the state.[36] We see here, at a patrimonial level, the kind of deficiency that we have seen elsewhere at the bureaucratic level of state administration: the professional limitations of their respective officialdoms.

It would be a mistake to think that the professional and bureaucratic principles imposed themselves over the avocational and corporative ones whenever they had the opportunity. The allegedly inherent superiority of rational forms stressed by Weber is not a universal and general rule. Such a view betrays an extremely simplified and mechanical conception of social change and is only correct when another *datum* is empirically posited, namely, the institutional presence of rational orientation according to ends (*Zweckrationalität*) as the typical form obtaining in the association.[37] It should also be born in mind that the development of status criteria fulfilled rational purposes in as much as the adscriptive foundations of rank tended to reinforce the corporate authority of the officerdom. In a sense, then, this vacillation between the two principles was a "cunning" of corporate reason.

The document below is a characteristic expression of such dynamics:

> I have the honor to inform Your Excellency that there are two senior captains of the battalion available for the Office of Major . . . , both with the same seniority, similar merit and talent, but although the first is wealthier, the second may better perform the role of Major, on account of his being more militarily minded. Your Excellency will, nevertheless, order whatever is considered fair.[38]

This vacillation is particularly significant in view of the fact that the office of major—one of the most technical in the hierarchy owing to its responsibilities in the area of training, discipline, accounting, and so on—was generally given to members of the professional army. This was not, however, sufficient cause to put aside the use of adscriptive and particularistic criteria. On the whole, these criteria took precedence over their polar types. Whenever they appeared together, the adscriptive criteria usually received more emphasis.[39]

A further manifestation of this pattern and, indirectly, of the relatively infirm development of rational orientation according to ends, was the appearance of expressive orientations that indicated a seigneurial spirit in the advanced stages of the corporation's history. These undercurrents pushing for "the enchantment of the world" would otherwise be a rather perplexing phenomenon. We will touch on that aspect presently, in our discussion of the *gaúcho* militias.

6

The *Gaúcho* Militiaman: "Lord of the Distances"

It is not possible to evaluate the historical importance of the Brazilian militias and their role in the process of state-building without focusing on the form they assumed in the southern province of Rio Grande do Sul, at the border of Uruguay and the Argentine. Most statements about the militias that apply to the Empire in general require qualification with regard to the *gaúcho* militias. They deserve an independent chapter because their institutional habitat, the *gaúcho* society, is an independent chapter in the historical development of Brazil. In order to obtain a better perspective, therefore, we will examine the nature of this habitat.

The Origins of *Gaúcho* Society

After the *bandeirantes'* destruction of the Jesuit experiment with missionary settlements in the first half of the eighteenth century, the Brazilian border with the Spanish Empire was a permanent theater of war with undefined political boundaries. Only with the Treaty of San Ildefonso in 1777 did the territorial boundaries acquire more definition, which gave some respite to the warfare between Spanish and Portuguese settlers in the area.

Gaúcho civil society was originally based on the economic organization of *mate* (a local tea) in the Missions area, and cattle-raising and cattle-processing enterprises spread throughout the vast fertile plains of the south-west of the captaincy, the *Campanha,* inhabited by itinerant cowboys, the native *gaúchos.*

The first *estancias* (cattle-raising estates) were established in the first quarter of the eighteenth century, founding the pastoral economy that became the backbone of the economic development of *gaúcho* society. For several decades, however, accompanying the process of territorial occupation, this economy was organized under a regime of *currais,** the basic form of economic appropriation. The social character of the *currais* was forged by the *gaúcho,* the pillager of semiwild cattle, the adventurous horseman attached to the lord of the *estancia.* Cattle-herding acquired a more economic form with the creation, around 1780, of the first *charqueadas,* the rural estates that produced jerked beef and other subsidiary products destined for the export market. Before this, the cultivation of wheat, begun by the first wave of settlers from the Azores Islands in the mid-eighteenth century, was the foundation of the provincial economy. But, unable to withstand the competition from Spanish producers across the border, the wheat economy crumbled in the 1810s, leaving the cattle-raising industry as the major source of work and wealth.

A provincial system of villages and towns arose, based on the cattle economy. It is important, nevertheless, to draw attention to the fact that well before the rational organization of the cattle economy as an enterprise system at the end of the eighteenth century, the military needs for the defense of the territory had already provided a foundation for an urban system:

> Contrary to what one might suppose, the great majority of villages and towns of Rio Grande do Sul did not have its origin in the cattle industry. . . . [Rio Grande do Sul] having from the start, and for many years, been the great theater of the Cisplatine campaigns, it is natural that the first settlements had their origin in military presidios, forts, posts, and camps.[1]

---

*The *currais* were temporary enclosures set up by wandering cowboys, who used them for the branding and slaughtering of roaming cattle.

It was thus that important cities such as Rio Grande, Rio Pardo, Bagé, Alegrete, Jaguarão, and Uruguaiana were created.

The militarization of *gaúcho* institutions and its overall social organization thus reached unparalleled levels, which set Rio Grande do Sul significantly apart from the rest of the Empire. One important difference lay in the nature of the process. In general, militarization north of Rio Grande do Sul was closely linked to patrimonial needs in the area of local government; in that sense, liturgical obligations were rationally exacted through the regimentation of patrimonial servants. Other conditions being equal, in the absence of a bureaucratic order, regimentation is an expedient method for the attainment of political goals. Within *gaúcho* society, militarization fulfilled a vital need in addition to regimentation, namely, defense of the national territory.

There was no "military enchantment of the world" possible for the *gaúcho* inhabitant, to paraphrase Weber's proposition about the opposite trend toward the sacralization of institutional life. That is, any genteel perversion of the rational use of the military institutions was out of the question, in so far as it would have endangered the very survival of the community in the face of the constant menace at the frontier. Militarized leaders who hated war because it spoiled the army had no place in the bellicose culture of the frontier. Up north, military institutions had a manifest value chiefly for the patrimonial state; down south, they had value both for the state and for the community. The northern militarized *honoratiores* could safely pervert the instrumental function of the militias and make of them a tool for the stylization of life; the southern militias could do so only at their own peril. The dilettantism of the north turned into the military virtuosity of the south.

The pastoral regime indirectly reinforced these contrasts. Generally speaking, it did not permit the accumulation of wealth on the same large scale that was possible for the agricultural estates of the northern economies. Not even wheat was a springboard to great accumulations of wealth. There are remarkable similarities between the *gaúcho* landlord and the colonial *estanciero* of northern Mexico. The Mexican also faced a fearful enemy, the Chichimecas; he was also, so to speak, at the periphery of the political and economic center; he also held vast tracts of land, but he was no match for the fantastic fortunes of the southern *ricos homes* of Nueva Galicia; and he was also imbued with a singular spirit of adventure and horsemanship. The total effect of these factors was twofold—a cultural orientation toward military values such as heroism, courage, and the ideal of military virtuosity, and the stifling of the urbane forms of gentility so desired by the northern landlords.

Another factor helped create a different military ethos in *gaúcho* culture, namely, the frailty of the patriarchal structure of the *estancia*. This facet is linked to the economic organization of the pastoral economy. The *estancia* conspicuously lacked the exuberance of the *gemeinschaftlich* relations characteristic of the northern rural estates. Its productive process was relatively simple; one cowboy could usually tend 1,000 head of cattle, and the work force needed was correspondingly small. This obviously led to the creation of a nonsedentary work force and a family structure lacking the density required for the creation of vigorous moral bonds. A similar pattern occurred in the Mexican and Argentinian *estancias*. François Chevalier remarks on the modernizing effects—the briskness of commercial relations and even speculation—produced by the lack of native "vassals" on the northern patriarchal estates; Tulio Halperin Donghi has also pointed out the Durkheimian idea formulated by Sarmiento concerning density of population and disaggregation of social bonds. All these factors point in one direction: the insurmountable difficulty of establishing in *gaúcho* society a patriarchal structure providing the objective possibilities for the development of a tradition-oriented culture with a seigneurial cast.[2]

The final factor was the influence of the professional military on the defense organization of the border. The operation of the professional army during the Empire was largely concentrated in Rio Grande do Sul. For reasons to be discussed below, the typical orientation of action of the professional officerdom was more rational and instrumental than elsewhere. This had repercussions within the *gaúcho* patrimonial corporation, which was subject to the continuous influence of its bureaucratic counterpart. Army and militias coalesced, on the southern frontier, into the war Minotaur of the bureaucratic patrimonial state.

Some Organizational Aspects of the *Gaúcho* Militias

Though formally the *gaúcho* militias did not differ from their northern counterparts, the distinction established in the two organic laws that structured the militias between detachments and detached corps assumed particular importance in this region. Detachments were meant to perform duties dealing with the day-to-day administration of government; detached corps had an entirely different function, namely, to assist the professional army in the defense of the frontier; they were, in other words, war detachments. The first type had relatively insignificant effects from an administrative standpoint, in as much as the state's obligation to defray the cost of the sustenance of the militiamen began, characteristically, after the third day of service. As this kind of service was generally limited to the jurisdiction of the local police officer or magistrate it rarely caused expense to the state.

The detached corps were another matter. Given the extraordinary duration of their service, the importance of their duties, and the considerable distance of their destinations, the state was forced to put its own bureaucracy into motion to attain the ends desired. Needless to say, the penchant of the incipient bureaucracy for enlisting patrimonial cooperation was, whenever possible, preserved. Thus both organic laws were explicit in the expectation that, in matters of equipment and uniform for these corps, the state would contribute for those members who did not possess the objects or the means to supply them for themselves, implicitly assuming that such units would be as far as possible self-equipped.

The defense task proved more complex and demanding than the legislators imagined. It called for an unprecedented degree of bureaucratic assistance because of the scale and duration of mobilization. And to meet this objective the state counted on its own professional army (permanently stationed, incidentally, in the right place).

The detached corps was not subject simply to the loose discipline of the *Guarda Nacional*. The law clearly and repeatedly stated that the detached corps should obey the same regulations and discipline as the professional army, and was entitled to receive the same remuneration. Furthermore, the frontier commanders were, together with all militiamen in war campaigns, subordinated to the professional army commanders. War was too serious a business to be left in the hands of dilettantes.

Out of this interaction between the two Imperial structures evolved a *modus operandi* that required their permanent cooperation. The rank of major of the corporation could be exercised by professional officers with at least the rank of captain, or by captains of the *Guarda Nacional* who had served for more than a year in the detached corps. Whatever the case, the officer was entitled to a salary. Commanders-in-chief of battalions or legions of the corporation, when in service in the professional army, were paid the salary of a colonel. Finally, the relative concentration of professional officers in Rio Grande do Sul frequently left the rest of the Empire without enough officers for other duties. This concentration led to a greater degree of closeness between the two agencies. Thus, militia officers could legally be invited to participate in military councils for the trial of privates garrisoned in the provinces.

Measures taken to ensure this cooperation were of particular importance in so far as they fostered the development of a professional and rational orientation in several sectors of the life of the corporation.

The province possessed its own militias. These made their appearance as swiftly as might be expected in a territory steeped in a long military tradition. In the first years after 1831, the three major regions—the eastern *Litoral*, the northern Missions district, and the western and southern *Campanha*—began to organize their own militias. The gap in the archives because of the provincial rebellion from 1835 to 1845 has made it impossible for us to reconstruct this movement. Its basic development, however, took place well within the first four years. Before the start of the rebellion practically the entire province was covered, and only the northern *Serra* lagged behind.

Let us now examine the characteristics the militias assumed.

The Private Foundations

Public funding of the *gaúcho* militias was chiefly geared to the satisfaction of defense needs. Therefore, other corporate needs connected with the patrimonial functions of local governments were, as far as possible, liturgically entrusted to the landlords.

We have noted that the satisfaction of these obligations depended in large measure on the weak distinction between private and public. Such was in fact the case in Rio Grande do Sul: "I well know how soldiers [sic] spoil their weapons," observes a commander, "but I think it is fair that they who spoil their armament should reimburse the Nation. This will cause them to be more careful." That is, private individuals in their capacity as public officials had to be held accountable for the repair of their service instruments. Probably the same kind of patrimonial ideology stood behind the compulsory character of liturgical services; he who could work for himself also had to serve the state: "As the crippled condition he alleges does not prevent him from using a lasso, therefore it should not prevent him from wielding a sword."[3] This was not a malicious rationalization, but a genuine principle in so far as it was invoked whenever applicable; in fact on the same grounds a veteran and impoverished captain, "overworked with the burden of a numerous family," was believed to have deserved dispensation.[4]

These documents reveal the existence in *gaúcho* society of the same pattern of consensual and communal cooperation that facilitated the cooptation of the local classes in the other provinces. Thanks to this cooperation, it was possible to establish the pattern of funding that we saw in Minas Gerais and Rio de Janeiro, whereby commanders advanced money from their own pockets to defray corporative costs, anticipating public reimbursement at a later date. Officers' contributions to the band, to the partial armament of militiamen, to the provision of office material for daily administration, the commander's loan of his estate as a parade ground and of his house as a headquarters and a store for archives—all these forms reappeared in *gaúcho* society. It would be tedious to document again a pattern that gained national uniformity. Yet one general remark is necessary: the rather subdued nature of private cooperation in the *gaúcho* case is worthy of note. The aspects discussed below will throw some light on this deviation.

A provincial rebellion (from 1835 to 1845) of the *gaúcho estancieiros* against the Crown brought the orderly functioning of the militias to a halt. Internal strife absorbed the attention of the state. There are no documents in either the provincial or national archives dealing with this critical period. Those available are few and scanty and do not permit a clear reconstruction of patterns. Little is known, then, about the first half-century of militia history. There is every reason to presume, however, that the domestic or administrative functions of government assigned to the militias were reduced to a bare minimum, given the prevailing critical circumstances. There was, consequently, probably little demand for liturgies and private resources from a stratum of lords thus divided. At the turn of the mid-century, a conflict with Uruguay led to the organization of the Cisplatine Campaign, and from 1864 to 1870 a bloody war against Paraguay took place. Peace had just come when the 1873 law deprived the militias of their liturgical obligations with regard to local government.

It is understandable that the almost permanently warlike state of the *gaúcho* territory (1835–1845, 1851–1852, 1864–1870) left little room for the involvement of its militias in the functions of local government. It is also natural, under the circumstances, that its officerdom did not become very involved in defraying the costs of functions that had been severely crippled. This general remark should not be taken to imply that the *gaúcho* landlord was an uncooperative servant. It is meant to partially explain why the pattern of cooperation through private funding that obtained in *gaúcho* territory was more similar to that of Bahia and Minas Gerais. Another cause had to do with the vicissitudes of the seigneurial project in the southern province; scant concern for aristocratic

values probably contributed to the pattern of the reduced
patrimonial funding of the militias, which was characteristic
of Rio Grande do Sul.

The *Gaúcho* Project

Corporate reason was as cunning with respect to *gaúcho* ideals as it had been in other provinces.

The most striking characteristic of the *gaúcho* ethos was
the relative absence of an aristocratic ideal. The *gaúcho* sense
of social honor was more linked to the ideal of military hierarchy than to that of social gentility. Status honor developed
essentially along military lines. Indeed, corporate identity
and rank integrity were chiefly related to military values. A
commander-in-chief expressed his indignation by not an-
swering a letter from a militiaman, just because the lieutenant
colonel of one of his battalions was described in that letter as
"you" (*Senhor*), whereas he himself, a still higher officer, was
addressed by the militiaman with a less ceremonious and
hierarchical "thou" (*tu*). The colonel, however familiar he
might have been with the informal and established forms of
address of the people, just could not stomach this lack of
tact.[5]

The need for hierarchical recognition was not limited to
the relationship among the members of the association. This
hypersensitivity applied to interaction with other institutions
as well. *Gaúcho* commanders submitted protests and developed grudges—unjustified at times from a strictly legal
standpoint—against local justices of the peace who requisitioned troops from the company commanders rather than the
corpos commanders. A commander-in-chief, incensed by the
inattention paid by the director of the war arsenal to his request for troops, asked for satisfaction and redress from this
director, who excused himself before the president, alleging
that the commander's request was not warranted.[6]

Hand in hand with the development of an acute hierarchical identity appeared an equally striking lack of concern
for genteel stylization. This trait may be abstracted from a
variety of sources, and is, generally speaking, reminiscent of
the pattern in Bahia and Minas Gerais.

In the case of Bahia, for instance, an analysis of the documentation of the first decade of the century—so rich in status qualifications and the like in the center of the Empire—revealed two uniform traits: the lack of status qualifications and the total absence of evidence to indicate that militarized *honoratiores* contributed economically to the routine administration of the militias. The practice of financing the musical band, institutionalized in Rio de Janeiro and the Court, did not exist in Bahia. The sources show, rather, that the local commands made all possible efforts to have the state satisfy the material needs of the corporation. This, along with the reduced number of cavalry units and the relative absence of transfer requests to that branch, may be taken as an indication of the infirmity of an aristocratic ideal.

Similar considerations hold good for Minas Gerais in the 1830s. The first mention of any private contributions is that made by the officers of the Diamantina battalion, and this occurred in the last year of the decade. There is no evidence that commanders or officers made a practice of buying the uniforms for their subordinates.[7] Nor were there many requests for transfers to cavalry units. Furthermore, analysis of electoral documents for officers in 1839 reveals that there was no concern with status qualifications, only with legal requirements.[8]

The 1840s essentially reproduced these traits in Bahia and Minas Gerais. Proposals from different districts were characterized, on the whole, by the absence of status qualifications. Observations accompanying these proposals pointed out that the candidate to office satisfied the legal requirements, and the intention was clearly *pro forma*. Civil status and profession were indicated, but there was no qualifying appreciation such as *proprietario abastado* (rich landowner), typical of the Court and its peripheral province.[9]

The remarkable point is that in this period attempts to erect a seigneurial culture with status group identity among the landlord stratum came chiefly from the Imperial authorities. It was these authorities, in fact, rather than the militiamen, who emphasized status qualifications.[10]

The seigneurialization of the militarized strata of landlords of Minas Gerais and Bahia took place at the turn of the mid-century. It was then that Bahian and *Mineiro* landlords finally caught up with the status orientation typical of the center of the Empire. It was then that the precocious legalism of the agrarian elite from Bahia (precocious, that is, when compared with the development of a legal rationality in the other provinces, not when seen from the perspective that for several centuries Bahia was the seat of the Empire and the higher magistracy) gave way to rank and social authority; it was also then that the Spartan values of moral virtuosism of the *Mineiro honoratior* succumbed to socially adscriptive elements. Only in Minas Gerais was it conceivable to find a dispatch of this kind: "When Your Excellency ponders well on what a [military] Instructor is, Your Excellency will have to select men who instruct not only in tactics but also in morals that do not scandalize the Public. An Instructor, Sir, is a Teacher; he must be a man of very good habits."[11]

This novel trend was reflected, for instance, in the proliferation of cavalry corps, in the sudden search for emblems and symbols, and in the attempts at prebendalization of office. Contrary to certain firmly established ideas of sociological theory, in which the center of the system is the seedbed of modernization and the rationalization of action, the Imperial centers in Brazil—the Court and the provincial capitals—favored the development of adscription and particularism. The new concern for status symbols and prerogatives occurred principally at the center. For instance, in the *sertão* of Minas Gerais there was no interest in finding out whether officers' sons should be considered first or second cadets, and whether they should wear this or that uniform. This occurred, on the contrary, in the central area of the oldest settlement, Barbacenas, a town in the mining region. Ouro Preto, the provincial capital, required moral virtuosity to be displayed by candidates for military instructorship in the first half of the century, but in the second half a candidate could be recommended because "he is considered very distinguished and qualified to instruct." The peripheral areas, by contrast, were just beginning to become familiar with the symbolic paraphernalia of rank and status; scarcely socialized into the corporate codes of pomp and circumstance, the newly appointed major commander in the "frontier" town of Serro addressed a letter to the local commander-in-chief, asking "if in the service of this Office I am permitted to wear the badges proper to Majors." Equally at a loss, the commander-in-chief is forced to relay the question to the provincial authorities. [12]

It is therefore possible to state that the 1850s saw the development of a status orientation among the dominant agrarian strata of the Empire. It seems correct to add, moreover, that the major sources of this development were the bureaucratic authorities of the Imperial nucleus of power.

The development in Rio Grande do Sul was, all the same, somewhat different. The lack of status qualifications, it is true, was a factor there during the first decades. This trait is in fact striking. Corporate membership was, however, variously based on pragmatic criteria generally lacking in the rest of the Empire. Local members of the community, for instance, were submitted as candidates to office "mainly because they reside at the locations of the Companies for which they are proposed." Characteristically, a legion major was proposed as instructor general not only because of his abilities, but also to avoid the inconveniences of job duplication. Only in Rio Grande do Sul, moreover, could corporate membership in the officer rank be denied for lack of the necessary strength and agility. [13]

But it was above all courage (*valentia*), the most characteristically *gaúcho* criterion, that set the virtuoso character of its officerdom. Thus, whereas it was the usual practice elsewhere for officers to buttress their requests for retirement with data on their liturgical contributions, *gaúchos* preferred to emphasize their military feats. One lieutenant colonel, for instance, not only neglected to submit evidence, officially required, to demonstrate the fulfillment of his patrimonial obligations, but he limited himself to describing an exploit that was for him reason enough to merit his dispensation. Needless to say, this conception of courage had very little to do with the classical *virtus* of the Roman notable; nothing in it suggested urbane and stoic strength of mind. It was closer to a notion of risk and fate, whose origin can probably be traced to the Islamic influence of eight centuries of Moorish domination on the Iberian peninsula. It is indeed significant

that this lieutenant colonel saw a worthy exploit in the fact
of being "attacked in 1857 by twenty-odd bandits, who fired
two volleys at him at close range, and chased him with intense anger and fury for over a *legoa*—as duly documented
by the provincial annals . . . [having as a consequence] of the
shots, one bullet received with five lead pellets in his back,
two in the head, and half a dozen in one leg, and a broken
arm."[14]

Courage, or what passed for it in that pastoral culture,
was not simply a desired ideal of virtuoso stylization. The
quasi-permanent warlike state of affairs provided ample opportunities for its material expression. *Valentia* was, in fact,
a qualification met with some regularity by the *gaúcho* officerdom. It ranked, together with service experience and talent for command, higher than social or economic status during most of the history of these militias. In practically all
proposals for admission to, or promotion within, the officer
rank in the first part of the century, social status was the last
qualification to be included—if and when it was.[15]

Instrumental values continued to be dominant in the
third quarter of the century. The warlike conditions of the
time could not permit a relaxation of pragmatic considerations. The major shift in the value orientations of the *gaúcho*
militias actually took place in the aftermath of the war with
Paraguay and after the passage of the 1873 organic law. It
was then, in fact, that the status orientation clearly appeared
in Rio Grande do Sul. Thus, in contrast to previous directives
that attempted to broaden the enlistment, the new measures
were issued "in order to exclude, from now on, from the
Guarda Nacional those individuals who do not possess sufficient income . . . to obtain the uniforms required by law."[16]

It is plausible, in fact, to assume that the avocational
foundations of the *Guarda Nacional* attracted the corporation
toward a seigneurial project, particularly after the war against
Paraguay. It should be kept in mind that the 1870s and 1880s
were the only period of peace in the province. As a result,
selective criteria of admission were implemented. Pragmatic
considerations could thus leave room for the first time for a
vicarious orientation reflected in the process of selection.[17]
The change, nevertheless, was too abrupt, and was out of
proportion to the development of previous decades.

As a matter of fact, given the peculiarity of regional conditions, any aristocratic project would have been doomed to
failure from the start. The very notion of horsemanship as a
genteel trait, in a province where "there is not one single individual who, however poor he may be, does not possess his
own horse," was chimeric, to say the least.[18]

The restriction of membership to citizens possessing incomes that met the required legal minimum, moreover, would
have meant a drastic reduction in the size of the corporation
and a perversion of its function: "Nobody ignores that the
Guarda Nacional of the *Campanha* is in very large measure
made up of citizens who do not have the income required by
law, but who are the most appropriate soldiers for the cavalry, due to their habits and professions. The corps commanders would do wrong to exclude them, because the corps
would consequently remain decimated."

It is important to add that the above opinion was, to all
intents and purposes, the official one, in so far as it came
from a provincial mandarin. The law was honored by being
constantly broken.[19] This consideration appears even more
decisive when it is born in mind that the Imperial commission, especially created to examine the military potential of
Rio Grande do Sul, saw in the *gaúcho* militias' cavalry,

the most essential arm in the organization of our Army in
case of war with our neighbors. . . . [In] the circumstances
of armed peace in which we must consider ourselves, it is
the Cavalry of the *Guarda Nacional* which constitutes the
most essential component of the Brigades ready to operate,
and which performs patrolling of the frontiers, communication services, etc. . . . [This] is the most adequate force
with which to oppose a fearful enemy.[20]

Additional factors were also at work. Decree 2073 of January 23, 1858, which dispensed from active service *estancieiros*
and estate administrators who branded over 100 head of cattle per year, not only further inhibited the objective possibility of establishing a seigneurial project, it also helped to
reduce the gap in social composition between the corporation
and the professional army, and to sap the possibilities of a
genuine avocational administration, in as much as the eco-

nomically dominant strata were dispensed from active service. The effects did not take long to show up; a year later, a commander-in-chief reported that,

> to comply with all the orders and dispositions of the Government concerning the *Guarda Nacional*, it would be necessary that the Corps and Company Commanders were wealthy Citizens who could perform only this service, but it is not in that class that the best servants of the Nation are always found, and this is why they are drawn from the class of those less favored by fortune, who cannot meet all the obligations imposed on them by the office [because] they have to take care of their future and their families.[21]

The reasons the postwar militias failed to become genteelly stylized did not lie only in the past. Any systematic attempt to develop a particular style of conduct depends very much on the vigorous institutionalization of a system of values. Such a process was not possible after the protracted conflict. The postwar period actually gave birth to an unparalleled degree of corporate anomie, which serves as a background to interpret the efforts at corporate gentility as a desperate move to restore some sense of value to the patrimonial project. This severe crisis was by no means limited to the *gaúcho* region; it extended to the extreme north, giving rise to rumors that the *Guarda Nacional* would be extinguished or substantially reformed. Some authorities went to the extreme of suggesting its "annihilation."[22]

The crisis developed with particular speed and scope in Rio Grande do Sul, where enlistment was practically suspended. The disaggregating effects of the Paraguayan conflict appeared even before it had come to an end, but only afterward did they burst out with virulence. Few areas escaped the affliction—Rio Pardo, Encruzilhada, Quarai, Livramento, Alegrete, Uruguaiana, Piratini, São Borja, Itacui, Cruz Alta— it is hard to find a local command that escaped the climate of despondency. The majority of officers coming back from the front avoided service at all costs on the pretext of illness or business; commands remained acephalous for years for lack of officers. The patrimonial charm had been broken; officers "in commission" who had received a rank in the professional army at the war front returned as "honorary" officers legally entitled to opt for the army and an official stipend. The crisis was so great that the dispatches acquired an almost surrealistic tone, because of the brutal discrepancy between the literal meaning of terms and the concrete context of their application. Ten years later a frontier commander-in-chief reported that "the *Guarda Nacional* of this County is still [*sic!*] disorganized."[23]

Two major changes in the postwar organization of the criteria of qualification further attest that the successful development of a status orientation was highly improbable. In fact, after ten years of tribulation and spectacular chaos, in the 1880s the corporation launched a new period of organization.

The spirit that guided this new militia appeared in two new patterns, both of which revealed the erosion of the hierarchical orientation typical of the *gaúcho* militias. The first, which illustrates the existence of external criteria, was the short-circuiting of career stages on the promotional ladder. The unprecedented practice appeared of submitting the names of individuals from the rank and file for posts of command (such as captains) as well as for other offices.

The second pattern, which revealed a still more radical break with the past, was the recommendation of private citizens who had no previous links to the corporation to the officer ranks. To fully appreciate the revolutionary nature of these new patterns, it is important to see them against the background of this province, considering its peculiar sense of hierarchy, discipline, and military rank.[24]

It is possible to see in these new practices the effect of a decimated and disintegrating corporation without sufficient members to replenish its hierarchical layers, without successfully socialized members, and without a sense of patrimonial mission. But it is probable that what lay behind this metamorphosis was the substitution of the hierarchical principle of selection for the factionalist one of political patronage.

Not that this was a uniquely *gaúcho* development. Bahia also experienced in the last decade of the Empire the same profanation of the notion of corporate continuity in promotion. In fact, many proposals contained no information about the candidates other than the fact that they were citizens, a new and republican attribute.[25]

The obvious question is, then, why, in the light of such a lack of liturgical obligations and patrimonial commitments, did the corporation continue as an active force? What was the use of the continuous mobilization of local and national energies and resources? What objective was served by a corporation that kept thousands of bureaucrats, commanders, and officers busy to no apparent purpose and without a practical agenda?

The *Guarda Nacional* did indeed continue to function even after the 1873 law, which transformed it into an essentially vicarious institution. It committed a great number of people to a variety of activities that extended to all corners of the Empire. The following dispatch is one of probably thousands of the same type. It reveals that even in its postpatrimonial stage there were citizens who invested considerable energy in the corporation. On April 10, 1885, the commander-in-chief of the county of Rio Pardo wrote an official letter to the President of the Province of Rio Grande do Sul. It was a lengthy, elaborate document, full of information as well as personal reflections. It reported the number of officers and guards in active service in the previous enlistment (32 and 1,694, respectively), the current number of guards (1,294), and the state of an infantry section; it suggested a reorganization of the corps in view of the number of companies and the extent of the region in order to facilitate the annual review; it proposed to the central government a specific scheme of organization; and it suggested the candidacy of two citizens as officers and justified the appointments with lengthy observations on their background and qualifications.[26]

This report was not unique. No doubt the amount of such correspondence was not as great as it had been in previous decades, but the fact that it persisted with some regularity is dramatic evidence that the *Guarda Nacional* continued until the end of the Empire as an institutional establishment, that is, a regular system of continuous action.

The general orientation of such a system of action was no longer liturgical; it was political. Politics had been an important element in the militias of all provinces in the second and third quarters of the century. But in the last quarter, after the war and the new law, politics became their most important if not the only concern of the corporation.

The political perversion of the *Guarda Nacional* began in earnest in the 1840s. In the previous decade, the only political consideration had taken place in those cases where a candidate to office had or had not rendered "valuable services for the cause of [monarchical] legality," as the phrase usually ran. In the next decade, however, local factionalism began to make political use of the corporation as systematically as possible. Just as some guards were transferred to the reserve as a reward for their electoral loyalty, others were penalized by the imposition of heavy liturgies. Admission into the officer rank and prospects for promotion were also subject to the contingencies of political factionalism. But the office of command—of a company, a batallion, or whatever—was the most valuable political conquest. A commander could torpedo the political ambitions of his personal enemies by, so to speak, liturgically harassing his opponent's patriarchal clientele or by promptly cooperating with the local authorities in eventually lawful moves against his enemies. On occasions the command became a crucial piece in the electoral process thanks to the commander's control of the mobilization of the militiamen and his other official functions. These and other forms of political patronage that the fertile imagination of ambitious commanders devised necessarily gave the *Guarda Nacional* a strategic function at the local and provincial levels. As a result, stability of command came to be linked occasionally to the political accidents of the provincial and national government.[27]

These circumstances were reproduced in the third quarter of the century. Those negatively affected by the ballot addressed local protests to the Court or the presidencies, concerning commanders who abused their authority by interfering illegally with the electoral process. The border conflicts offered these commanders a new and dreadful means of coercion, namely, the enlistment of militiamen of the opposed faction into war service.

State authorities, in a fruitless effort to neutralize this influence, began to issue regular instructions prohibiting corps and company commanders from gathering or reviewing the rank and file in periods of electoral activity. The most effective measure in fact came at the end of the third quarter of the century, with the transformation of the *Guarda Nacional* into a *de facto* corporation of officers. The elimination of ordinary liturgical duties and the radical reduction of the power to regiment gave the corporation the semblance of a club.[28]

Despite its critical function as the major organ of national defense, the *Guarda Nacional* of Rio Grande do Sul could not escape the influence of factionalism. The second quarter of the century, indeed, was marked by the effect of the *Farroupilha* rebellion (1835–1845) on the organization of the corporation. Entire battalions were dissolved whenever the behavior of their members was considered disloyal or opposed to the interests of the central state. This was, for instance, the fate of the infantry battalions of the provincial capital.[29] Admission into the officership was, as might be expected, primarily contingent on the candidate's stand in regard to the regional dispute. Moreover, its effects were felt for some years after the conflict. The provincial commander-in-chief gave instructions not to admit to active service persons who had served on the side of the rebellious forces.[30]

These were not the only ways in which the corporation was subject to the impact of politics. Immediately after the pacification of the province, the militias became a major factor in electoral politics involving both local and provincial authorities. It was a practice for corps commanders to solicit cooperation from their subordinate officers in favor of electoral rolls; disobedient officers were likely to be separated from the corps after a presidential change, obviously on the initiative of the commanders.[31]

The third quarter of the century saw a new outbreak of factionalism in the organization of the militias. The war campaigns were no obstacle to using the corporation for political ends. The extraordinary processes of enlistment dictated by the needs of war, for instance, were used as instruments of electoral coercion and postelectoral retaliation. To rid these processes of political maneuvering, the presidents of the provinces issued instructions to execute enlistment orders during nonelectoral periods. Similarly, during peaceful years, enlistment into the reserve was frequently considered a form of political protection to be granted to the electoral clientele.[32]

Corporate leadership, moreover, was to some extent dependent on the vicissitudes of national politics. For instance, the end of the year 1862 was also the end of a relatively long period of provincial administration, which was characterized by its opposition to the *comandante superior* of Cruz Alta. The new year began with a new president, who did not have to wait long to receive from the commander a "Proposal to improve the state of the Higher Command corps . . . of Cruz Alta." It could not have been more drastic; the list contained fifty-eight candidates, literally altering the entire local structure of corps command.[33]

But at the end of that quarter and throughout the next one the effect of political factionalism on the corporation was felt most intensely. The erosion of patrimonial orientation had already appeared in the final year of the war; then for the first time in the documented history of the militias officers refused to serve their liturgies, as a means of manifesting their political opposition to a party in power. There had existed in the past political maneuvering *with* the corporation, never *against* it. The corporation assumed a political identity that was altogether novel. One commander reported that he would not be able to obtain cooperation and service "because all [my officers] are political partisans involved in a coalition with the liberal party." And a year later his successor confirmed "the reluctance of the majority of Officers of the *Guarda Nacional* of this County to render any service, so as to oppose the established situation."[34]

Nevertheless, not until after the war was the climax reached. The partisan—as opposed to the patrimonial—definition of liturgies was delineated more sharply and in such a way that officers felt obliged to serve only when their political party was in power. The connection between local commands and party politics was reinforced by the overt role played by commanders in electoral struggles. Thus, after relaying the list of candidates who had to be strategically appointed for electoral maneuvering, a commander added: "The approval of these proposals, as well as those which Your Excellency has allegedly requested of the Imperial Government, will guarantee the victory of the conservative party in the next elections, in those parishes where we have jurisdiction. In view of the trust and support which Your Excellency and the Government have given us, it [the victory] is almost a foregone conclusion."

The local strength and success of a political party was now interpreted as a function of the *Guarda Nacional* as a matter of course: "The liberal party is strong in Sao Borja, especially because the other party lacks a person of official position in the *Guarda Nacional* who can organize and take charge of things."

The enthusiastic conviction that control of the *Guarda Nacional* was the key to electoral victory occasionally led to extremes that were, in all likelihood, tacitly accepted, but whose explicit mention was in bad political taste; a local supporter of the provincial administration suggested the appointment of some local notables as a means of winning the forthcoming elections, and then added: "if Your Excellency cannot make these appointments before September, just give me orders and send me the necessary troops because I shall win, with the help of arms if need be."[35]

It was probably this constellation of factors that led a provincial president to express in a confidential letter to the Court that "great value is given in the Province to the pronouncements of the *Comandantes Superiores.*" The saliency of the corporation as a political instance in the postwar period transpires in the role that the provincial authorities wanted it to play when republican ideas appeared among the professional military. Just after the war the president communicated to the Court its concern with the activities of certain prominent officers, who were trying to find a liberal solution, capitalizing on the growing discontent among the professional military in the *Campanha* and the garrisons at the frontier. He observed that in order to neutralize the pernicious activities of officers with a republican orientation, all that was needed was to detain them at their posts and then relocate the corps to the frontier before election time. It is significant, however, that the *Guarda Nacional* was represented as a force of contention against a convulsive army. Along with the police, in fact, it was supposed to act as a decisive influence in neutralizing army officers.[36]

Finally, the corporate climate of the postwar period and of the end of the Empire was vividly illustrated by the appearance of a new value as a qualifying attribute for would-be officers, namely, reliability or trustworthiness. Trustworthiness had been considered important in other provinces in previous decades but not in Rio Grande do Sul. There it appeared in the 1870s with a frequency that was as radical as it was novel. This is indicative of how deeply political factionalism had reached into the corporation as one of its major constitutive principles.[37]

The Frontier Commander: the Expert Dilettante

In the Imperial history of patrimonial administration, the frontier form is unquestionably the most uniquely *gaúcho* development.

It is indicative of the patrimonial orientation of the Imperial state organization that it had enlisted and relied as much as possible on the private cooperation of its subjects for critical tasks associated with territorial integrity. Previously we have noted the major role assigned by the central state to the local militias. No war effort was, indeed, conceivable without them. "I must warn Your Excellency," the provincial president informed the War Ministry, "that if we have to invade the Oriental State [Uruguay], I intend to add to the Army the frontier Corps of the *Guarda Nacional* . . . because these Corps, accustomed to constant detachments, are exceptionally mobile, especially for the said objective."

On the other hand, the state authorities soon realized that because of the magnitude of private liturgies, the corporation required exceptionally rational administrative assistance in order to be successful. "I just have to express to Your Excellency," writes the provincial president on the eve of reorganization, "that it is not possible for the President of Rio Grande do Sul to adequately look after the minutiae of organization, discipline, economy, bookkeeping, and fiscalization of the amounts spent on the service of the *Guarda Nacional*, its equipment and horses, without the assistance of an intelligent inspector in the said *Guarda Nacional*."[38] The *gaúcho* officer was supposed to be a special breed of man; as an ideal patrimonial servant, the state expected that he "combine the talent for war service along with [his] influence in his place of residence, not forgetting [i.e., when considering him as a candidate for office] his political stance favoring the Government."[39]

There was in all these remarks a recurrent *Leitmotiv* that contributed to set the peculiar tone of the *gaúcho* corporation, namely, the urgency of rationally adapting the liturgical association of freemen to the requirements of a bureaucratic enterprise.

It is true that army officers were frequently required by the *honoratiores* of other provinces to initiate them into the arcana of rational administration that the officers were so well versed in, and occasionally to replace "landlords with little knowledge of military service, dwelling in more or less distant places and busy with their agriculture and business." But the professionalization of the corporation went no farther than this.[40]

The *gaúcho* case was different; the bureaucratic impact of the professional military on the corporation was more permanent, more systematic, and more generalized. An army commander of a division could also serve as a frontier commander-in-chief of the *Guarda Nacional*; patrimonial commanders were, moreover, exposed to military instructions from professional officers of a higher rank, which further enhanced professional expectations; and even nonfrontier commands demanded a pattern of performance that was dictated by the urgency of needs at the front.

Generally speaking, the pattern of performance was exceptionally good in view of the demands behind war liturgies. The document below is particularly relevant for two reasons. On one hand, it reveals the considerable amount of private initiative necessary in the corporate routine of the *gaúcho* setting; on the other hand, it reveals a vacillating and timid cast of mind that was very seldom found in the militarized *gaúcho* culture. At the beginning of the war against Paraguay, the commander of the twenty-third cavalry corps of Rio Pardo was ordered to campaign service, and was expected in Bagé with the entire effective force. The commander, apparently taken aback by the imminence of the presidential order, replied with a volley of questions. Exactly what was the number of guards that made up an effective contingent? Was the corps to head for the front with or without a surgeon, a fiscal overseer, and a secretary? Who catered, and where, to the guards? He needed to know the number of guards, he added in justification, in order to plan for the purchase of horses and so on. These questions indicated his acting status and the obstacles of dilettante warfare.[41]

The efficient execution of the corporation's manifest goals was also obstructed in part by the officer's own material needs in Rio Grande do Sul. The virtual tension between these goals and these needs was pointedly observed by a commander who had been instructed to comply with regulations calling for a quarterly review of the different units under his jurisdiction. After mentioning the great distances between the different corps and so on, he added that if the regulations were strictly obeyed, "The Chief of the General Staff of this Higher Command would not have time to remain at home one single day, and such a situation is not compatible with an officer who is not salaried and who receives no remuneration."

Others, particularly residents at the frontier, occasionally assumed a rather defiant attitude. One captain, instructed to proceed as urgently as possible to a local district with the officers of his command for a corporate meeting, enumerated his reasons for not complying: "(1) . . . I have my interests in the Oriental State [Uruguay] and I must arrange them . . . ; (2) I must get ready to leave for a Campaign, perhaps a very long one." And he concluded with obvious sarcasm, "As soon as these considerations cease to obtain, I will punctually obey orders."[42]

On the whole, however, such tension was less critical in Rio Grande do Sul, since the *gaúcho* corporation received from the state a more active contribution for the satisfaction of its needs, and, in particular, thanks to the presence of the professional military within the administrative hierarchy of the militias. These factors, allied to the peculiarity of provincial location and to the military tradition reigning there, gave birth to frontier commanders with a remarkable degree of initiative and an enterprising spirit that set them off from the typical patrimonial dilettantes.

In a way, the *gaúcho* militia officer was a commander used to an immense scale of organization in comparison with the smaller scale of the northern servant. The commander of the *Guarda Nacional* of Cruz Alta, for example, was commissioned by the provincial authorities to buy, on behalf of the state, 10,000 horses in his district and deliver them to the army 250 miles away. It would have been beyond imagination to entrust such a complex errand to a northern *honoratior*. No doubt this was not a routine purchase, but all the same it indicates the characteristic scale and context of operations by *gaúcho* commanders. Above we saw how an inexperienced acting commander of a Rio Pardo cavalry corps prepared his unit for war detachment in a relatively short period of time, which also included the time spent awaiting official answers to entirely rational logistic questions.[43]

It is interesting in this respect to note that, although at the Court and in Rio de Janeiro and elsewhere the commanders viewed the democratic election of officers as deleterious for the corporation on the grounds that it might bring to positions of leadership ordinary individuals without social authority, the *gaúcho* commanders argued that elections were deleterious because those chosen may "entirely ignore the military praxis." These are two contrasting forms in which early indiscipline was explained away. In one case, obedience is thought to follow from social authority, in the other, from practical knowledge and expertise.[44]

This emphasis on rational competence was obviously a pragmatic requirement for frontier duties. To be an *official de campanha* demanded an instrumentally oriented frame of mind that judged the militias from a utilitarian point of view. Frontier commanders alone occasionally disbanded entire company-sized contingents of guards for lack of competent officers. The swiftness and relative efficiency of this organization was considerable and, what is more, was assumed as a matter of course. There is nothing extraordinary in the instructions given by the commander-in-chief of the Misiones frontier requesting the presence of the commander of Cruz Alta, over 200 miles eastward, for 300 horsemen to be enlisted on notice and due in fifteen days. It would be incorrect, moreover, to think that this climate of permanent mobilization and the concomitant pragmatic frame of mind of the *gaúcho* commander existed only in periods of open conflict. They were, on the contrary, rather pervasive and permanent traits of *gaúcho* militarized society.[45]

The overall effect of this development was the creation of an *aficionado* commander with an unparalleled degree of private initiative, which was reinforced by the need for organizational autonomy in making quick decisions. One frontier commander decided to sidestep the commander-in-chief and the commander of his legion and to request instructions from a higher authority, otherwise, as he said, "I'll never accomplish anything as I'm always in the same predicament," namely, always waiting for instructions. This and other instances clearly reveal that substantive considerations of defense prevailed over formal legal requirements without much hesitation. This was tersely put by one commander in São Borja who had enlisted unqualified individuals: "I would rather assume responsibility for disobedience to the [organic] law than leave the garrisons without manpower for service and for any emergency that might take place.[46]

This picture indicates the extent to which the central state left the responsibility for assuming initiatives in the hands of its patrimonial officers, justifying this by the organization of the territory. It is conceivable that, without the spirit of initiative displayed by these militarized *honoratiores*, the corporate structure—with all its irritating proclivity to pass the buck to the bureaucratic authorities, as was the case in the north—would have proved an inadequate instrument of military administration on the frontier.

Fully conscious of the above circumstances, the state encouraged the enlistment of enterprising dilettantes, in so far as frontier commanders received special faculties vis-à-vis local bureaucrats. The commanders were given the power to enlist neighborhood inspectors, police delegates and subdelegates, justices of the peace and municipal judges who were not exercising office. Thus, in contrast to the rest of the Empire where the militarized *honoratiores* were at the service of the magistrates and the police, here the local bureaucracy of government was, to a large extent, subordinated to defense needs as defined by frontier commanders. The commanders, by the way, did not hesitate to make use of this power.[47]

All these circumstances favored the emergence of a *gaúcho* commander with a sharp awareness of the value of his patrimonial services to the state. When this awareness was asserted, it splendidly but imperceptibly contributed to the state's institutionalization of its own normative obligations. When a provincial president refused to credit the salaries and rations of a detached corps because he had not authorized them, the local commander replied that such detachment was made by virtue of dispositions to which he was legally entitled, and concluded:

> If Your Excellency does not give orders (as I expect Your Excellency will do) to pay for that detachment as soon as possible, Your Excellency may at once start giving Your orders to another *Comandante Superior* appointed by Your Excellency, because I cannot accept that Your Excellency will not pay the consideration which I am entitled to demand from all my Superiors, and that the great trust which I deserve from Your Excellency should be reserved only for political elections.[48]

This concludes our examination of the major patrimonial structure of government in Imperial Brazil; we have identified those aspects that obstructed the execution of its tasks and perverted its manifestly established functions. The *Guarda Nacional*, however, did not deal with a fully developed bureaucratic state; had this been the case, it would not have had a *raison d'être* in the first place. The state it served was in the process of intense metamorphosis; the transformations taking place in its midst had noticeable repercussions in the state's interaction with the agrarian militias. We will now turn to this development and attempt to define its significance for the institutionalization of a new, modern, rational, and bourgeois social order.

7

The Modern State:
From Patrimonial Maxims
to Bureaucratic Principles

L'anatomie de l'homme est la clef de l'anatomie du singe.

Marx, *Contribution à la Critique de l'Economie Politique*

The transition from patrimonial to bureaucratic domination does not imply simply the establishment of a new administrative order. Above all else, bureaucratic domination requires a new legal order within which the public sphere is subject for the first time to a set of norms entirely different from those obtaining in the private sphere. Historically, the lord and his household managed to impose the standards of the patriarchal order on the patrimonial "public" domain, which became genuinely public only with the institutionalization of its own legality. The sociological literature has generally called attention to the first problem, the administrative one. It has seldom paid attention to another, more complex question, namely, the creation of a legal order for the legitimation of political coercion. This last chapter will examine the changes brought about in the system of administrative officials and servants of the Brazilian Imperial state. I will attempt to trace the shifting patterns of legitimation of authority and, in particular, the development of legal rational authority.

Before that, I will discuss some of the major structural changes that were taking place in the overall institutional order.

The Luddites of the Backlands

> [C]'est précisément la systématisation, c'est-à-dire le fait
> d'élever à l'universel, qui est la tendance infinie de notre
> époque.
>
> Hegel, *Philosophie du droit*, par. 211, Gans' *Zusatz*

Kant concludes his *Critique of Practical Reason* with some brief but splendid reflections on the sublime character of the moral law within us. Profound admiration and respect for this moral law, he comments, is no substitute for its scientific investigation. Of all the major sociologists, Durkheim was the only one to take up Kant's program and to convey the awesome Kantian sentiment toward the moral order. At about the time that Durkheim began his sociological work, a moral order was crumbling and a new one was coming into being in agrarian Brazil. Society no longer commanded the respect of the rural Brazilian; old habits, practices, and institutions were being brusquely changed and replaced by new and unfamiliar canons. In the early 1870s two new laws exacerbated this intolerable sense of drift experienced by the poor freemen—a law of universal and compulsory conscription for military service ("the blood tax due to the army") and another adopting the metric system of weights and measures. This sense of disorientation became unbearable, and it eventually led to a mass protest of short but intense virulence, which encompassed four provinces of the Empire and lasted a little over a month. The movement took the name of the central activity of those involved, the *quebraquilos* (scales-smashers). Bands of rural inhabitants, varying in number from fifty to several hundred, in spontaneous yet simultaneous concert, would enter towns and burn the notary's office, the local post office, and the public archives, liberate the convicts from the municipal jails, and intrude into the commercial establishments to smash the instruments of measurement. Significantly, they acted on market days; "the seditionaries would assume control of the market place and start to destroy the weights snatched from the merchants, to shatter to pieces the measuring cups of retail grocers, picking up standards of all sizes, to throw them immediately away."[1]

A few days after it first appeared, the movement spread like wildfire to seven counties; in less than a month four provinces were burning. Several bands would get together to occupy large cities. The public authorities were impotent and could not effectively resist. Although they did not follow premeditated and centralized planning, the peasants struck as though following a preestablished command. A chief of police stated in his investigation that many counties rose up "as one single person, under the impulse of one single objective, on the same day, against every established principle, manifesting determined opposition to the laws and the established authorities."[2] The flame burnt out as quickly as it had started.

The general and collective character of the movement makes implausible any attempt to explain it away as a mere episode; it had, in fact, the dimensions of a social fact of which the overall significance was the desperate effort made by the bearers of a dying order to negate the actuality of a new one. The conventional view that the *quebraquilos* movement was the product of religious fanaticism (the country was at that time witnessing a very delicate confrontation between the Catholic hierarchy and the state) is insufficient and unsatisfactory; it does not account for the wide spectrum of institutions against which the rural freeman violently protested. In fact it was the religious aspect of the movement that had a more episodic character. The protest was addressed against both public and private institutions, and with particular vehemence against the system of weights and measures. It was a conscious but intuitive and ineffable protest against bourgeois rationality, against the abstract notion of rational calculus that was subjecting the whole society to a unified system of laws. Just as the British Luddites protested two generations earlier against a new industrial order, the Luddites of the Brazilian *sertão* were now protesting against a new social order.

Sine Ira et Studio . . . but Still Passionately

The political institutionalization of that order and its new legality was no easy matter. The state was slow to build up an effective repressive apparatus. The highest authority of an important province confessed the powerlessness of the state apparatus to put a stop to the invasion of public lands in a rather central district: "As the Government and the Legislature know, today the Public Administration has few or no means to put a stop to such illegal and dangerous invasions of lands belonging to the Nation due to the absolute lack of the necessary force to protect them." Ten years later in the same province, a court judge questioned not only the probability of adjudicating justice but even the continuity of office,

> without being able to guarantee my permanence, given the absolute lack of personal security and the inexistence of means to make it effective, even when there is good disposition on the part of the local Authorities . . . [The district is under the reign of terror of a family and] nobody dares to annoy them, no Authority has the courage to prosecute them, and no witness would show up to testify, such is the terror they impose.

Two years later, in a clumsy dispatch, a provincial chief of police had "the honor" to declare that "moral repression" was jeopardized because more than thirty towns had no jails and the state and security conditions of those that existed were deplorable.[3]

But it was not just the relative absence of armed forces, penitentiary institutions, or magistrates that made the institutionalization of a normative pattern difficult. The process was equally obstructed by the immense power of the local landlords and their patriarchal clienteles. The official correspondence of provincial presidents to the Court frequently betrayed a mixed feeling of amazement and incredulity at the amount of power held by this stratum of landlords. Thus, the President of Sergipe reports: "This man is the terror of the *sertão* of Bahia and his malefic influence reaches into this Province. In Campos, a boundary district with Itapicuru, you will never find a police officer who, in the fulfillment of his duty, dares step into [his] fief."

Three months before the date of the above report, the same authority realized that governing the province was, in his words, like governing hell. "It is not a custom of this province," he adds, "to take action against landlords who hide criminals. It is enough to rid them of their moral force by having their estates besieged and rounding up the criminals." He had, interestingly, given a vigorous description of what was locally meant by "moral force"; powerful landlords, he said,

> believe that they must get everything from the Presidents in order to preserve what they call their moral force, moral force which consists in protecting delinquents and murderers; hiding them on their properties; filling up their *engenhos* with vagrants and criminals during recruitment periods; grabbing convicts from the hands of justice; buying witnesses to testify in fantastic trials; and protecting friends at the expense of the public coffers by the most undignified ways and without hesitation.[4]

There is an almost Tocquevillian tone to the denunciative yet poised manner in which this analysis is presented.

The precarious character of the order arising from this set of circumstances cannot plausibly be explained away just by the disturbing impact of local forces on the development of an institutional political *order*. As far as the state was concerned, there was not so much political weakness as political calculation. The notion of a firmly established politically guaranteed legal order was radically compromised as long as the central state actively enlisted the cooperation of local oligarchies to control the local instruments of government. It is not the recurrent issue of centralization and decentralization that is referred to here. Such an issue is entirely compatible with a preestablished legal order. What is being discussed is the problematic effect of private yet nonrepresentative forces, patrimonially coopted, on the development of a central state possessing the legitimate monopoly of coercion. The impertinent influence of private forces on the behavior of public authority can be viewed in terms of the Gulliverian representation of a state entangled in a private net; this led a provincial president to describe his own predicament as follows: "You cannot say to a man whose arms are fettered 'Be energetic'."[5]

This political calculation is revealed in the processes of cooptation of, and alliances with, local heads of patriarchal clienteles engineered by provincial presidents. Thanks to this cooptation, and making the best of the electoral results that redefined the power of the political factions, the apparently weak state gave way to fulminating acts of government which were able to dissolve bureaucratic caucuses and local oligarchies. It was this awareness of the private foundation of political order that frequently led provincial presidents to sentiments of studied prudence. Thus, after giving his version of the popular idea among presidents that one's own province was the least governable ("because there are absolutely no neutral people with influence or education to employ for any office"), a president added that a Court's request to appoint a candidate for office could not be satisfied

> because the southern machine is very well established here and it is not convenient to scandalize so soon all these partisan, sympathetic people who hold in their hands all the power of the Province, and from whom we have received immense favors (deputations, dinners, dances, etc.) and who would all stand against me if they knew whence the proposal came. I would resign myself to this sacrifice, but it would be of no benefit to the Province.[6]

This matter-of-fact acceptance of the private limits of the state is not consistent with the idea of political authority. It is tempting to suggest that perhaps it is the very notion of state *authority* that is missing here. The state wields power, yes; but it is still not authoritative. It does not automatically entail obedience; it persuades, it coopts and bargains.

The Militão affair dramatically illustrated how severe these limits could be, and consequently, what a colossal effort was needed to establish a new political order. Militão was a landlord in the Bahian *sertão* who for six consecutive years ruled the central districts of the province, particularly Pilão Arcado and Sento Se. The state was literally powerless before this lordling. The first document concerning the affair appeared in July 1843, when he had already killed, among others, the local parson and his brother, a doctor, and a lieutenant colonel of the *Guarda Nacional*. Conscious that Militão went unpunished because the local court judge was either intimidated or bribed and because the municipal judge had not been appointed, the provincial president dispatched in July

1842 a contingent of sixty soldiers commanded by a captain and a new judge. Only a year later the president was informed that now both judges had been coopted by Militão, who was also the president of the local legislature and the man who selected the jury that passed sentence. Repeated instructions to bring order into the area were sent, followed by a force of 100 policemen and a police delegate with two decrees, one removing the incumbent judges and another appointing their substitutes, with instructions to initiate prosecution.

Several months later, in the face of the new magistrates and the repeated disorder created by Militão, who at this time was reported to have counted on 600 to 700 men, the local commander of the *Guarda Nacional* asked for police assistance. Whatever the outcome of this request, the fact is that by the end of 1844, no *bacharel* had the temerity to accept the office of municipal judge that had been vacated. The situation dragged on for some time, with occasional raids by Militão bands on neighboring places, resulting in the reactivation of requests for energetic official assistance. The central government then decided to take more decisive measures and sent a military contingent with several hundred men under the command of a major who, once in the field, estimated that he needed at least 600 men; so a militia detachment was added.

Militão emerged unscathed from this long episode. Possessing not only secret information about the moves of official units, but also the connivance of local authorities and militia officers, Militão managed to smother the legal forces. Gradually the *imperium* of this landlord grew firmer and bolder; navigation of the major river of the *sertão*, the São Francisco, became subject to systematic interception by his retainers; transit by land was equally subject to inspection; and hordes of disaffected landlords were not allowed free movement. These activities were at times accompanied by bandit raids on neighboring villages and towns. The provincial authorities reported their matter-of-fact conviction that the official repressive apparatus was simply inadequate to deal effectively with the lordling. The local authorities had prudently fled to the capital of the province, and the state characteristically continued to be unable to staff the offices necessary for local administration and government.

It is significant that the preoccupation voiced by the highest provincial authority consisted not so much in annihilating Militão, but in containing his authority so that the pernicious effects that were being felt did not become endemic in a wider geographical radius. Archival sources do not permit us to discover the *denouement* of the Militão saga. He was probably shot by one of his private enemies as a consequence of a protracted and bloody war he and his family waged, successfully, against another family in the area. All we know is that at the end of 1848, after six uninterrupted years of personal rule, in a mock trial staged in Villa do Juazeiro, Militão was "uproariously absolved" of a criminal vendetta against twenty-odd persons, together with his men. The president of Bahia asked rhetorically in a letter to an unidentified political patrician at the Court (probably a senator),

> But, Your Excellency will say, what inspires such audacity in an ignorant backlander [Militão] who has not exercised Public offices and does not even possess those great riches which give power and prestige. I will reply that [it is] the impunity of his first crimes due to the distance of 150 *legoas* from the Capital; a long and familiar knowledge of the *sertão* wilderness when he knows that he is going to be pursued; the impunity, cowardice, or corruption of those who should punish him; and, above all, the protection of those Deputies to whom he gives his votes, who here as at the Court itself, resort to all the means that their ambitions recommend—either through one of the public Gazettes of this City, or through pledges and promises to Detachment Commanders not to persecute him. [7]

It is apparent that the Militão episode was not an exceptional affair; it was, rather, a structural phenomenon, the like of which appeared throughout the Empire, made possible not only because of the feebleness of the repressive apparatus and the inability of the bureaucracy to restore a political and administrative order, but also to a large extent because of the form in which the state apparatus defined its *modus operandi* in interaction with private groups. The predictability a bureaucratic state needs, in order to design a rationally planned administrative course of action, was jeopardized by the constant interference of private forces acting within the structure of the state bureaucracies.

Regardless of the actual power of these forces, there is little question that the way in which the state dealt with them helped to retard the development of the legitimacy of its rule and to strengthen the position of the landed groups. The state's awareness of its precarious position was dramatically conveyed by the case of an official envoy, sent to the *gaúcho* frontier to find out whether certain apprehensions as to the monarchical loyalty of one *fazendeiro* were justified or not. This caution was justified by the rebellion of a local baron against the Imperial authorities, which was taking place at the same time.[8]

The institutionalization of a legal order, bureaucratically administered by the state, was further obstructed by the weak differentiation between public and private. The notion that society as a political body could be subject to an objective system of norms different from the norms that oriented the actions of its members in the private sphere was certainly retarded by the patrimonial representation of the political community. The Hegelian concept of penalty, as an objective assertion of society's own rights, did not have a place in the normative order of the *sertão*. The rational and abstract notion that the political rights of society as an institutional order emerged from, but were not identical to, the private rights of its individual parts was antipathetical for the reigning patrimonial normativity, that is, for the prevailing canons giving validity to the institutional order. Any attempt on the part of the bureaucratic agencies to redress a private wrong was then condemned to be interpreted by those negatively affected as a vindictive reaction. Vengeance was perceived behind any penalty. A major of the *Guarda Nacional* was ambushed and shot to death with one of his slaves and three militiamen by the very men whom he had just summoned by order of a local judge. The bureaucratic execution of the law, the assertion of an impersonal code transcending the particularism of the vendetta, made no sense in the privatized universe of the backland.

Not even the higher authorities of the state could escape from a normative pattern, which was, after all, part of the cultural orientation of the time. A provincial president fore-warned the Minister of Justice at the Court of the imminence of trouble; a local *bacharel* and municipal judge was "living scandalously and publicly" with the wife he "stole" from an-other *bacharel* and, as Your Excellency knows, "the Laws [even with a capital L] . . . are not enough to put an end . . . to such a revolting scandal."[9]

Whereas penalty reconciliates and restitutes, vengeance is an offense that reproduces itself indefinitely. Herein lies a key for the understanding of the daily existence of family vendettas in the Brazilian *sertão*, of which the Militão affair was but an inconspicuous instance.[10] In a context where legal penalty was likely to be interpreted as a vindictive reaction, what was meant to be extirpated was actually fostered, and institutionalized means of redress were not considered res-titutive actions but further crimes. Such obstacles began to yield, of course, with the gradual development of organic solidarity, which was maturing along with the bourgeois or-ganization of society.

From God to Petersen in a Few Decades

Thus the patrimonial structure of the political bureaucracy and its form of association with the larger society indirectly retarded the organization of a new social order, insofar as it was caught up in the whirlwind of vindictiveness stimulated by repressive justice.

The attempts to overcome such a *status quo* were, con-sequently, linked to the consciousness of a new legal stance emphasizing persuasion and reason over repression and tra-dition. Against this background of violence and disorder, a provincial president, disappointed by the failure of repressive measures to restore public tranquility, observed, "If the gov-ernment could command by affection the hearts of these men [the criminals], it would be able to bring about the reform of certain habits fatal to society."[11] Behind this apparently awk-ward statement coming from a higher bureaucrat, was the need to search for a new principle of legitimacy on which to build the new order. The consciousness that rational persuasion was needed—albeit awkwardly formulated as "affection"—was, of course, the end of the principle of traditional authority. [12] It was, moreover, a far cry from the political philosophy of the magistrate who two decades before saw in a strong police apparatus, together with the use of force, the foundation of political obligations. [13]

The need to examine the development of a legal rational consciousness is here seen not just as an answer to the broad question, how was a *bureaucratic order* created in nineteenth-century Brazil? The discussion of the development of a rational legality and of the structural consequences it entailed in terms of the creation of specialized, functionally differentiated, and technically rational patterns of administrative work is sufficient to answer such a question. This need, rather, emerges from the consideration that a thorough discussion must not be limited to the examination of a bureaucratic order simply as a system of norms—legal/rational in this case—but must include the degree of *validity* of that order.

The above distinction, followed by Weber in *Economy and Society* and abandoned by Talcott Parsons in so far as he does not conceive of the social order other than in terms of its institutionalized (that is, valid) character can be traced back to and clarified by the Kantian distinction between legality and morality as two forms of legitimate action. There is legality when action is performed *in accordance with* norms; morality when it is performed *in obedience to* norms. It is this last type of action that validates order for Max Weber; such a concept is, however, despite its special relevance for an understanding of the problem of order, rather the limiting case for Weber, in as much as order in terms of typical action founded on legality is less exacting and more frequent than order based on morality. Conversely, Parsons has refused to accept the former type as a genuine class of social system. To him, all social systems are based on morality as defined above. Those based on legality would be, for him, cases of imperfect institutionalization of norms. [14]

For this reason an examination of the development of a bureaucratic order in Imperial Brazil should take into account the transformation of the patrimonial normativity as a requisite for a valid and consciously defined new social order. The neglect of this dimension runs the risk of transforming the reconstruction of that momentous development into a purely mechanical and formal evolutionary process.

Administrative dilettantism and the avocational approach to the tasks of organization of government were obviously a serious obstacle to the development of bureaucracy. The document below shows, nevertheless, that the economic and market orientation had already made some inroads into an area that had been greatly colored by the status principle:

> Only at a time when jobs and offices are just considered from the perspective of the return that they produce and, what is more, of that which they can produce, would a request like this one [submitted by a Captain about to be discharged because of the distance between his residence and his service district] appear. There we have a necessary consequence [of the new political principles] that, destroying all the standards of duty and justice, the only ones with which well-established societies may exist, entitle the citizens to judge public obligations as objects of commodity, to be discharged as, when and where, they so desire.

> I do not dare to pass judgment on that request as I am well advanced in years; and having received an education entirely based on the principles of honor and duty, I must candidly confess to Your Excellency that I do not understand the language spoken nowadays: therefore, Your Excellency, decide as is judged convenient. [15]

This is patrimonial normativity at its best. There was a categorical repudiation of the concept of office as an "object of commodity"; this was a value orientation that did not disappear easily. Even in the 1870s, the decimated condition of the militias was attributed to the "unscrupulous" appointment, during the war, of officers "who aspired to those offices as a means of livelihood." [16]

A bureaucratic consciousness was also hindered by the obstacles created by patrimonial normativity to the effective institutionalization of positive law, which is necessary to rational bureaucratic rule. A characteristic of this law is that its obligatory character is independent of whoever happens to demand its execution. In a patrimonial conception of law the "correct" interpretation of the legal norm does not rest on the understanding of its principle, but rather on hierarchical instance, in other words, on patrimonial discretion. This is one of the most constant traits that appears in the official correspondence between the patrimonial officers and the Imperial authorities in Brazil. It shows up in the vast majority of documents, almost as a literary formula for concluding official letters containing legally valid requests or recommendations. For instance, a commander fully entitled by law might, say, have requested some clerical supplies, or have proposed an appointment satisfying all the legal requisites. He almost invariably concluded his letter with the following formula or one of its variations, "Your Excellency will, however, order as Your Excellency wishes," or "Your Excellency will, nevertheless, be judge of whatever is just."[17]

We can observe here the persistence of an element of patrimonial discretion, attributed to bureaucratic authority, that was formally out of place and no longer indispensable. A system of action based on the revindication of objective rights—even when legally posited—was still not firm. It could be argued that such patrimonial servants, in giving priority to the person of the bureaucrat over the norm on the definition of objective rights, were simply giving room to hermeneutics, to an authoritative and unambiguous interpretation of the norm. No doubt that was in fact the case in many instances. But it is not a plausible overall interpretation for a generalized practice that had a permanent expression and even a literary formula.

This normative consciousness changed gradually. It persisted throughout the first half of the century and remained practically unchanged during the 1850s. It is not possible to detect significant changes in the typical legal consciousness of patrimonial servants until toward the end of the third quarter of the century. The first change was the decreasing use of the above formula, which began to drop noticeably during the middle 1860s. A second and more significant change appeared as a subtle but relevant shift in the terms in which the formula acknowledged the superior and discretionary bureaucratic instance. The characteristic phrasing was no longer, "Your Excellency will, however, order as Your Excellency considers *just*" or "what is of *justice*," but "as Your Excellency considers *best*" or "more *convenient*."[18]

This shift should not be dismissed as a mere literary nuance. There is a meaningful and adequate affinity between it and the orientation of the structural changes simultaneously taking place in the larger society. The new formulas, which gained wide literary currency in the 1870s and 1880s, no longer required that the definition of what was justice or positive law depended on the particular bureaucratic instance. Bureaucratic discretion was now restricted simply to the convenience of its application. The legal instrumentality of authority was no longer arbitrarily defined, just arbitrarily used, so to speak.

Of course, a legal rational consciousness did not belong exclusively to the fully developed bureaucratic order appearing at the end of the Empire. It had striven to assert itself from the beginning of the Empire. The remarkable fact is that, as noted elsewhere, it developed with the assistance of the patrimonial *honoratiores* themselves.

For reasons that merit an independent inquiry, it was in Bahia that this new legal consciousness first developed. The revindication of legal rights appeared there with some frequency, which necessarily contributed to the firmer stereotyping of orderly patterns into the 1830s. Illustrative of this— and reminiscent of the *gaúcho* commander—is the position assumed by a commander of the *sertão* of Bahia in response to the president's silence toward his repeated requests for equipment for the militias. He observed that he had not had an answer, which appeared very strange to him, considering that the mail was a safe medium. Moreover, he remarked with unconcealed forwardness, that he could not believe "that Your Excellency had the temerarious idea of disregarding [the letters] in view of the . . . law which stipulates [the answers] in such cases."[19] This is remarkable; here is a patrimonial servant addressing himself to the highest bureaucratic authority of the province in the 1830s.

This trait was also extended to other provinces, but its development there appeared later. We have already recorded its incidence in Rio Grande do Sul, where commanders would occasionally reassert the execution of the positive law against its arbitrary interpretation by bureaucratic authorities.

Yet the development of a legal rational representation of the norm became a generalized occurrence in the Empire only toward the end of the third quarter of the century. It then ceased to be an idiosyncratic trait associated with the penchant for legal virtuosity of the Bahian public servant or with the pragmatic needs of the militarized *gaúcho* commander. We can also find it at the center of the Empire. This may be illustrated in the modification of the objection of the *comandantes superiores* to the policy of the central bureaucracy concerning service dispensations. The typical objection, as noted, had so far been of a substantive, material nature; those groups more in need of dispensation in view of their precarious means of livelihood—the poor freemen—were precisely the ones who had to bear the brunt of the liturgies. The paternalism and particularism of this objection were replaced by a rational and universalistic objection. It was repugnant, a commander remarked, "to be severe with some [poor freemen who neglect their liturgical service] when others . . . find the means to avoid the discharge of duties that the law imposes on everybody." The law is no longer spelled with a capital L, but is more of a valid principle. [20]

The new legitimacy of power and its gradual institutionalization as a genuinely normative orientation did not come by itself. In a general sense, the final years of the Empire also saw the breakdown of certain forms of social solidarity and their replacement by others more in tune with *Gesellschaft*. Significant in this sense was the effect of these new forms on the values of kinship, which—when excessive to the point of bordering on perplexity—must be understood as a rather gauche expression of new canons insufficiently tried out. This was, indeed, the case in the episode of the local commander who dutifully reported to the bureaucratic authorities that the ensign and secretary of two corps under his command had abandoned their corporate obligations to live at the distant Court. That such incidents were detrimental to legal obligations is not what strikes one in this dispatch. The amazing element is, rather, the commander's remark "that

these two . . . officers are tied to me by bonds of kinship
[that] I declare as a testimony of my credibility."

However excessive—and, therefore, more likely to be
considered episodic than typical—the above incident was, it
was nonetheless prompted by the intimate acceptance of
standards that had a cultural rather than a personal origin.
Similar standards had, in fact, prompted a Bahian commander-in-chief to prefer to nominate for another post of
command a candidate with "literary education" and "military
knowledge," over the head of his own son.[21]

Finally, again in the literary formulas of the correspondence of an emaciated corporation, we perceive in splendid
synthesis the force of the secular values that had eroded a
type of normativity and questioned the priority of kinship
solidarity; in the 1880s, letters are no longer concluded with
a worn-out "May God keep Your Excellency," but with a
brisk and resonant "Health and Brotherhood."[22]

The Administrative Patterns

The adoption of a set of rational patterns by the state bureaucracy was to some extent based on the adoption of the
normative canons discussed in the previous section. These
new canons, however, were not entirely successful in erad-
icating the legacy of a well-established tradition. Just as the
patrimonial structure of government was not immune to the
influence of the formal legality of the bureaucracy, neither
was this latter altogether successful in preventing the emergence of patrimonial orientations in its midst. That pattern
may be illustrated as follows: in 1869, a provincial president
dismissed a local commander-in-chief and a commander from
official duties without communicating to the Court the specific reasons for his decision. The Court mandarins—routinely in charge of the elaboration of the comments based on
legal norms and jurisprudence that would serve the Minister
as a basis for his decision—expressed a rather adverse recommendation concerning the confirmation of the president's
decision. They went about it with characteristic caution. The
dismissal, one mandarin stated, may be approved "unless
the Imperial Government wishes to have prior knowledge of

the reasons justifying it, something that will be demanded
if Your Excellency so orders." He carefully added that even
state authorities of unquestioned reliability should not be exempted from stating the justification of their decisions, and
he reinforced the remark, adding that according to a legal
decree, the president was supposed to give a *reasoned account*
(the mandarin's emphasis) to the Imperial government, but
he concluded with a consideration that he unquestionably
disliked and that arbitrarily opened the door that he had legally closed in the previous sentences, "I repeat, however,
that they [the dismissals] may be approved right away if Your
Excellency wishes to prescind from the reasons they might
have."[23]

It would be hard to find a better example. The discretion
is so presumed that the mandarin restores it after having first
legally negated it, and despite his obviously manifest preference against it. The mandarins not infrequently suspended
judgement on matters that to their eyes were blatant cases
of illegality, just to have the final decision depend on their
superior. The full normative force of legal principles, however rational they were as a source of legitimacy, had not yet
been obtained. There was, unquestionably, a bureaucratic legal order, but it was not yet sufficiently valid.[24]

The fact that such a bureaucratic order was suffused with
political values contributed, in turn, to weaken the process
of the elimination of particularism and discretion from the
patrimonial structures of government. In other words, the
political content of the decision negatively affected the im-
personality and formalism of the legal norm. The obstacles
created by this situation with regard to the institutionalization of a bureaucratic order were, of course, evident. A local
commander-in-chief, instructed by the provincial president
to give posts to officers who had not yet received the necessary *bona fide* commissions, resignedly replied that in view
of the superior order, and despite determinate legal dispositions to the contrary, he had given them their posts, "thus
fulfilling the obligations of a subject whose only business is
the most passive obedience."[25] It was this very tension that
led the same commander to express in a moment of despair
his confusion with regard to another incident two months

later, "If my information is false, why does not Your Excellency dismiss me? If it is true, why is wrong not prevented instead of being increased?"[26]

It is no wonder, then, that part of the daily routine of the central bureaucracy consisted precisely in revising its own previous decisions provoked by the changes in the bureaucratic organization that came with new political cabinets. No confrontation between local *honoratiores* and central authority could be wisely considered susceptible to a categorical and definitive solution. The political misfortune falling accidentally on the *honoratiores* by a decision from the center, discharging or removing a notable from his position, was more often than not tomorrow's matter of political redress for the new cabinet made up of his political allies.

The deleterious repercussions of these factors on the establishment and institutionalization of a new order need not be further stressed. They were compounded, finally, by other factors having to do with the precarious character of the institutional channels of communication of the state apparatus.

The development of these channels was jeopardized, in turn, by two kinds of obstacles. The first obstacle was the scarcity of material resources at the disposal of the state, and the effect of this on the erection of a unified and centralized bureaucratic command. An order, for instance, though transmitted, might not reach all the agencies necessary for its implementation. Regardless of the will to cooperate on the part of those agencies, there was here a material problem to be solved. Similarly, to a conscientious patrimonial servant who requested copies of new regulations that he by chance knew had been issued concerning the militias, a bureaucrat suggested in a senseless and vague reply that the applicant had to "try to obtain them [by himself] having in view that the Presidency has no copies for distribution."[27]

Second, as a result of the above predicament the bureaucrat typically entertained the notion that the norms at his disposal were perhaps no longer in effect, thereby further disturbing the structure of the bureaucratic code and its chances for institutionalization. Indicative of this situation is a dispatch from a militia inspector to a provincial president concerning the payment of salaries to professional majors: "[There] may exist on this matter modern governmental instructions which are often printed only after a very long delay. Perhaps the Military Paymaster's Office may better clarify each and every doubt on this subject."[28] These factors, in summary, worked against a prompt delineation of a standard system of administrative norms, that is, against the very notion of an administrative order. The state needed first to establish clearly the professional and rational grounds of that order before it could contemplate the possibility of validating and institutionalizing it.

In this respect, the central state and its representatives frequently displayed the awareness that the task of efficient government was to some extent compromised by the avocational and liturgical contributions of its patrimonial servants. Patrimonial administration lacked the continuity, dependability, and predictability that were becoming indispensable in the vast and complex administrative enterprise under the state's responsibility. In a report to the Court, a provincial authority complained about the inconvenience of the lack of a police force to cooperate with the magistrates in the administration of justice. And he added:

> These inconveniences cannot be removed with the provisional service of the *Guarda Nacional*. As it is not possible to give to it a regular organization, nor to have its discipline wholly observed, the sudden appeal to National Guards represents obstacles and difficulties of a sort that almost all the commissions of justice done through that means either fail entirely or are performed with great delay and paralyze the regular course of the Administration."

Indicative of this awareness of the avocational limits of efficient administration was, for instance, the change in the organic law with regard to official priorities. Whereas the law of 1831 left it to the patrimonial officer to decide whether to accept an appointment as magistrate instead of his militia office, the law of 1841 deprived him of that privilege. Corporate office had to be sacrificed in favor of professional service as a magistrate.[29]

This is a clear indication that the central state was now much more concerned with the bureaucratization of its legal apparatus than with more patrimonial forms of administration.

In previous chapters we discussed the genesis of the bureaucratic impetus behind the Brazilian process of state-
building toward the mid-1840s. At that time, the incipient
process of administrative centralization was reflected—as far
as the militias were concerned—in the reallocation of the
responsibility of supervising the local corps of the *Guarda
Nacional*. This responsibility passed from the hands of the
municipal *camaras* to those of the provincial president. The
examination of the official correspondence sent by the provincial presidents to the Court in the period 1830–1890 reveals that, generally speaking, the provincial presidents essentially mediated between the ministerial bureaucracy and
the provincial corps. Their functions generally were, on the
one hand, to relay to the patrimonial commanders the instructions issued by the Court's bureaucracy, and, on the
other, to refer to the Court the demands of the corps concerning the payment of *per diem* for militia detachments and
salaries for the musicians of the bands, the provision of armament and military equipment as well as clerical material,
and proposals for the appointment of commanders-in-chief.
The president was, of course, instrumental in the selection
of the provincial officer corps and to that extent it was an
influential office. There is no indication, however, that this
office tried to wrest from the central state its control over the
Guarda Nacional.

The degree of centralization to which the militarized corporation was submitted was, moreover, so impressive that
it bordered on the absurd. Not only were the most irrelevant
and procedural issues referred to the Court for a decision, but
it was the minister himself who personally took care of these
inanities. He might, for instance, receive a request from a
distant command to the effect that instructions be given to
the corresponding local legislature to have the lamps of the
local jail lit; or he might receive a request from another battalion for permission to fire a salute on a ceremonial day. The
central bureaucracy in a way encouraged these grotesque
demands by displaying much care in preparing its elaborate
answers. It is necessary to understand, all the same, that
there was more to it than the centripetal feature of the central
bureaucracy; equally important were the economic indigence

of the state, which transformed practically any request into a well-meant attempt to save resources, and the heteronomy of a corporation of notables, which offered very little in the way of private initiative.[30]

The development of bureaucratic patterns within the patrimonial militias—made virtually possible by the corporate legal code—thus found occasional obstruction in the deadlocks that this heteronomy fostered, in so far as it stimulated an exasperating practice among patrimonial commanders of elevating all matters requiring any kind of decision to the higher echelons of the central bureaucracy. There is every reason to suppose that the *honoratiores'* vacillation and timidity with regard to the process of decision making was in part conditioned by the novelty of the administrative experience. It must, in fact, be born in mind that in contrast to the colonial militias, the *Guarda Nacional* represented a vast extension and systematization of the scope of administration by *honoratiores*. This, in the long run, led to the recrudescence of the trend toward administrative centralization that had gained momentum just a few years after the creation of the new militias. Ironically, although consistently with the developments we have been discussing throughout this work, the Brazilian patrimonial experiment during the Empire strengthened the organization of the central bureaucratic apparatus rather than the power of the local stratum of notables.

It is a mistake, however, simply to associate the exacerbation of the process of centralization with the bureaucratization of the modern Brazilian state. Such a colossal concentration of administrative initiative at times helped paralyze both local decisions and measures of some importance to the creation of a national system of institutions. The vicissitudes experienced for more than three decades by the Municipal Legislature of Rio Pardo, which asked to have a budget approved to build a bridge, were not exceptional. A careful search of the relevant sources would probably yield hundreds of similar cases. Also, we have already identified some patrimonial values operating within the bureaucracy of the central state itself that stood in the way of a valid bureaucratic order. Given this set of circumstances, any organic connection between the process of state-building in the nineteenth century and the process of administrative centralization is in need of some qualification. Without satisfactorily established rational norms, such centralized forms carry with them the mildew of the past.[31]

It is, in fact, indicative of the amount of dead weight and irrationality of this style of centralization that, when the efficient organization of the national resources was actually needed more urgently (e.g., during war periods), the decision-making process under direct control of the central apparatus was subject to a countermovement of decentralization. Contrary to other national experiences in which the efficient organization of wartime mobilization went hand in hand with more centralized forms of bureaucratic command, the Brazilian nineteenth-century experience suggests that the movement toward more rational patterns signified the relative decentralization of the administrative apparatus. This may be seen as a recognition that this style of centralization was not any the more conducive to the attainment of the ends—calculability, efficiency, rationality, and so on—that centralization is supposed to lead to.

It is possible to detect this countermovement in the militias themselves. To start with, it is significant that the official defrayal of the corporate costs of contingents sent to satisfy domestic liturgies was taken care of by the Ministry of Justice. However, when those contingents were designed for war service, the whole operation came under the supervision of the Defense Ministry and its agencies on the southern frontier. This trend was reinforced by the local or provincial authorities. The general demands of mobilization, for instance, worked in favor of the trend. A provincial president complained that garrisoning and other needs could hardly be achieved if the provincial authorities were not granted a wider scope of autonomy to overcome all the obstructive administrative minutiae demanded by the Court. Another president reported the otherwise extraordinary episode that he had decided by himself to allot to the different *comandantes superiores* the number of guards each one must enlist. (The minister, of course, felt in need to reply that he approved such a decision.) Provincial presidents, moreover, gained in war what they could not obtain in politics: the right to suspend from office wayward commanders-in-chief. It is hard, in this respect, to evaluate what is more significant: that the provincial authorities circumstantially gained more power, or that they were conscious to the end that this prerogative was of a provisional character. Equally indicative of the patrimonial residues of the pattern of administrative centralization was the *gaúcho* frontier experience discussed above. Again, when pressing needs demanded that the administrative apparatus function as a rational enterprise, the pressures toward a countermovement came into effect.[32]

Given, then, the relative ambiguity of the trend toward centralization as an expression of the growth of the modern bureaucratic Brazilian state, it is advisable to look for its appearance in another area, namely, the process of rationalization of administrative work. Unlike the forces toward centralization, this other process did not run the risk of carrying with it undercurrents of patrimonialism. Rationalization is, unquestionably, a reliable manifestation of the process of bureaucratization.

It is again possible to detect some of the major moments of the rationalization of the new state apparatus by looking at the history of the militarized corporation.

It is interesting to observe that the official concern for the rationalization of the administration of the *Guarda Nacional* began at the time the central state was launching its new policy of centralization, that is, around the mid-1840s, as discussed in Chapter 2. Before that, interest in rationalization was rather sporadic, and it was characteristically expressed by commanders who had had some experience with the professional army.[33] But in the 1840s these sporadic instances turned into a general trend with a more systematic character. A general headquarters was created to supervise the provision of armaments, ammunition, and other resources of the corps; a standardized form was distributed among the corps for statistical information on their state and organization— the number of companies, guards, subofficers of each branch and service, the composition of the officership, and so on. For the first time, the legal instruction with regard to the creation of Administrative Councils for the corps was taken seriously. These and like measures were taken with a view to establishing a uniform and standard administration.[34] Nonetheless, these initiatives did not alter the characteristic heteronomy of the corporation. As discussed previously, major as well as minor decisions affecting the life of the corporation were not made by the corporation itself.

The efforts at rationalization were carried over to the new militias organized around the middle of the century, when they were reinitiated with invigorated impetus; new models were created to establish uniform and homogeneous administrative procedures throughout the Empire.[35] These changes were typically felt with more emphasis in the southern militias. Of course, the pressures toward a rational organization began there during the first years of the effort. Rio Grande do Sul was the only province that created Administrative Councils for its militias in 1833. These pressures were to a large extent accounted for by two factors: in the first place, its commanders frequently had some military background and were familiar with the bureaucratic practices of the professional army, practices that were carried over to the patrimonial militias. Second, unlike the situation in the rest of the Empire, the responsibility for the defrayal of costs of corporate administration was, generally speaking, not liturgical. As discussed previously, the central state assumed a considerable role in the satisfaction of the fiscal and material needs of the *gaúcho* corporation. As a result, the presence of bureaucratic agencies of fiscal control in direct and frequent contact with those commands further reinforced the trend. These factors, together with the practical demands exerted by the predicament of war, brought into being a corporation with a keen sense of professional and rational orientation.

But it was in the 1880s that the first signs appeared of more secular, profane, and rational values. Nothing was more suggestive of this new climate than the otherwise "irreverent" simplification of the pompous uniform of the militiaman. Instead of both a gala and a service uniform, there was from now on only one uniform. This measure was taken for economic reasons, but only when it is interpreted against a long cultural tradition emphasizing status and rank and seigneurial stylization does its full significance become clear.[36]

The process of the decay of the *Guarda Nacional* during

the mid-1870s and 1880s ran parallel to the constitution of a more solid bureaucratic form of political domination. The liturgical employment of freemen, the essential premise for the patrimonial organization of the political community, was constantly losing its normative and legitimate ground. The 1873 law excluding the corporation from the local circuit of police and justice was an institutional expression of the new individualism and the new form of solidarity on which *Gesellschaft* was now being built.

The central bureaucracy was, however, slow to accommodate itself to the new legal reality it was responsible for; on the one hand, it redefined the role of the militias by demobilizing them and reducing them to emaciated political clubs of citizens rather than patrimonial associations of servants, but on the other hand, it kept intact the habitual—and now ritualized—expectations with regard to their capacity for mobilization. To summarize, it was slow in realizing that the corporate sense of mission and obligation could not simply be rekindled with central bureaucratic orders. In October 1873, the Ministry of Justice sent a circular to the provincial presidents requesting that they demand from the militia commanders maps of their respective corps, together with proposals for the reorganization of local commands. This same request was persistently and successively addressed in January 1874, April 1874, April 1876, January 1877, July 1877, December 1877, and May 1878. The request always had an urgent character though a progressively more laconic wording. It went unheeded. This was a mute testimony to the end of an era.[37] The old order was extinct, having passed quietly away.

Conclusions

We have come to the end of a broad examination of the process of state-building in nineteenth-century Brazil. In a span of two generations, Brazil underwent a rhythm of change of an intensity unmatched during the colonial period. It is no exaggeration to state that the institutional physiognomy of the Brazilian social structure changed more during the second and third quarters of the nineteenth century than throughout the entire colonial period.

The general process of change assumed, of course, a variety of facets. At the risk of oversimplification, it is possible, nevertheless, to abstract three important trends in the general transformation: first, the expansion of government agencies toward the periphery of the political community and the creation of a national bureaucratic web; second, the shifting in the relative contributions of the bureaucratic and the patrimonial structures of government to the creation of an administrative order, in other words, to the establishment of an institutional routine for the organization of the state; and third, the emergence, consolidation, and institutionalization of a new normativity, a new way of giving bases and validity to the daily administrative routine and decision making processes.

None of these trends was historically as neat as they appear analytically. The erection of a bureaucratic order did not entirely sweep away the value orientations typical of patri-

monialism; the bureaucratization of office met some resistance from officials used to a diffuse and particularistic
definition of administrative functions; and the expansion
of bureaucracy toward the frontier was hindered by the
lack of qualified personnel and monetary resources. The
creation of a modern bureaucratic state was, then, by no
means an easy task.

Yet, despite the apparent continuity with the past, the
Brazilian state began to change substantially toward more
bureaucratic forms at the same time as it inaugurated a systematic program of patrimonial administration in the early
1830s. While patrimonialism had always been a component
of political organization during the colonial period, it assumed a more institutional and systematic expression only
when the state decided to enlist thoroughly the private cooperation of the dominant patriarchal classes in the 1830s. In
this antagonistic coexistence of traditional and rational forms,
of patrimonialism and bureaucracy, lies one of the most peculiar traits of the institutional organization of the Brazilian
political community.

Two trends may be singled out as characteristic of this
process of state-building in the last century: first, the sheer
expansion of the bureaucratic apparatus of government. That
expansion took place in two different movements, one of
which was the growth of the bureaucratic apparatus at the
center of the Empire, at the Court. The second movement,
which took place chiefly in the latter part of the century, was
an extension of this growth to the provincial periphery of the
Empire.

The second trend involved the creation of a bureaucratic
system of authority divorced from its previous patrimonial
foundations. Again, this trend took place in two different
movements, one of which involved the replacement of patrimonial officers in charge of the functions of local government by bureaucratic officials. Professional administration
replaced local administration by *honoratiores* and dilettantes.
The second movement involved a gradual shift in the normative ground of administrative actions.

This movement toward a different normativity was expressed in different ways—first, in terms of the emergence

of a political order that began to be institutionalized with different boundaries from those of the household and second, through development toward more impersonal and universalistic forms of social action that took place at the same time as the decharismatization of princely power, together with the institutionalization of bureaucratic principles founded on a new rational legality, not on patriarchal particularism.

As a result of these trends, the last quarter of the nineteenth century began with a state organization considerably different from that of previous decades—more modern, more bureaucratic, more rational. But it would be a mistake to think that the process of state-building ended with the end of the century. The bureaucratic state established some continuity with its patrimonial heritage. A strictly legal rational principle of authority could not entirely eradicate the influence of the traditional forms of legitimation of power, which in fact managed to survive within the state apparatus until the end of the Empire.

When appraised from the comparative perspective offered by the political history of its Hispanic-American neighbors, the Brazilian process of state-building is an extraordinary development. None of its neighbors, indeed, embarked as thoroughly and systematically as did Brazil on a patrimonial project of administration.

Brazilian patrimonialism did not develop fully, however. The notion of patrimonialism is predicated on the institutionalization of traditional forms of authority and, ideal-typically, also on the establishment of a status order, namely, a social order where rights and obligations are primarily allocated according to status groups. We saw that these traditional forms and a status order did not become institutionalized aspects of the social structure of nineteenth-century Brazil. Although the predominant patriarchalism of the agrarian society favored the establishment of traditional forms of power, their legitimation was obstructed by the institution of slavery from which it, dialectically, received at the same time so much stimulus. Similarly, while the reigning landlordism was virtually an instrument for the development of a status order because of its stress on collective obligations, a status order was obstructed by the rational economic orientations encouraged by the agrarian capitalism on which, in turn, landlordism was in large measure based.

As things were, the development of patrimonialism was bound to display a checkered course. The interpretation of the role played by the *Guarda Nacional* is significant for the understanding of patrimonialism. A synthesis of its development is reflected in the history of the corporation of freemen that was held institutionally accountable for the patrimonial liturgies of Brazilian society. The vicissitudes of the *Guarda Nacional* are not, consequently, accidental. They are a necessary expression of the institutional and structural difficulties involved in developing genuinely patrimonial forms of organization, in a society that was progressively more bourgeois and capitalist in its orientation. As we have shown, the tensions and contradictions that led to the perversion of the manifest goals of the militias were inextricably bound up with its antagonistic principles of orientation. These tensions evolved around a basic antagonism; on the one hand, there was the corporation's demand for traditional subordination on the part of its members; on the other hand, there was the members' inability or unwillingness to meet these traditionally defined obligations because of the insufficient institutionalization of a status order, and because of the progressive institutionalization of rational orientations of action.

Despite these shortcomings, the contribution of the *Guarda Nacional* to the creation of a modern bureaucratic state in Brazil was impressive. Although the freemen's liturgical obligations with regard to the prince and the state were not always met satisfactorily, the administrative assistance provided by the local *honoratiores* proved to be indispensable in filling the gaps that the indigent state was in no position to fill. The relevance of the militias to the process of state-building lay, among other things, in their participation—at times exclusive—in the creation and maintenance of an administrative routine of local government, which was a necessary condition for the development of an institutional order beyond the confines of the patriarchal society. The continuity of public administration that the militias made possible for two generations was a very important element in the process of state-building. The militia experience was equally crucial, dialectically, in helping delineate a public order transcending the particularism of the patriarchal society from which it itself emerged. Indeed, the daily habituation of rural freemen to certain practices and routines, the legitimacy of which had to be searched for beyond the household, was a training ground for the socialization of the Brazilian citizen into alternative forms of legitimation of power and authority. When seen from this perspective, the apparent paradox behind the fact that the Brazilian landlord and poor freemen were inadvertently major actors in the development of legal rational authority vanishes, and the paradox becomes a splendid synthesis of their political participation during the nineteenth century.

References

Introduction

1. Leibnitz's epigraph of Bodemann's edition was taken from Louis Couturat, "On Leibniz's Metaphysics," in Harry G. Frankfurt, ed., *Leibniz: A Collection of Critical Essays*, p. 25 and note 15 for another version.

Immanuel Kant, *Critique of Pure Reason,* especially part 2, division 2, "The Transcendental Dialectic."

2. "The Social Psychology of the World Religions," in *From Max Weber: Essays in Sociology,* H. H. Gerth and C. Wright Mills, eds., pp. 299–300.

This is not a pertinent place for a thorough discussion of the implications of that strategy for causal imputation. There is no question, however, that it eliminates Weber's most original contribution, namely, the transformation of pure ideal types into tools for causal imputation. On this general question, see Chapter I of his *Economy and Society: An Outline of Interpretive Sociology,* Guenther Roth and Claus Wittich, eds., vol. I; and " 'Objectivity' in Social Science and Social Policy," in his *Methodology of the Social Sciences,* Edward A. Shils and Henry A. Finch, eds.

The discursive usefulness of this notion should not be denied. Hans Rosenberg's otherwise excellent *Bureaucracy, Aristocracy and Autocracy* regrettably suffers from the lack of a synthetic concept of this sort. See particularly the provocative Introduction, where it is clear how useful such a concept would have been.

3. From a strictly analytical point of view, the contribution of this book to the discussion of that concept lies in what might be called a topological outline of its structure, an outline that Weber neglected to work out in his historical monographs. Throughout the chapters it will become evident, in fact, that the bureaucratic apparatus of the Brazilian state originated in the political center of the community and developed from that base outward, whereas the major *locus* of the patrimonial apparatus lay in the political periphery of the Empire, that is, in the domain of local patriarchal society.

185

4. Hegel, *Logic: Being Part One of the Encyclopaedia of the Philosophical Sciences (1830)*, par. 140, von Henning's *Zusatz*.
Also, Hegel, *The Philosophy of History*, pp. 26–32.
The conviction that values should be taken seriously in sociological analyses does not alter the problematical relationship between means and ends. In fact, the wide chasm between idealist philosophy and sociological thought lies in the latter's recognition of a tension between the actual and the ideal, between the factual and the normative. The unveiling of those tensions is one of the major sources of interpretation in this book.

Chapter I

1. Euclides da Cunha, *Rebellion in the Backlands: Os Sertões*, p. 68.
2. Eulalia Maria Lahmeyer Lobo, "Conflict and Continuity in Brazilian History," p. 269.
3. Caio Prado Jr., *Formação Econômica do Brasil*, p. 127, *apud* Alberto Passos Guimarães, *Quatro Séculos de Latifúndio*.
4. Antonio E. de Camargo, *Quadro Estatístico e Geográphico da Província de S. Pedro do Rio Grande do Sul*, p. 78.
5. It supplied the consumer centers of Rio de Janeiro and São Paulo after the organization of the *charque* (dry meat) industry, the main line of operation having been the export of hides.
6. Cf. Caio Prado Jr., *The Colonial Background of Modern Brazil*.
7. Raymundo Faoro, *Os donos do poder: Formação do patronato político brasileiro*, p. 52.
8. Nestor Duarte, *A ordem privada e a organização política nacional*, pp. 23–24.
9. Stuart B. Schwartz, "Free Labor in a Slave Economy: the Lavradores de Cana of Colonial Bahia," pp. 164–165.
10. "As a result, secondary towns in the Reconcavo did not develop until the late seventeenth century, almost 200 years after the original settlement of the area. The *engenhos*, so dependent on the primary port cities of the coast, prevented the growth of secondary towns in the interior and served as poor substitutes for them." Schwartz, "Free Labor," pp. 165–167.
The function of the *"hacienda-plantación"* complex as a type of settlement rather than as a type of enterprise is also advocated for Latin America by geographers like Ward Barret, as reported by Magnus Morner, "La hacienda hispanoamericana en la historia: Un esquema de reciente investigación y debate," p. 756, note 111.
11. Faoro himself agrees to this privatized aspect of the process of occupation.
12. Tulio Halperin Donghi, *Politics, Economics and Society in Argentina in the Revolutionary Period*.
13. Caio Prado, *Colonial Background*, p. 357.
14. C. R. Boxer, *Four Centuries of Portuguese Expansion, 1415–1825: A Succinct Survey*, p. 75.

15. Cf. Jose Maria Ots Capdequi, *Instituciones de gobierno del Nuevo Reino de Granada durante el siglo XVIII*.

16. "The Crown's policy of promotion, privilege and reward, which was designed to bolster the authority of the magistracy, also fed the ambition and pride of the bureaucrats, who at times assumed the attitudes and aspirations of the nobility of the colonial elite. Once created, the bureaucracy had a life of its own, and magistrates sometimes sought collective or individual goals beyond those prescribed by the law. The crown, however, maintained control over the state bureaucracy. Through the system of education and promotion, rotation in office, and institutional checks, the magistracy remained tied to royal interest and dependent on the crown. This was a major feature of the Portuguese administrative and social structure. Despite family traditions of bureaucratic service, we cannot properly speak of a nobility of magisterial office, a *nobreza da toga*, which came to regard bureaucratic posts as their exclusive domain or office as an extension of social rank. The magistracy was open to all. . . . *Desembargadores* and lower magistrates did not own their offices nor could they pass them to others of their choosing. . . . Thus, unlike the French nobility of the robe or the Prussian judicial nobility, the Portuguese magistrates remained a professional elite rather than a distinct social class, although there was always a tendency for them to become one." Stuart B. Schwartz, *Sovereignty and Society in Colonial Brazil: The High Court of Bahia and its Judges, 1609–1751*, p. 362. See also pp. 215–216 and p. 274.

17. "The complexity of the administrative tasks and the sheer expansion of their scope increasingly result in the technical superiority of those who have had training and experience, and will thus inevitably favor the continuity . . . of at least some of the functionaries." Max Weber, *Economy and Society: An Outline of Interpretive Sociology*, vol. 3, pp. 951–952.

18. Erving Goffman, *Asylums: Essays on the Social Situation of Mental Patients and Other Inmates*, p. xiii. Mitchel Gurfield has suggested this characterization as a total institution, but is not clear whether he is thinking also in terms of Goffman's scheme. See his "Class Structure and Political Power in Colonial Brazil: An Interpretative Essay in Historical Sociology," p. 69. Despite the contemporary origin of the concept of total institution, it is useful to bring into focus the basic characteristics of colonial institutions. The following applies as aptly to an asylum as to the barracks life of the *engenho:* "First, all aspects of life are conducted in the same place and under the same single authority. Second, each phase of the member's daily activity is carried out in the immediate company of a large batch of others, all of whom are treated alike and required to do the same thing together. Third, all phases of the day's activities are tightly scheduled, with one activity leading at a prearranged time into the whole sequence of activities being imposed from above by a system of explicit formal ruling and a body of officials. Finally, the various enforced activities are brought together into a single rational plan purportedly designed to fulfill the official aims of the institution." Goffman, p. 6.

19. In this sense, the *engenho* and the *fazenda* of the colonial epoch bring to mind the now inadequate seventeenth- and eighteenth-century "box-

within-box" theory of development, according to which the original already contains in actual but miniaturized and Lilliputian size the subsequently differentiated elements. See Hegel, *Logic: Being Part One of the Encyclopaedia of the Philosophical Sciences (1830)*, par. 161 and von Henning's *Zusatz*.

20. One landlord's proud remark, "This household buys only iron, salt, powder, and lead," is illustrative in this connection. Oliveira Vianna, *Populações meridionais do Brasil*, pp. 123–124.

Alcantara Machado also observes: "Within his domain the *fazendeiro* has the meat, bread, wine, and cereals that nourish him; the hides, wool, and cotton that cover him; the peanut oil and wax that light his nights; the wood and tile that protect him against the inclement weather; the bows that give him protection. He lacks nothing. He can challenge the world." *Vida e morte do bandeirante*, p. 57.

21. In this as in other comparative statements appearing in this work, it is important to bear in mind that they represent trends and accentuations of processes of a rather general nature.

22. C. R. Boxer, *The Golden Age of Brazil: 1695–1750: Growing Pains of a Colonial Society*, p. 223 and Passos Guimarães, *Quatro séculos de latifúndio*, p. 17.

23. "The attacks by Indians are so frequent and ferocious that the *engenhos* become actual fortresses with their own militia bodies and arsenals. Friar Gaspar writes about contemporary family heads with fortifications 'as many as used to exist in yesteryear, with enough people to fight back against the assaults of the enemy.'

Organized in the middle of a wild milieu, the domain assumes its own defense. Besieged all round, it is forced to adopt a military constitution. It thus creates within its wall a small and permanent army—ready, agile, swift, a faithful reproduction of the enemies'." Oliveira Vianna, *Populações meridionais do Brasil*, p. 78.

24. Oliveira Vianna accurately interpreted this colonial ruralization over half a century ago. He traced its origin to the ineffective artificial formation of towns: "The creation of towns and cities was always an act of official initiative—of the Metropolitan authorities, the Governors of the *capitanias*, the *governadores-gerais* or vice-roys, not an initiative coming from the people." Oliveira Vianna, *Instituições políticas brasileiras*, vol. 1, p. 135.

25. "That remarkable economic independence of the seigneurial estates exerts a powerful simplifying action upon the entire structure of our rural populations." Oliveira Vianna, *Populações meridionais*, p. 124.

26. Oliveira Vianna, *Populações meridionais*, p. 125.

27. A clear manifestation of this is to be seen in the timid and distorted "convention" of commensality that vainly struggled to emerge in the artisan's participation at the landlord's table. This commensality was, of course, restricted to artisans and assumed an entirely atypical expression in so far as the artisans would sit as mute spectators, reminiscent of Erving Goffman's nonpersons. The institutionalization of this "convention" extended well into the nineteenth century; Lins do Rego's fictional reconstruction of the memories of a lord in his puberty—(Lins do Rego himself was the grandson of a landlord)—suggests what Julio Bello's biographical recollections as a *senhor*

de engenho confirm. Jose Lins do Rego, *Menino de engenho*, pp. 11 and 71; and Jose Maria Bello, *Memórias de um senhor de engenho*, p. 104.

28. Carvalho Franco has brilliantly shown the predatory intrusion of economic interests on the delicate structure of moral association, in *Homens livres*.

29. For a discussion of tribe, see Max Weber, *The Religion of India: The Sociology of Hinduism and Buddhism*, chap. 1, and *Ancient Judaism*, chaps. 1 and 2.

30. Cf. Weber, *The Religion of China: Confucianism and Taoism*, chap. 3.

31. Cf. Clifford Geertz, *Peddlers and Princes: Social Change and Economic Modernization in Two Indonesian Towns*, chap. 2.

32. Weber, *The Religion of China*, p. 157, my italics.

33. The contrast between representation and cooptation has been well brought out by Simon Schwartzman in his article, "Representação e Cooptação Política no Brasil." See also his *São Paulo e o estado nacional*, and S. N. Eisenstadt, *Traditional Patrimonialism and Modern Neopatrimonialism*.

34. See, for instance, Eul-Soo Pang and Ron L. Seckinger, "The Mandarins of Imperial Brazil," and Roderick James Barman, "Brazil at Mid-Empire: Political Accommodation and the Pursuit of Progress under the Conciliação Ministry, 1853–1857."

35. Weber, *Economy and Society: An Outline of Interpretive Sociology*, and *The Religion of China*, p. 14.

36. C. B. Macpherson, *The Political Theory of Possessive Individualism: Hobbes to Locke*, pp. 46 ff.

37. Georg Lukacs, *History and Class Consciousness: Studies in Marxist Dialectics*, p. 59, his italics. In the same work, Lukacs has appropriately emphasized the stifling effects that a noneconomic integration of society has on the development of class consciousness: "[For] precapitalist epochs and for the behavior of many strata within capitalism whose economic roots lie in precapitalism, class consciousness is unable to achieve complete clarity and to influence the course of history consciously.

This is true above all because class interests in precapitalist society never achieve full (economic) articulation. Hence the structuring of society into castes and estates means that economic elements are *inextricably* joined to political and religious factors." Moacyr Palmeira has proposed a similar diagnosis of the predominance of "political" forms in his "Latifundium et Capitalisme au Brésil: Lecture Critique d'un Débat," pp. 151–152.

38. André João Antonil [João Antônio Andreoni], *Cultura e opulencia do Brasil*, Book 1, p. 139.

39. Saint-Hilaire, *Segunda viagem do Rio de Janeiro a Minas Gerais e a São Paulo*, p. 17.

40. Alcântara Machado, after examining legal records covering the period 1578 to 1700, draws a social profile of the paulista colonist which stands in sharp contrast to the genteel stylization that only a "delirious imagination" (*fantasia delirante*) could create: what appears is "a poor and illiterate *bandeirante* [frontier explorer], of ordinary allure and meager possessions, living almost indigently, tough with himself as well as with others, austere and elementary" as stated by Sérgio Milliet's Preface to Alcântara Machado's *Vida*

e morte do Bandeirante. Cf. also Passos Guimarães, *Quatro séculos,* pp. 75–76 and 62–63, and Euclides da Cunha, *Rebellion in the Backlands: Os Sertões,* p. 95. The statement above is confirmed by Boxer, perhaps the most well informed historian of that period. "There were," he says, "of course, many and obvious contrasts between the captaincy of São Vicente [São Paulo] and the rest of Brazil. Whereas the settlers and sugar-planters along the coast had their interest concentrated on the maritime trade with Portugal, and their eyes fixed on the Atlantic, the inhabitants of this remote highland plateau turned their faces and their footsteps to the unexplored hinterland. There was nothing corresponding to the luxury and easy living of the planters of Bahia and Pernambuco to be found among the settlers in the backwoods of São Vicente, whose way of life was certainly on the frugal side." *Salvador de Sa and the Struggle for Brazil and Angola: 1602–1686,* p. 27.

41. Cf. Roderick J. Barman, "Uma nobreza no novo mundo: A função dos títulos no Brasil Imperial," pp. 4–21.

42. Jerome Blum, *Lord and Peasant in Russia: From the Ninth to the Nineteenth Century,* and Vatro Murvar, "Patrimonial-Feudal Dichotomy and Political Structure in Pre-Revolutionary Russia: One Aspect of the Dialogue between the Ghost of Marx and Weber."

43. Cf. Weber, *The Religion of India,* p. 66.

44. Carvalho Franco, *Homens livres,* p. 201.

45. Ibid, p. 204.

46. Saint-Hilaire, *Segunda viagem,* p. 103.

47. On commensality, cf. Lins do Rego, *Menino de engenho,* pp. 11 and 71, and Bello, *Memórias,* p. 104; on the adjudication of justice, see Lins do Rego, pp. 36, 42–44, 60; on schooling, see Lins do Rego, p. 33, Bello, p. 65 and chap. 3, Lins do Rego, p. 60, Bello, pp. 55 ff., 197, 205.

48. G. C. Homans, "The Rural Sociology of Medieval England," p. 155 and *passim.* See also his *English Villagers of the Thirteenth Century,* pp. 323 and 414.

49. *Rebellion,* p. 380, and "Like the majority of those hamlets whose names are pompously inscribed on our maps, it (Uaua) was a sort of cross between an Indian camp and a village, consisting of an ugly-looking cluster of a hundred ill-made houses and dilapidated shanties," p. 184.

50. Weber, "Capitalism and Rural Society in Germany."

51. The following remark by a contemporary historian indicates that economic orientation. It is pertinent to our analysis that such an orientation is—incorrectly—seen as exceptional: "Despite the rudimentary techniques of the time [early eighteenth century], it may be perceived in the description of Antonil [of the organization of the *engenho*] the concern of the sugar entrepreneur to rationalize production according to a rigorous time diagram— *quite surprising for the epoch.*" Mircea Buescu, *História econômica: Pesquisas e análises,* p. 179 (my italics).

52. Weber suggested in this work how the lack of an urban market had negative consequences for the creation of *Grundherrschaft:* "A certain number of towns upon a given area was necessary to inspire the mass of the peasants with at least such a degree of interest in production that the lord was enabled to draw from them the means necessary for his sustenance, of using them

as 'funds for interest.' Where these influences of culture, which cannot be replaced even by the best labor and best will, were lacking, the peasant frequently lacked the possibility and always the incentive to raise the yield of his land beyond the traditional measure of his own needs." *From Max Weber*, p. 379.

53. Henri Pirenne, "Stages in the Social History of Capitalism," pp. 97–107, and Karl Marx, *Contribution à la Critique de l'Économie Politique*, p. 167.

54. See Nelson Werneck Sodré, *História militar do Brasil*, p. 28.

55. See Caio Prado, *Colonial Background*, p. 361 ff.

56. See F. W. O. Morton, "The Military and Society in Bahia: 1820–1821." This is a valuable research report conducted in the local archives. It gives support to the findings of John N. Kennedy's "Bahian Elites 1750–1822," in his contention that no representatives of the merchant classes were found among the officers.

57. See Rui Vieira da Cunha, *Estudo da nobreza brasileira: I-Cadetes*.

58. For a discussion of the status of the military in war and peace time see Stinchcombe, "Some Empirical Consequences of the Davis-Moore Theory of Stratification."

59. The most important strategy designed by the king to entice this stratum into his royal professional army was the institution of "cadetship," established by Dom Jose in 1757. The young cadets "would dress in the uniform of officer rank and would be introduced by the colonel of the regiment before the troop in formation. They would be allowed to frequent the officer's club without being compelled to wear the moustache; they would be excused from stable and sentry duties; and would compete with sergeants for external services. They could be promoted without a fixed term as privates." João Batista Magalhães, "História e evolução militar do Brasil," in *Anais [do] IV Congresso de história nacional*, R.J.: IHGB, 1950, vol. 6, p. 501, n. 45. Actually, this royal policy had begun much earlier—at the beginning of the eighteenth century—with constant efforts to staff the royal army with persons of "[a] melhor nobreza, cristandade e desinteresse," as phrased by a Royal Order of 1709, *apud* Magalhães, p. 502, n. 49. There are grounds to believe that this policy, which lasted with a remarkable degree of social homogeneity until the end of the colonial period, first had its corporative front cracked in Rio Grande do Sul.

60. It is interesting that the *gaúcho* military actively engaged in the southern process of state-building also made more noticeable efforts to develop a militaristic ethic.

61. According to Faoro, "[that] troop played the role of a pretorian guard of governors to be employed in extraordinary missions (*missões de confiança*)," *Os donos do poder*, p. 99.

62. Cf. Caio Prado, *Colonial Background*; Sodré, *Formação histórica*; Morton, *The Military and Society*; and Gustavo Barroso, *História militar do Brasil*, pp. 24–25.

63. "Without fear of exaggeration, it can be said that the *ordenanças* made possible the maintenance of law and order in this vast territory, with its scanty population and paucity of proper officials." Caio Prado, *Colonial Background*, p. 379.

64. Cf. Caio Prado, *Colonial Background,* pp. 378 ff.

65. Marques de Lavradio, "Memórias públicas e económicas da cidade de São Sebastião do Rio de Janeiro para uso do Vice-Rei, Luis de Vasconcelos, por observação curiosa dos anos de 1779 até o de 1789," *apud* Caio Prado, *Colonial Background,* p. 380.

66. Caio Prado, *Colonial Background,* p. 381.

67. "We speak of *status liturgy,* if the obligations are linked to monopolistic groups in such a manner that the members cannot withdraw unilaterally and hence remain collectively liable for satisfying the needs of the larger political unit." Weber, *Economy and Society,* vol. 1, p. 350.

68. For an analytical discussion of these concepts, see R. Aron, "Social Class, Political Class, Ruling Class."

Chapter 2

1. Vicente Barretto, *A ideologia liberal no processo da independência do Brasil,* pp. 110, 147, and *passim.*

2. "[The] only political and economic meaning attached to the movement [of independence] was precisely the meaning implied by the word; that is, political and economic *autonomy* from a colonial power. It *did not* mean that Brazil would attempt to build a Rousseaunian society by accepting the premise that all men are socially and politically equal. As a matter of fact, the only commitment made by the Brazilian elite during the Independence movement pointed to another developmental line. The statement of independence was issued by the son of the Portuguese king, himself Portuguese born, who was immediately acclaimed Brazil's first Emperor. It *was not* clear, however, whether Brazilian monarchy was to be absolutist, constitutional, parliamentary, or what." Wanderley Guilherme dos Santos, "Liberal Praxis in Brasil," p. 14. See also, Barretto, *A ideologia liberal,* pp. 87, 91, 93 and *passim.*

3. José Murilo de Carvalho, "Elite and State-Building in Imperial Brazil," chap. 8, p. 12, and in "As forças armadas na Primeira República: O poder desestabilizador."

4. Halperin Donghi, *Politics, Economics and Society,* p. 149 and *passim.*

5. This is Halperin Donghi's synthesis of Pueyrredon's views forwarded to San Martin in 1816, from *Politics, Economics and Society,* p. 195 (my translation).

6. *Politics, Economics and Society,* pp. 204–205 and *passim.*

7. I do not mean to imply that the opposite is false, namely that the army had nothing to do with Brazilian politics or the military organization nothing to do with, say, Argentinian politics. This comparative statement is principally meant, of course, to synthesize contrasting *trends,* as are other comparative materials brought into this work. A more qualified presentation would contrast the pattern of integration of military and political institutions at the local and national levels, characteristic of the Gran Colombia and the Argentine, to the Brazilian pattern, where such integration is principally valid for the local level only.

8. Henri Bergson, *Les deux sources de la morale et de la religion*, chap. 1. This is a "sociological" rendering of Bergson's text.

9. The statement belongs to Armitage according to Euclides da Cunha, *À margem da história*, p. 229.

10. Testimonies abound to the effect that Dom João VI took particular care to provide his semi-exiled dependents with the necessary prebends for personal sustenance: "There was not," according to a living witness, "one single person among all who went voluntarily into exile for love of their sovereign who did not receive from his liberal hands a reward for so great a sacrifice, according to status, dedication, and abilities." Luiz Gonçalves dos Santos, *Memórias para servir a História do Reino do Brasil*, 1825, quoted from Max Fleiuss, *História administrativa do Brasil*, p. 70.

It was also said that "he provided pensions to noblemen and fidalgos; [that] he promoted Army and Navy officers; [and that] he generously distributed prebends and offices for priests, military, and civilians." The city of Rio de Janeiro, with a population of about 100,000 inhabitants, suddenly had to make room for 1,000 royal officials and another 1,000 royal favorites. A few years later, when Dom João IV returned to Europe, leaving his son Pedro as Emperor of Brazil, the royal retinue returning to Portugal is said to have numbered about 4,000 individuals including fidalgos, rich merchants, and capitalists. Fleiuss, *História administrativa*. According to E. da Cunha, *À margem da história*, the population of Rio at that time was just 45,000, whereas according to Calogeras, *A History of Brazil*, it was 130,000.

11. "For all practical purposes, the budget did not exist. Dom Pedro [I] was wont to give direct orders to the treasury for the payment of such and such expenses, for which in many cases no legal authority existed. Nominations within the competence of the ministers were made by the Emperor himself, without regard for the results of such a deplorable practice." Calogeras, *A History of Brazil*, p. 112.

12. These percentages were computed with data from *Exposição do estado da Fazenda Pública*, pp. 40 ff.

13. For these figures, see *Exposição do estado da Fazenda Pública*.

14. "Fully aware that they had no means of resisting attacks from their rivals for power, the rulers of the house of Aviz adopted in their transatlantic enterprises one consistent policy of defense: absolute secrecy. It was forbidden to publish maps, portolanos, or accounts of voyages. If it were absolutely necessary to commit anything to writing, it was done in such a manner that no information of value could become public property." Calogeras, *A History of Brazil*, pp. 1–2.

15. Ibid., p. 96.

16. AN, Seção de Doc. Hrica, *caixa* 771, *pac.* 4. There is no indication of the official source or its date. It was issued, at any rate, after October 1831.

17. Cf. BPER [*Guarda Nacional:* Maricá e Itaborai: 1853], off. let. from the loc. com. to the cs on July 21, 1853; also BPER [*Guarda Nacional:* Sto. Antonio de Sá e Rio Bonito: 1853], off. let. of the loc. com. to the cs on August 26, 1853. I have purposely selected these two sample letters from the province closest to the influence of the charismatic emperor and his Court, namely, the Province of Rio de Janeiro. It goes without saying that the trend was stronger in more distant provinces like Rio Grande do Sul or Minas Gerais.

18. See, for example, Nelson Werneck Sodré, *Formação histórica do Brasil*, pp. 224–225.

19. The more divergent case, Rio Grande do Sul, with a growth rate of 1.20 can be explained by the fact that the base year for that rate, 1852, showed a rather high expenditure in defense compared with the amount spent at the end of an already pacified empire. The volume of military expenditure—not even including the maritime—dropped from 77.97 percent in that year to 62.40 percent in 1888. Clearly, Riograndense growth was actually higher than it appeared.

20. *Evolução do povo brasileiro*, p. 264. See also p. 244.

21. *Evolução*, pp. 204, 208, 215, and *passim*.

22. *Os donos do poder, passim*.

23. See, for instance, Nelson Werneck Sodré, *Formação histórica do Brasil*, and Maria Isaura Pereira de Queiróz, "O mandonismo local na vida política brasileira".

24. See, for instance, João Camilo de Oliveira Torres, *A democracia coroada: Teoria política do Império do Brasil*, pp. 439–440; and Sergio Buarque da Holanda, *Raízes do Brazil*.

25. José Murilo de Carvalho, "Elite and State-Building." An evolutionary perspective may be found in the work of a nineteenth-century thinker; see Justiniano José da Rocha, "Ação, reação, transação: Duas Palavras acerca da atualidade política do Brasil," pp. 161–218.

26. Rodrick James Barman, "Brazil at Mid-Empire: Political Accommodation and the Pursuit of Progress under the Conciliação Ministry, 1853–1857," p. 71 and *passim*.

27. Francisco Iglesias, *Política econômica do governo provincial mineiro: 1835–1889*, p. 20 and *passim*.

28. Iglesias remarks that, during the entire Imperial rule, the average presidential tenure in Minas Gerais was six-and-a-half months. *Política econômica*, pp. 40–41. Cf. also Heitor Lyra, *História de Dom Pedro II: 1825–1891*, vol. 2, p. 35.

29. Heitor Lyra, *História*, p. 34.

· 30. Cf. Oliveira Torres, *A democracia coroada*, chap. 12.

31. da Cunha, *À margem da história*, p. 281.

32. In 1852, for instance, members of the cabinet officially declared to the emperor that, however much they might desire conciliation on the national level, they could implement such a policy at the local level only at the expense of their local support. Barman, "Brazil at Mid-Empire," pp. 70–71. See also José Murilo: "In the Brazilian circumstances, with a small urban population, with most of the rural population under the slave system, no central state could maintain itself without some sort of compromise with the landowning groups," in "Elite and State-Building." Also, Aspasia Alcântara de Camargo, "Autoritarismo e populismo, bipolaridade no sistema político Brasileiro," pp. 22–45. Finally, Fabio Wanderley Reis also regards the relative privatization of power as a form of state-building, not as a dispersion of power. See his "Brasil: 'Estado e Sociedade' em perspectiva."

33. For instance, AN, IJ[1] 770 off. let. from pp of Rio de Janeiro to MJ on March 13, 1843; also AN, IJ[1] 616 off. let. from pp of Minas Gerais to MJ

on January 5, 1848. This problem dragged on for a long time. Thus, at the end of the Empire the problem still existed. Cf. AN, IJ¹ 661, ms. addressed to pp of Minas Gerais by a private citizen on March 4, 1879, termo da Prata, requesting a court judge (*Juiz de Direito*) for the district.

34. See, AN, IJ¹ 450, pp to MJ, March 17, 1848, for instance. For Minas Gerais see AN, IJ¹ 612, pp. to MJ, July 25, 1843. Usually these conflicts of competence took place between the police and the judiciary, among the judiciary, and between the judiciary and the municipal legislatures.

35. AN, *caixa* 783, *pac.* 1, pp of Ceará to MJ on November 8, 1849.

36. AN, *caixa* 783, *pac.* 2, pp of Sergipe to MJ, n.d. [1851]. Emphasis in the original.

37. AN, *caixa* 783, *pac.* 2, pp of Parahyba do Norte to MJ on November 21, 1851. See also off. let. of December 15.

38. See, for instance, AN, *caixa* 783, *pac.* 2, pp of Minas Gerais to MJ on January 20, 1851.

39. For the English case, cf. Lawrence Stone, *The Crisis of the Aristocracy: 1558–1641*, chap. 5, and J. H. Plumb, *The Growth of Political Stability in England: 1675–1725*, chap. 3.

40. "Elite and State-Building," chap. 6, p. 24.

41. The political career of the *coronel* remained at the prefecture level. Cf. Antonio Octavio Cintra, "A integração do processo político do Brasil: algumas hipóteses inspiradas na literatura," p. 19, n. 29. The origins of "coronelism" will become clear with the examination of the *Guarda Nacional* in the following chapters.

42. Emil Farhat, "O genro, o grande culpado," in *Diário de Notícias*, February 16, 1946, *apud* Victor Nunes Leal, *Coronelismo, enxada e voto: O município e o regime representativo no Brasil*, p. 194, n. 2.

43. Gilberto Freyre, "Social life in Brazil in the Middle of the Nineteenth Century," p. 230.

44. Max Weber, *The Religion of China*, chap. 5.

45. See, for instance, Barman, "Brazil at Mid-Empire" and Pang and Seckinger, "The Mandarins of Imperial Brazil."

Chapter 3

1. AN, Seção de Documentação Histórica, *caixa* 771, *pac.* 2: (a) ms. addressed to the Camara de Paranaguá on November 30, 1841 by forty-three signatories; (b) ms. addressed to the Diocesan Bishop of São Paulo on November 30, 1841 by sixty-nine signatories; (c) off. let. from the said *camara* to the President of the Province of São Paulo on March 13, 1842; (d) off. let. from the said *camara* to the Minister of Justice on May 4, 1842; (e) off. let. from the said *camara* to the emperor on May 4, 1842; (f) ms. with public statement by twenty-six signatories on August 2, 1842; (g) off. let. from the provincial president to the *camara* on March 4, 1842.

2. AN, IJ⁶ 459, *Acta da Apuração dos Votos para Eleitores desta Parochia de S. João d'El-Rei*, January 4, 1861, annexed to Despacho Imperial no. 440,

Minas Gerais, *Guarda Nacional:* Pedido de Reforma: July 2, 1878. The remaining six were two *comendadores*, two doctors, one senator, and one priest.

3. AN, IJ[6] 456, *Acta de apuração geral dos votos para vereadores deste Município [da Capital de Pernambuco]*, March 7, 1873.

4. They constituted, moreover, primarily a market of buyers, a fact which may attest to the resilience of this process of militarization. See Arquivo da Prefeitura de Valença, vol. 147, *Registro de escrituras públicas de compra e venda [de terras e escravos]*, 1856–1867.

5. AN, IJ[6] 465, cf. Despacho Imperial no. 65: *Guarda Nacional:* Reforma, March 25, 1875 and annexes.

6. I am indebted to Rafael Bayce who drew my attention to the relevance of the distinction discussed here.

7. See José Murilo de Carvalho, "As forças armadas na Primeira República: o poder desestabilizador," p. 141.

8. Army troops could, however, be assigned military missions for the domestic pacification of the Empire.

9. For the number of enlisted men in the National Guard at the end of the 1830s, a few years after its creation, see AN: Seção de Doc. Hrica, *caixa 777, pac.* 1, ms., *Informação sobre as Guardas Nacionaes das Províncias, desde a sua criação até 24 de Março de 1841, organisada segundo os officios, e Mappas recebidos.*

10. "O povo em armas: Guarda Nacional 1831–1850." Mrs. Castro conducted extensive archival research. Her work provides a comprehensive introduction to the organization of the *Guarda Nacional* during the first half of the Empire; her scope is broad and gives special attention to the *Guarda Nacional paulista*. It is very rich in information which in part regrettably distracts the author from a contextual discussion of the corporation and a more theoretical treatment; without this the discussion loses some of its value. There is, to my knowledge, no other single monographic discussion of the corporation. Brazilian historiographic introductions give a brief and passing reference to it. So far it has not deserved, inexplicably, even a chapter. There are a scattered half-dozen independent discussions in the relevant literature, but they are without particular value.

11. Law of August 18, 1831, art. 1.

12. Castro, "O povo em armas," p. 24.

13. Ibid.

14. Law of August 18, 1831, art. 2.

15. Art. 6 of the above law.

16. APM, *cod.* 391: Ofícios do Governo aos Comandantes da Guarda Nacional: 1846–1848, off. let. from the president of the province to the commander of the Ouro Preto Legion in May 30, 1846.

17. APM, *cod.* 391: Ofícios do Governo aos Comandantes da Guarda Nacional: 1846–1848. Off. let. of the provincial president to the commander of the First Batallion of the County of Ayuruoca in March 27, 1848.

18. The previous summary is based on the organic law and the decree of October 25, 1832, which first altered it.

19. As above; see also law no. 602 of September 19, 1850, and Castro, "O Povo em Armas," chaps. 3 and 8.

20. Samples of these licenses may be found in AN, IJ⁶ 466. Licenses for less than two months were granted by the company commanders with the possibility of appeal to the *comandante superior*, who could, in turn, grant up to four-month licenses to officers and militiamen under his command, but only on the Court's or the provincial president's approval. See decree no. 1354, April 6, 1854.

21. Archival records for the decades 1840 and 1850 do not abound in these *guias*. For the period see, for instance, BPER [*Guarda Nacional:* 3a. e 4a. legiões: 1838], from the chief of the legion to the pp in October 6, 1838.

22. There were periodic laws and decrees regulating this process. The most important were decree no. 1130 of March 12, 1853 and that of November 25, 1865. For a model of a *guia de mudança* see BPER [GN: Angra dos Reis e Parati, 1854].

23. For instance, BPER [*Guarda Nacional:* avulsos sem classificar], off. let. from the cs of the Barra Mansa *Guarda Nacional* to MJ on February 4, 1893 relaying a request for a *guia* for a captain under his command to move to the state of São Paulo.

Chapter 4

1. The information above was drawn from the organic laws of 1831 and 1850, as well as from other decrees like no. 99 of October 1, 1841. For the quotation, see the law of 1850, art. 80, par. 3.

2. Off. let. from the pp of Bahia to the MJ on September 5, 1861 in AN, IJ¹ 412.

3. See decree no. 1354 of April 6, 1854, and *Despacho da Secretaria dos Negocios da Justiça,* April 18, 1877, in AN, IJ⁶ 433, Ms. By an *aviso* sent by the Ministry of Justice to the provincial presidents on March 31, 1874, all expenses with the *Guarda Nacional* would cease except for the salaries of the *comandantes superiores* who were Army officers.

4. For such a view see, for instance, T. H. Marshall, *Sociology at the Crossroads and Other Essays,* and Reinhard Bendix, *Nation-Building and Citizenship: Studies of Our Changing Social Order.*

5. For illustrative cases on the absence of magistrates and public tranquillity for Minas Gerais in the 1830s, see AN, IJ¹ 763.

For complaints against justice administration by dilettantes, see, for instance, AN, IJ¹ 450 for the late 1840s, in the Province of Rio de Janeiro. Particularly, pp to MJ on July 8, 1848; aldermen of the city of Campos de Goitacazes to pp on July 13, 1848; and court judge of the village of Cantagallos to pp on May 27, 1848. For Bahia, two telling cases are found in AN, IJ¹ 400, off. let. from pp to MJ on July 12, 1843, and off. let. from the municipal judge and delegate of Caetité to pp on July 19, 1843. Also, AN, IJ¹ 707, pp to MJ on February 28, 1832, and court judge of Caravellas to pp on March 10, 1832. For the lack of jails in the mid 1850s in the Province of Bahia, see AN, IJ¹ 410, off. let. from the police chief of the province to MJ on March 31, 1855.

6. AN, IJ¹ 412, off. let. from pp of Bahia to MJ on October 15, 1861.

7. AN, IJ¹ 612, off. let. from the court judge of Barbacenas to the pp of Minas Gerais on March 15, 1843, annexed to off. let. from pp to MJ on April 20, 1843.

8. AN, IJ¹ 400, off. let. from the pp of Bahia to MJ on June 11, 1842.

9. The failure to do this is at the root of "feudal" readings of Brazilian history, such as Nestor Duarte's.

10. See, for instance, AN, IJ⁶ 420, particularly off. let. from cs to MJ on August 29, 1837, and *Acta do processo de desobediência contra José Bernardino de Sá, 2.° Distrito da Candelária* on June 10, 1837 for a law suit against a militiaman who refused to be imprisoned for not providing service on account of having paid the music contribution. See also AN, IJ¹ 416, off. let. from the commander of the Third Battalion to the colonel chief of the Third Legion of the court on March 30, 1835. Also, IJ⁶ 417, off. let. from the acting commander of the First Battalion to the commander of the Second Legion of Rio de Janeiro on May 24, 1835. And AN, IJ¹ 410, off. let. of the cs of the capital to the pp of Bahia on August 13, 1856 for the compulsory character that such contributions might have.

11. See, for instance, AN, IJ⁶ 415, off. let. of cs of Court to MJ on September 11, 1834 and September 13, 1834.

12. AN, IJ⁶ 443, off. let. from the commander of the company of cavalry of the G.N. of Parahiba do Sul to MJ on April 29, 1833.

13. AHRGS, *lata* 428, off. let. from the colonel chief of staff to the cs of Quarai e Livramento, Jiquiecuá, December 27, 1864 annexed to off. let. from cs to pp on January 14, 1865 suggesting the approval of the request, provided the said corps be subject to the command of the local garrison.

14. It is interesting, moreover, to remark that these sites were not chosen by the commanders, but were determined by the Imperial authorities. Apart from these *campos de fazenda,* other habitual places selected for parades were the public squares and in front of churches. See, for instance, BPER [*Guarda Nacional:* 1854] Ordem Presidencial on February 8, 1854. Even in 1883 it was possible to find proposals for the establishment of company parades in front of private households. See, for instance, AHRGS, *lata* 422, cs: Cruz Alta: 1850–1884, off. let. from the com. of the 67.° Corpo to the cs on August 8, 1883.

15. AN, IJ⁶ 424, off. let. from cs of the Court to MJ, June 2, 1842. This *ad hoc* solution had been previously employed in other commands to compensate those officers whose means of livelihood became jeopardized somehow by their avocational duties. For significant cases regarding the commanders' defrayal of administrative costs, see AN, IG¹³ 672, off. let. from cs of the G.N. of Porto Alegre to pp of Rio Grande do Sul on March 16, 1858; and AHRGS, *lata* 442, cs of Cruz Alta to pp of Rio Grande do Sul on May 28, 1874. General instructors, it is to be remembered, were appointed from the pool of officers of the bureaucratic, salaried Army.

16. AN, IG¹³ 672, off. let. from the cs to the pp on April 8, 1859.

17. Commanders were particularly sensitive to and impatient with the bureaucratic authorities' reluctance to give full credit to their words. Sometimes they just could not make out the latter's refusal to accept them on their

merit. A local commander from Minas Gerais once sent a bill covering six years of personal funding of clerical expenses and costs of transportation. The higher commander relayed the petition to the provincial president, recommending payment "because [the bill] is quite correct." APM, *cod.* 228, off. let. from the commander of the First Battalion of the G.N. of Queluz to the cs of the same place on March 1, 1839; and off. let. from the same cs to pp on April 19, 1839.

A *gaúcho* commander, in a protracted move to recover money he spent to fund a detachment, alleged the existence of official documents at the bureaucratic archives that bore out his command of the said detachment, and he concluded with indignant exasperation: "If that is not enough, I have a record of 42 years of very honorable services that will doubtless constitute a proof that [those expenses were paid by me]. I reckon that in view of all I have said above, Your Excellency will not allow that I degrade myself requesting certificates from my subordinates." In AHRGS, *lata* 422, off. let. from cs of Cruz Alta to pp of Rio Grande do Sul on June 30, 1866.

18. *Capitalismo e escravidão no Brasil meridional: O negro na sociedade escravocrata do Rio Grande do Sul*, p. 97. My italics.

19. *Capitalismo e escravidão*, p. 119, n. 61.

20. Militia officers, for instance, were denied the same military honors given to deceased military officers. See AN, IJ[6] 419, off. let. from cs of the Court to MJ on August 8, 1836. There are other official letters with similar content. There were political reasons for this, to be discussed later.

21. Hegel, *The Phenomenology of Mind*, pp. 229–240. The development of this mode of consciousness, rigorously speaking, depends not only on work but also on fear: "For this reflexion of self into self the two moments, fear and service in general, as also that of formative activity, are necessary: and at the same time both must exist in a universal manner. Without the discipline of service and obedience, fear remains formal and does not spread over the whole known reality of existence. Without the formative activity shaping the thing, fear remains inward and mute, and consciousness does not become objective for itself." p. 239.

22. The officialdom of a local district in Bahia sent a complaint to the higher commander concerning the injurious and disrespectful way in which an ensign had been taken to jail by the justice of the peace, and asked that the necessary measures be taken not only to avoid the repetition of acts of this kind, but also to get satisfaction for the offense. They added that such a procedure was not commensurate with the dignity of the corporation to which they belonged, with the significant remark that although the law did not grant them military *foro*, the corporation deserved it. AEB, *Guarda Nacional: maço* 3528, off. let. from officers of the *freguezia* of Nossa Senhora da Conceição da Praia to ch. of the First Legion on August 6, 1832.

23. The prosecutor of a council of discipline ignored formal procedure in the judgement of some bandmen of the local battalion "because he takes it that, as they serve for a wage, they are not in the circumstances to be tried in the same way as the qualified citizen-guards." AN, IJ[1] 707, pp of Bahia to MJ on December 20, 1834. The government's answer was "that the band-

men must not be tried in the same way as the citizen militiamen, but that they must be held accountable," (Manuscript comment in the margin of the document).

24. BPER [*Guarda Nacional:* Campos e São João da Barra: 1862], off. let. from the major chief-of-staff in Campos to the Vice-p of Rio de Janeiro on June 11, 1862 and annexed documents. The law gave the militiamen the same privileges given the professional military. Cf. organic law of 1850 and *aviso* of November 30, 1861, of the MJ.

25. BPER [*Guarda Nacional:* 10a. e 11a. Leg.: 1844], off. let. from colonel ch. of 10th. leg. to the *Juiz de Direito* (court judge), Angra dos Reis, May 9, 1844.

26. AN, IJ⁶ 422, off. let. from the lieutenant cel. ch. of the 5th. bat. of the Court to the cs on January 2, 1839. The candidate for rank was a tavern owner. For another interesting opinion, see APM, *cod.* 228, off. let. from the com. of Ipiranga to the colonel ch. of. leg. of the G.N. of Queluz on January 9, 1839: "as long as the Officers of the *Guarda Nacional* be chosen by popular election, it will never be possible to attain with them the goals for which it was created."

27. The lack and inadequacy of prisons was a permanent headache for the Imperial authorities. Official commissioners who occasionally made inspections were aghast at the general conditions under which prisoners— usually of both sexes—were confined. A common enquiry of the commanders to the Ministry of Justice was where to confine the militiamen who had been sentenced. The common answer was to leave it to the commander's own discretion to find an *ad hoc* place. See, for instance, AN, IJ⁶ 443 and IJ⁶ 415.

28. For the fisherman's case, see AN, IJ⁶ 423, off. let. from the lieut. col. ch. of the 5th. bat. of the Court to the cs on October 11, 1841, annexed to off. let. from cs to MJ on October 15, 1841. For the tailor's case, see AN, IJ⁶ 421, off. let. from the lieut. col. ch. of the 5th. bat. of the Court to the cs on December 7, 1838.

29. AN, IJ⁶ 450, off. let. from the cs of the G.N. of the Court to MJ on April 21, 1838, and annexed documents.

30. AN, IJ⁶ 414, off. let. from the cs of the G.N. of the Court to the MJ on March 6, 1834.

31. For the contrasting pattern of discipline and organization, see the report in AN, IJ⁶ 443, off. let. from the col. ch. of the leg. of the G.N. of Valença, Vassouras, and Parahiba do Sul to the MJ on September 10, 1833. For the election of officers, AN, IJ⁶ 443, off. let. from the justice of the peace of the parish of the Sacra Familia in Macaé, Province of Rio de Janeiro to the MJ on September 11, 1832.

32. For the 1858 affair, see AN, IJ⁶ 430, off. and confidential let. from the cs of the Court to the MJ on March 6, 1858. Status was so much taken for granted for the constitution and organization of the militias that a *comandante superior* saw no incompatibility between his use of the criterion of seniority for the promotion of his officers and his simultaneous rejection of an ensign candidate who had a tobacco shop and could not enjoy "a status convenient for an officer of the Guarda Nacional." AN, IJ⁶ 429, off. let. from

the cs of the Court to the MJ on November 6, 1857. This incongruity is the more striking as the commander in the same letter justified the candidacy of other officers on the basis of seniority, which the Ministry of Justice had tried to invigorate by the recent circular of August 18, 1857. For the last case, AN, IJ⁶ 430, off. let. from the com. of the artillery bat. to the cs at the Court on September 28, 1863.

33. BPER [*Guarda Nacional:* Vassouras e Iguassu: 1862], off. let. from the cs to the vice-p of Rio de Janeiro on July 17, 1862.

34. By parental status I mean the notion of legitimate as opposed to natural parenthood.

35. See, for instance, BPER [*Guarda Nacional:* Promoções: Vassouras e Iguassu: 1860] and [*Guarda Nacional:* Magé e Estrela: 1860], and [*Guarda Nacional:* Campos: 1870].

Chapter 5

1. In AN, IJ⁶ 444. August 14, 1834.

The quotation from the Bahia President about buying more arms may be found in AN, IJ¹ 709, off. let. on April 14, 1847.

The quote on sticks and clubs may be found in BPER [*Guarda Nacional:* 1a. Legião: Niteroi: 1838], off. let. from the col. ch. of the leg. to the pp on July 30, 1838.

On public ridicule, see, for instance, AN, IJ⁶ 442, off. let. from the com. of the cav. company of Itaguahy to the MJ on February 1, 1833. See also this commander's off. let. to the MJ on September 19, 1833, reporting that the seventy-odd members of his company needed armament, which had been requested several times and which had been promised more than seven months before. The service was frequently performed with unarmed men. The following statement from a local newspaper is illustrative: "The detachment of the 1st. infantry battalion . . . which was garrisoned to auxiliate the police force . . . was headed for the barracks with a simulacrum of armament, that is, with forty old shotguns." *A Reforma*, March 30, 1870. See also the following statements: "As far as the arms are concerned, I am sure that they will not even shoot one single shot," in an off. let. from the cs of the *Guarda Nacional* of Campos to the pp on June 27, 1870, BPER [*Guarda Nacional:* Avisos do Ministério da Justiça: 1870]; and "I have been informed that the armament is so ruined and old that it does not do even for very simple parade firing." in AN, IJ 400, off. let. from the pp of Bahia to MJ.

For Minas Gerais, see very illustrative cases in APM, *cod.* 768, off. let. from the com. of the bat. of S. Romão to pp on January 8, 1859; and off. let. from the com. of the G.N. of Januaria to pp on January 27, 1859.

2. AN, IJ¹ 456, off. let from the cs of the G.N. of Itaborahy and Maricá to the vice-p of Rio de Janeiro on May 4, 1854.

On the "illusory" organization, see AN, IJ⁶ 443, off. let. from the com. of the G.N. of São João do Príncipe in the Province of Rio de Janeiro to the MJ on July 16, 1833.

On the need for professional instructors, see, for instance, off. let. above on May 4, 1854; also AN, IJ¹ 466, off. let. from the pp of Rio de Janeiro to MJ on September 9, 1864: "Considering how the lack of those assistants strongly contributes to the lack of discipline, training and bookkeeping." For more correspondence on the issue see, for instance, AN, IJ⁶ 413, off. let. from the cap. instructor of the G.N. of the parish of S. Salvador (Campos) to the lieut col. and general instructor of the G.N. of the county on September 21, 1833. Also AN, IJ⁶ 414, off. let. from the instructor of the G.N. of Santo Antonio de Sa to the general instructor at the Court on January 6, 1834. Both these letters are reports on the question.

More of this in AN, IJ¹ 708, off. let. from the pp of Bahia to MJ on September 5, 1837 and BPER [Guarda Nacional: Macaé e Barra de São João: 1864, Avulsos], off. let. from the cs to the pp on December 6, 1864; and BPER [Guarda Nacional: Relatorios e Qualificação: 1858], off. let. from the cs of Macaé and Capivari to pp on June 4, 1858.

3. AN, caixa 783: Pacotilha 2, off. let. from MJ, to the pp of Minas Gerais on November 1, 1851.

4. BPER [Guarda Nacional: Avulsos], off. let. from the cs of Niteroi to the vice-p of the province on April 21, 1866. Also AN, IJ⁶ 427, off. let. from the cs at the Court to MJ on July 21, 1851.

Commenting on the dispensations from service, a commander observes: "These dispensations are always revolting for those who, for lack of patronage, are forced to bear all the burden of service." AN, IJ⁶ 417, off. let. from the cs at the Court to MJ on September 25, 1835. See, again, off. let. from cs to MJ on November 8, 1835. As indicated, the commanders frequently thought it ironic that dispensations were given precisely to those people who received a regular income from the state, whereas those who depended on their own daily labor were not excused. See, for instance, AN, IJ⁶ 424, off. let. from the cs at the Court to the MJ on May 18, 1842. See also BPER [Guarda Nacional: 1839: 5a. Legião], off. let. from the com. of the 1st. batallion of Cabo Frio to pp on March 11, 1839.

The justices of the peace tended to reinforce the pattern of service discussed above insofar as they usually requisitioned infantrymen. See, for instance, BPER [Guarda Nacional: 1a. e 2a. Legiões: 1835], off. let. from the ch. of the leg. of Itaborahy to pp on October 19, 1835. And AN, IJ⁶ 443, off. let. from the com. of the G.N. of Itagoahy to MJ on September 13, 1833. More documents relevant for this general issue may be found in that lata.

5. The state of indiscipline is amply documented in the relevant archival sections. For significant statements, however, see AN, IJ⁶ 419, off. let. from the cs at the Court to the MJ on October 11, 1836 and AN, IJ⁶ 429, off. let. from the cs at the Court to the MJ on October 12, 1857, and IJ⁶ 416, off. let. from the acting com. of a bat. of the 4th. leg. at the Court to the col. ch. on April 16, 1835, and documents below.

On the preference for cavalry service and transfer requests, see AN, IJ⁶ 443, off. let. from the col. ch. of the leg. of Valença, Vassouras e Parahiba do Sul to the MJ on September 10, 1833; and IJ⁶ 433, off. let. of the com. of São Gonçalo, Rio de Janeiro, to the MJ on August 10, 1833. Also, AN, IJ⁶ 415, off. let. from the lieut. col. instructor of the G.N. at Irajá, Rio de Janeiro on October 10, 1834. For the "general and great preference for the Cavalry Arm, [and the] almost insuperable antipathy toward that of the Infantry," See AN, IJ⁶ 444, off. let. from the com. of the G.N. in Barramansa in Rio de Janeiro to the MJ on January 2, 1834.

On the renting of horses for disguising status, see AN, IJ⁶ 29, off. let. from MJ to acting cs on February 11, 1836.

On the arbitrary wearing of uniform, see AN, IJ⁶ 443, off. let. from the col. ch. of the leg. of Valença, Rio de Janeiro, to MJ on December 28, 1833.

On vocational courses, see AEB, *Guarda Nacional, maço* 3529, off! let. from the major acting ch. of the G.N. in Cachoeira, Bahia to pp on December 1, 1834, where mention is also made of the practice of obtaining canonical offices just to avoid service. This appeared documented, characteristically, only in Bahia.

For the ironical observation about the lyceum, see AEB, *maço* 3529, off. let. from the cs of the capital of Bahia to pp [?] on November 12, 1839.

On fictitious change of residential districts, see AN, IJ⁶ 420, off. let. from the general secretary of the G.N. at the Court to MJ on December 6, 1833, and AN, IJ⁶ 443, off. let. from com. of the G.N. of the parish of São Gonçalo to the MJ on September 4, 1833.

On the appointment of neighborhood inspectors, etc., see AEB, *Guarda Nacional: maço* 3528, off. let. from the acting cs of the G.N. to the pp on August 3, 1833: "Your Excellency well knows that if this profusion of Inspectors and other officials keeps growing to reach all the Districts, the *Guarda Nacional* will disappear," and AN, IJ⁶ 444, off. let. from the com. of the G.N. of Barramansa, Rio de Janeiro, to the MJ on January 2, 1834.

For the quotation on consensual service, see AN, IJ⁶ 422, off. let. from the cs at the Court to the MJ on October 30, 1839. For the quotation on the militiamen's attitudes: AN, IJ⁶ 414, off. let. from the com. of the 4th. bat. to the acting cs of the G.N. at the Court on April 10, 1834.

On the general resistance to service, see documentation above and especially also AN, IJ⁶ 444, off. let. from the ch. of leg. of the G.N. in São João do Príncipe, Rio de Janeiro to MJ on March 15, 1834. For the refusal of indoor clerical service in exchange for dispensation from other services: AN, IJ⁶ 428, off. let. from the com. of the 1st. and 2nd. bats. of reserve at the Court to MJ on June 27, 1833.

For the quotation on confinement rather than service, see APM, *cod.* 391, off. let. from pp of Minas to the col. ch. of the leg. of the G.N. of Serro on March 30, 1848.

For the quotation on the need for a legal principle, see AN, IJ⁶ 416, off. let. from the cap. com. of the 6th. comp. of the 1st. bat. of the G.N. at the Court to the com. of that bat. on February 26, 1835.

6. APM, *cod.* 768, off. let. from the *Camara Municipal* of Villa das Dores do Indaiá to pp on January 17, 1859.

7. Save for Minas Gerais, all provinces had organized their militia corps by the mid-1830s.

8. See, for instance, BPER [*Guarda Nacional*: Campos e S. João da Barra: 1856], off. let. from the cs to the vice-p on September 4, 1856 relaying a request for the change of location of a local company's parade. A reference

is there made to a locality with the name of Quilombinho which, since its transformation into the parade of a local unit "has very much grown . . . as well in population as in commerce, being the reason for the construction of more buildings which is very positive for the comfort of Citizen Guards who go there for training."

9. These conclusions were reached on the base of the documents dealing with elections to be found in the bibliography. See also Fernando Uricoechea, *Patrimonialism, Electoral Patterns and Social Stratification in Imperial Brazil.*

10. This generalization is based, among other things, on the relative frequency or absence of status qualification for corporate membership. Such qualifications reached an almost obsessive point in the status-oriented culture of the political center of the Empire and reached their lowest ebb in the Province of Bahia. See, for instance, the very significant and altogether typical off. let. from the pp of Bahia to MJ on September 12, 1839, AN, IJ[1] 708, submitting the names of candidates for the top commands of the counties of Itaparica, Jagoaripe, Macaubas, Urubu and Carinhanha; there is no mention whatsoever of the social status or the economic position of the candidates.

11. See, for instance, APM, *cod.* 229:1839, off. let. from the cs of Sabará to the pp on June 4, 1839, where it is observed that the commanders did not make personal contributions for the uniform of their subordinates. The first mention of a contribution of private money for the corporation refers to the officers of a batallion in Diamantina: characteristically, it was for the music band. See also off. let. from the col. ch. of leg. to pp on July 10, 1839. It is not common to find cases in the Province of Rio de Janeiro of commanders requesting the restitution of money spent on the administration of the unit. See for the opposite pattern in Minas Gerais, APM, *cod.* 391, off. let. from pp to ch. of leg. of Oliveira on October 3, 1846.

12. See documents in note 5 and also AEB, *maços* 3528, 3529, 3535.

13. AN, IJ[1] 709, off. let. from pp to MJ on March 30, 1846. See also AN, IJ[1] 400, off. let. from pp of Bahia to MJ on June 12, 1844 showing the impossibility of regularly sending the statistical tables of the militias because of "the bad organization in which is still found the *Guarda Nacional,* principally that of the center [not administrative or political] of the Province." And AN, IJ[1] 709, off. let. from pp of Bahia to MJ on April 10, 1847: "The *Guarda Nacional* of the hinterland of the Province is in the most inorganic state possible . . . [its] officers not caring for the organization of its corps."

14. BPER [*Guarda Nacional*: 2a. 3a., 7a. e 16a. Legiões: 1846], off. let. from the cs of those legions to pp on April 21, 1846.

15. See law 2395, September 10, 1873, especially articles 1, pars. 1, 5, 6, 10, and 12.

16. AN, IJ[1] 879, off. let. from pp to MJ on March 12, 1880. The trouble taken by officers to comply with their obligations was chiefly in relation to their *patentes* (certificates of appointment): why they had delayed the request for the *patente,* or asking for an extended deadline to pick it up, etc.

17. AN, IJ[6] 420, off. let. from cs at the Court to MJ on April 4, 1837. See this off. let. for a case of dissolution of a company whose members had, in defiance to the Imperial authorities, reelected unapproved officers.

For the case of the eight officers: AN, IJ⁶ 421, off. let. from the cs at the Court to MJ on October 15, 1838.

18. For the quotation about the three substitute lieutenant colonels, see BPER [Guarda Nacional: 8a. e 13a. Legiões: 1845], off. let. from cs to pp on February 1, 1845.

For the quotation on the reason for refusal, see BPER [Guarda Nacional: 4a. e. 5a.; 6a. e 14a. Legiões: 1845], off. let. from the lieut. col. ch. of 2nd. bat. of inf. of the 5th. to col. ch. of the leg. on June 4, 1845.

For quotation on the militias as a contrived vehicle of the government, see BPER [Guarda Nacional: 8a. e 13a. Legiões: 1848], off. let. from cs to pp on November 22, 1848.

For significant remarks on the state of disorganization of the above command, see off. let. from cs to pp on November 17, 1848: "The state of the Guarda Nacional, deprived of its better officers for reasons that only the Provincial Government may judge and which I ignore." It also discusses the reigning uncertainty of tenure and so on. More of this in BPER [Guarda Nacional: 10a. e 11a. legs.: 1848], off. let. from cs to pp, S. João do Príncipe, on July 11, 1848.

19. BPER [Guarda Nacional: 9a. e 12a. legs.], off. let. from cs of 9th. leg. to pp. Rezende, on May 4, 1849. The said "vacancies were deliberately kept since 1844 to be gambled with at Election times, each of the vacant offices being promised to 10 or 20 men provided they submitted themselves to the violence and arbitrariness characteristic of that time."

20. For the first quotation, see BPER [Guarda Nacional: 8a. e 13a. legs.: 1845], off. let. from cs to pp on February 1, 1845. For the second, AN, IJ⁶ 417, off. let. from act. cs at the Court to MJ on December 3, 1835. He suggested forcing the elected to accept.

21. See, for instance, the case of the indiscipline of the acting command of an infantry company in Valença, Rio de Janeiro: AN, Seção de Doc. Hrica. cod. 112, vol. 6, let. addressed by the acting com. of the 3rd. comp. of inf. to the Lieutenant José de Souza Werneck on September 14, 1865. See also the let. addressed to the said lieutenant by the com. of a detachment, Valença, December 3, 1865. Also the already quoted off. let. from cs of Paraty and Angra dos Reis to the vice-p. of Rio de Janeiro on May 20, 1861, BPER [Guarda Nacional: Avulsos sem classificar] commenting on the rank and file's lack of respect for the lieutenant com. of the art. comp.

22. For three dramatic cases of drastic change of economic status with repercussions on the corporate status of the affected, see (1) AN, sec. de doc. hrica., caixa 777, pac. 1, petition for transfer by Manoel Diaz Teixeira, Irajá, October 31, 1834; (2) BPER [Guarda Nacional: 6a. e 14a. legs.: 1848], cs to pp on April 20, 1848; and (3) BPER [Guarda Nacional: Campos e S. João da Barra, 1856], off. let. from cs to vice-p. on August 15, 1856.

23. The exceptional use of a legal-rational legitimacy will be explained in other chapters. For this quotation, see AHRGS, caixa 210, maço 3, off. let. from the com. [s. of the city of Porto Alegre] to the cs of the province on June 10, 1834.

24. For the militias' cooperation with the police forces in the repression of the slave traffic, see BPER [Guarda Nacional: Angra dos Reis e Parati: 1854],

off. let. from com. of the 28th bat. of Parati to cs on May 25, 1854. Several contingents were sent to the coastline; others reinforced or substituted for the police force in their functions of local vigilance and patrol of the captive inmates and local inhabitants. The commander complained that the requisitions of guards made by the police delegate went against the economic interests of the local economy inasmuch as they divested the agriculture of the "hands which it so dearly needs."

For the quotation on the commissioner, see AN, IJ[1] 477, off. let. from cs of 8th. and 13th. legs. to pp on February 21, 1842.

For the request of the officers of the neighboring legion, see AN, IJ[1] 447, off. let. of officers and commanders of the G.N. of Rezende to the Emperor on March 7, 1842. The functions of these commissioners were regulated by Decree A on October 15, 1837.

25. BPER [Guarda Nacional: 8a. leg.: 1839], off. let. from the cel. ch. [Valença] to vice-p on September 11, 1839.

26. For quotation on jeers, see AN, IJ[6] 428, off. let. of the lieut cel. com. of the 6th. bat. of the Court to cs on September 30, 1852.

For quotation on prison orders, see AN, IJ[6] 428, off. let. of the cap. of the 2nd. comp. to the com. of the 6th. bat. annexed to off. let. above.

27. AEB, Guarda Nacional: maço 3612, off. let. from the cs of Ilheus to the pp on November 11, 1867. This maço contains further documents, revealing the landlord's protection of local inhabitants, thanks to the protection provided by the Guarda Nacional to some immigrant families by instructions from, allegedly, the vice-president of the province.

28. For quotation on the stillness of time, see Euclides da Cunha, Rebellion, p. 111.

For the congratulations to the provincial president, see AEB, Guarda Nacional: maço 3646, off. let. from acting cs of Caetité to pp on April 10, 1870.

For the lack of civilization, see AEB, Guarda Nacional: maço 3605, off. let. from cs of Caetité to pp on October 13, 1865.

For the quotation on the bases of solidarity, see AN, IJ[1] 710, off. let. from the pp of Bahia to MJ on October 24, 1848.

29. BPER [Guarda Nacional: Relatórios e Qualificação: 1858], off. let. from cs of Campos to pp on June 19, 1858.

30. For this case, see BPER [Guarda Nacional: 6a. leg.: 1836], let. from Manoel Pinto Neto Cruz to pp, Fazenda de São Francisco, Campos dos Goitacazes, February 21, 1836. See also off. let. from act. ch. of the leg. of Campos to pp on August 12, 1836. And BPER [Guarda Nacional: 6a. leg.: 1839], let. from Julião Baptista Coqueiro to Luiz Antonio Muniz dos Sanctos Lobos [vice-pp?], Campos, May 18, 1839. The command was accepted by the justice of the peace on July 7, 1839.

31. APM, cod. 228: 1839, off. let. from the secretary of the com. of the G.N. of Villa da Campanha annexed to off. let. from the cs of Campanha to pp. I apologize for not having at the time registered the exact date of this document. See also APM, cod. 228: 1839, off. let. from the lieut. cel. com. of the 1st. bat. of Curvello to pp on August 9, 1839, asking for demission after five years of command as it interfered with his occupation (mail chief) and his obligations toward his large family.

32. AN, IJ⁶ 414, off. let. from the act. cs of the G.N. to the MJ on January 31, 1834. This is a general report on the state of the militias. Besides the remarks noted see: "the colossal Number of those dispensed is one of the great obstacles hindering the perfection of regular service."

33. BPER [*Guarda Nacional*: Angra dos Reis e Parati: 1857], off. let. from the act. com. of the 30th. inf. bat. of Ilha Grande de Fora to act. cs of Angra dos Reis e Parati on December 22, 1857.

34. See, for instance, the case of the craftsman and company commander with regard to a guard and son of a capitalist in AN, IJ⁶ 420, *Petição do G.N. João Luiz da Silva Valladares dirigida ao Imperador em* [9] *setembro de 1837*.

35. AN, IJ⁶ 417, off. let. from cs at the Court to MJ on December 7, 1835.

36. AN, IJ⁶ 443, off. let. from Manoel Joaquim Rangel, Juiz de Paz of Saquarema to MJ on October 2, 1832; and off. let. from the lieut. com. of the sect. of Saquarema to MJ on October 19, 1832.

37. To avoid misinterpretation, it is necessary to remark here that Weber is free from this criticism thanks to his methodological, ideal-typical strategy.

38. BPER [*Guarda Nacional*: 7a. leg.: 1839], off. let. from cel. ch. to pp on February 12, 1839.

39. The following example of a proposal for the office of lieut. cel. commander is typical: "[The candidate] has the precise qualities to be confirmed in the Office he fills by Election, not only because he enjoys wide esteem in the district and is one of the wealthy landowners, but also because of the good performance of that command." AN, IJ⁶ 422, off. let. from cs at Court to MJ on November 12, 1839.

Chapter 6

1. Florêncio [C.] de Abreu [e Silva], "O gado bovino e sua influência na antropogeografia do Rio Grande do Sul," *A Provincia de São Paulo*, no. 11, 1948, p. 38, *apud* Cardoso, *Capitalismo e escravidão*, p. 84, n.1. The brief historical survey presented in this section was elaborated with the help of the above work by Cardoso as well as Joseph L. Love's *Rio Grande do Sul and Brazilian Regionalism: 1822–1930*, chap. 1; Antonio Eleutherio de Camargo's *Quadro estatístico e geográphico da Província de S. Pedro do Rio Grande do Sul*; and Florêncio C. de Abreu e Silva's "Retrospecto economico e financeiro do Estado do Rio Grande do Sul: 1822–1922," as well as his "O gado bovino," quoted above but in a different edition. The title of this chapter is taken from E. da Cunha, *Rebellion in the Backlands*.

2. For the phrase on the hatred for war because of its destructive effects, see Alfred Vagts, *A History of Militarism: Civilian and Military*.

For the contrast with the Mexican *estanciero* see Chevalier, *Land and Society in Colonial Mexico: the Great Hacienda*, chap. 5. For the modernizing effects, see pp. 150–151.

With regard to the Argentinian *estancia*, see Halperin Donghi, *Politics, Economics and Society in Argentina in the Revolutionary Period*, pp. 35, 63, and

70 for the organization of work, the family, social density, and moral bonds. These pages correspond to the Spanish edition.

3. AHRGS, *lata* 448, off. let. from cs of Alegrete to pp on February 28, 1849.

AHRGS, *lata* 432, off. let. from cs of Rio Pardo to pp on October 1, 1850.

4. AHRGS, *lata* 422, off. let. from cs of Cruz Alta to pp on July 14, 1859.

5. AHRGS, *caixa* 210, *maço* 3, off. let. from cs [Porto Alegre] to pp on June 20, 1834.

6. For the justice of the peace, see, for instance, AHRGS, *caixa* 210, *maço* 3, off. let. from cs [Porto Alegre] to pp on July 19, 1834.

For the War Arsenal incident, see AHRGS, *lata* 448: com. sup. da *Guarda Nal:* 1833, off. let. from cs to pp on November 25, 1833.

7. For the evidence of Diamantina, see APM, *cod.* 229: 1839, off. let. from cel. ch. of leg. to pp on July 10, 1839.

For the unobserved practice regarding uniforms, see the above *cod.*

8. For the lack of requests for transfer, see APM, *cod.* 391:1839; and AEB, *Guarda Nal: maço* 3534, where appears the first request for transfer we found. See off. let. from cs of 5th. bat. [Capital] [to cs?] on August 28, 1838. Incidentally, the intention of that request was simply to avoid enlistment into a detached unit.

For the lack of status qualifications, see APM, *cod.* 229:1839. See that source for the insignificant character of cavalry.

9. See, for instance, AEB, *Guarda Nacional: maço* 3563 and *maço* 3554.

10. See, for instance, AN, IJ[6] 449, ms, "Proposta para os Postos das Guardas Nacionais da Província da Bahia, cuja nomeação pertence ao Governo" from pp of Bahia [to MJ] on March 26, 1832. Also AN, IJ[6] 450, off. let. from pp of Bahia to MJ on September 23, 1836.

11. With regard to the legal consciousness of Bahians, it should be remembered that several of the incidents relative to the *foro* institution took place there. See the two cases quoted in a previous chapter: AN, IJ[1] 707, pp to MJ on December 20, 1834, and AEB, *Guarda Nacional: maço* 3528, off. let. from a group of officers from the parish of N.S. da Conceição da Praia [Capital] to ch. of 1st. leg., on August 6, 1832. Moreover, the only systematic reflection on the changing climate of legality found in the documents examined was written by a Bahian notable. This was by no means accidental. It is a beautiful text that will be used in the final chapter in the discussion of the development of a rational legal mentality.

With regard to the *Mineiro* emphasis on moral principles, it was only in examining these provincial documents that we were struck by the salience of this feature. It appears, but very tenuously, in some areas of the Provinces of Rio and Bahia. Only in Minas does it appear with sharpness. For the quotation, see APM, *cod.* 228, off. let. from the cel. ch. of the leg. of Queluz to pp on October 10, 1839. The only qualification likely to be found in the early decades in Minas Gerais apart from the legal ones is probity.

The *Mineiro* emphasis on moral virtuosism has a stoic ring that is characteristically reflected in the following episode. A candidate for the office of instructor was supposed to submit—apart from a report on his professional experience—certificates of good moral standing from local authorities. The president of the local legislature observed that the candidate lived honestly and was appreciated for "his prudence and good behavior"; the parson commented, "[He] lives with probity and performs his duties as a useful and peaceful citizen." See APM, *cod.* 231, off. let. from ch. of leg. of Diamantina to pp on December 11, 1839 and annexed documents.

12. On the question of cadets and uniforms, see APM, *cod.* 768, off. let. from cs of Barbacena to pp on January 10, 1859.

For Ouro Preto's qualifications for the instructor, see APM, *cod.* 768, off. let. from cs to pp on January 30, 1859.

For the Serro case, see APM, *cod.* 768, off. let. from the major to the cel. com. of Serro bat. on January 22, 1859.

13. For evidence on the lack of status qualifications, see, for instance, AHRGS, *lata* 448, leg. da G.N. de Porto Alegre: 1835. There can also be found the reference to job duplication: see off. let. from act. cs to pp on January 14, 1835.

For the quotation referring to candidates living close to the company parades, I apologize for not having recorded its archival location; the locale, though, is AHRGS, off. let. from act. leg. com. to pp on December 8, 1850. It is a proposal for officers of the cavalry corps of the legion.

For requirements of strength and agility, see AHRGS, *lata* 422, ms note annexed to off. let. from instructor general of Cruz Alta to pp on November 28, 1850.

14. AN, IJ⁶ 460, ms, Despacho Imperial no. 499, R.G.S.: G.N. Pedido de Reforma do Ten. Cel. do Corpo de Cav. no. 41 da G.N. de R.G.S., June 18, 1879.

Clifford Geertz has sketched some basic components of Islamic culture that, not surprisingly, help make sense of some cultural traits of the Iberic—and by extension Latin American—tradition. See his *Islam Observed: Religious Development in Morocco and Indonesia.* Bravery was not a value shared by other areas under the influence of a pastoral economy. It did not show up in the pertinent areas of Bahia or Minas. In Campos, in the Province of Rio de Janeiro, a request for retirement was supported by the information that the candidate always was "quiet and peaceful," certainly a disqualifying virtue for a *gaúcho* militiaman. BPER [G. N.: Campos, S. João da Barra e São Fidelis: 1855], letter of recommendation (*atestado*) from the act. com. of the 7th comp. of the 13th. bat., Campos, November 9, 1854, annexed to request for retirement from the cap. of the 5th. comp. on January 24, 1855.

15. Proposals that illustrate the above pattern may be found in AHRGS, *lata* 431: G.N., ms, *"Propostas para oficiales comandantes,"* annexed to off. let. from cs of Rio Pardo to pp on March 25, 1848.

Also AHRGS, *lata* 448, proposal to fill the offices of the districts of Capivari, Encruzilhada and São José do Patrocinio, 1849; see also proposal of October 3, 1848 annexed to proposal included in off. let. from lieut. col. of the G.N. of Rio Pardo to pp on January 3, 1849. All the above documents stress courage, command experience or ability, services rendered, intelligence, and (occasionally) local prestige or economic status.

For a proposal without the slightest mention of social status or background, see, AHRGS, *lata* 431, proposal from the cavalry corps of Cachoeira on June 24, 1849, and from the cavalry corps of the county of Rio Pardo on July 12, 1849.

16. For proposals without status qualifications in the 1850s and 1860s, see AHRGS, *lata* 422, proposals for the officers of the cavalry corps of Cruz Alta on November 27, 1868; November 15, 1859; November 16, 1859; October 30, 1859.

For quotations, see AN IG[13] [still unclassified], off. let. from pp of Rio Grande do Sul to cs of the G.N. of that province on April 25, 1872.

17. For illustrative cases, see AN, IG[13] 676, off. let. from cs of the city of Rio Grande to pp on July 24, 1885; AN, IG[13] 674, off. let. from the cs of the county of Rio Pardo to pp on April 10, 1885; and AHRGS, *lata* 428, off. let. from the cs of Quarai e Livramento to pp on August 24, 1881.

18. AN, IG[13] 672, off. let. from cs of Porto Alegre to pp on June 29, 1858.

19. AHRGS, *lata* 422, cs: Cruz Alta, comment put down by a bureaucrat of the Secretaria do Governo of the pp on November 6, 1862.

20. AN, *caixa* 783, *pac.* 2, off. let. from pp of Rio Grande do Sul to MJ on December 31, 1850, reporting on the *Inspectoria* created for the evaluation.

21. AHRGS, *lata* 432, off. let. from cs of Rio Pardo to pp on January 3, 1859. For a more detailed report see, for instance, AHRGS, *lata* 442, off. let. from the Presidente of the Qualifying Council of Bagé to pp on June 26, 1860; in each parish of the *Campanha* 100 to 300 citizens were dispensed—"precisely . . . the most courageous and intelligent and . . . those who could get their uniforms and equip themselves with more promptitude and gallantry on account of their possessions."

22. See AN, IJ[1] 418, off. let. from pp of Bahia to MJ on December 3, 1869.

23. AHRGS, *lata* 428, off. let. from cs of Quarai e Livramento to pp on June 23, 1880.

For more evidence on the general disorganization, see, for instance, AHRGS, *lata* 428, off. let. from cs of Quarai e Livramento to pp on March 1, 1874; AHRGS *lata* 435, off. let. from cs of S. Borja e Itacui to pp on January 3, 1872; November 9, 1872 and April 20, 1875; AHRGS, *lata* 432, off. let. from act. cs of Rio Pardo to pp on June 4, 1870; June 10, 1870; May 16, 1870; off. let. from com. of Encruzilhada to cs of Rio Pardo on May 10, 1870 (there are two dispatches with the same data above: both are relevant). Also AHRGS, *lata* 441, off. let. from act. com. of Piratini to pp on February 14, 1871; AHRGS, *lata* 422, off. let. from cs of Cruz Alta to pp on February 4, 1879.

Official status in the professional army as an "honorary officer" for those commissioned in it during the war could be maintained thereafter if the officer so chose, according to an *aviso* of February 13, 1872 of the Ministry of Justice. This further contributed to the dismantling of the *gaúcho* officership as war promotions were very rapid and the individual received, naturally, the salary equivalent to his new bureaucratic position. For further effects, before the *aviso*, see AHRGS, *lata* 422, off. let. from cs of Cruz Alta to pp on December 12, 1870.

24. See, for instance, AHRGS, *lata* 428, cs: Quarai e Livramento, proposal for the 56th. Cavalry Corps on July 19, 1880; *lata* 422, cs: Cruz Alta, proposal for the 61st. Cavalry Corps on March 20, 1880; and for the 62nd. on April 7, 1880; and for the 60th. on April 16, 1880.

25. It was not possible to confirm this pattern for Minas Gerais because the regional archive has classified sources only up to the early 1870s. The sources for the Province of Rio de Janeiro in the archive in Niteroi are very scanty for that period as well. There is, however, little doubt that the development was uniform.

26. In AN, IG^{13} 674.

27. For especially significant documents see AN, Seção de Doc. Hrica, *caixa* 777, *pac.* 1, ms. sent by 82 notables of the county of Itaborahy, Rio de Janeiro, to the emperor protesting against the abusive retaliations of the representative authorities of the new cabinet against the judicial, police, and militia representatives of the cabinet in power during the early 1840s.

Also, BPER [G.N.: 8a. e 13a. legs.: 1844], off. let. from act. cs to pp on March 12, 1844 and annexed off. let. from act. lieut. cel. of the 8th leg. to act. cs on March 5, 1844.

And BPER [G.N.: Avulsos sem classificar], off. let. from cs of Rezende to pp on August 6, 1846 (a splendid piece that is not possible to reproduce here because of its length). It reveals how political calculation lay behind an apparently patrimonial orientation of service. See also IJ^6 446, ms from officers of the G.N. of Sergipe to the Emperor on October 22, 1842.

28. For some interesting documents on commanders, party politics, and elections, see AN, IJ^1 466, off. let. from pp of Rio de Janeiro to MJ on October 19, 1864; AN, IJ^6 14, off. let. from MJ to cs at the Court on October 28, 1856; AN, IJ^6 464, off. let. from pp of Ceará to MJ on September 21, 1872; and off. let. from pp of Minas Gerais to MJ on September 9, 1869; BPER [G.N.: Avulsos, 1867], off. let. from cs of Rezende, Rio de Janeiro, to pp on October 15, 1867; and BPER [G.N.: Avulsos sem classificar], off. let. from cs of Parahiba do Sul to pp of Rio de Janeiro on November 20, 1885.

29. See AN, IJ^6 419, off. let. from pp of Rio Grande do Sul to MJ on August 17, 1836.

30. See, for instance, AHRGS, *lata* 432, off. let. from cs of Rio Pardo to pp on November 25, 1850.

31. See AHRGS, *lata* 435, cs: S. Borja, off. let. from cs of the *comarca* of Missões to pp on November 2, 1849.

32. For typical instances, see AHRGS, *lata* 435, cs: S. Borja, off. let. from cs of Missões to pp on February 3, 1861, and AHRGS, *lata* 422, off. let. from cs of Cruz Alta to pp on July 28, 1868.

33. The proposal is annexed to the off. let. from the said commander to pp on April 7, 1863 in *lata* 422, AHRGS. For an equally illustrative case, see the vicissitudes of the frontier commander-in-chief of Quarai and Livramento, David Canabaro, in the mid-1860s in AHRGS, *lata* 428, cs: Quarai e Livramento.

34. For the quotations, see respectively, AHRGS, *lata* 428, cs: Quarai e Livramento, off. let. of cs to pp on December 5, 1869 and on March 14, 1870. It is important to observe that one of the four basic goals of the Liberal

Manifesto of 1869 was the abolition of the *Guarda Nacional*, side by side with the emancipation of the slaves, an electoral, and a judiciary reform.

35. For the partisan definition of liturgies see, for instance, AN, IG[13] 674, off. let. from act. cs of Rio Pardo and Encruzilhada to pp on February 24, 1871.

For the first quotation, see AN, Seção de Doc. Hrica, *caixa* 781, *pac.* 2, off. let. from cs of Alegrete to pp on June 24, 1872.

For the quotation about the liberal party in São Borja, see AN, *caixa* 781, *pac.* 2, ms., memorial annexed to report of the vice-p on October 20, 1871.

For last quotation, see AN, *caixa* 781, *pac.* 2, letter from Amaro Ferreira de Camargo Bueno to pp, Passo Fundo, on May 11, 1872.

36. The source of the first quotation is AN, IJ[6] 464, a confidential letter from pp to MJ on April 20, 1872.

For the communication of the president, see AN, *caixa* 781, *pac.* 2, off. let. from pp [to MJ?] on December 9, 1871.

37. For other places before the 1870s see, for instance, AN, IJ[1] 412, off. let. from pp of Bahia to MJ on November 21, 1861. For Rio Grande do Sul, see AHRGS, *lata* 422, cs: Cruz Alta, [*pac.* for 1873], lists of conduct on January 31, 1873. Trustworthiness being a political property it was, consequently, particularly expected for offices of command.

38. For the first quotation, see AN, Seção de Doc. Hrica, *caixa* 823, *pac.* 2, off. let. from pp to the Min. of War on March 2, 1851.

For the second quotation, see AN, *caixa* 783, *pac.* 2, off. let. from pp to MJ on December 31, 1850.

39. Ibid.

40. BPER [G.N.: Maricá e Itaborahy: 1854], off. let. from act. cs to vice-p on May 4, 1854.

See also, BPER [G.N., Maricá e Itaborahy: 1858], off. let. from cs to pp on September 14, 1858; and [G.N.: Campos e S. João da Barra: 1862], off. let. from cs to pp on January 20, 1862.

41. AHRGS, *lata* 432, off. let. from act. cs to pp on January 9, 1865. The corps was ready to march on March 5, 1865 all the same.

42. The first quotation is from AHRGS, *lata* 422, off. let. from cs of Cruz Alta to pp on June 14, 1859. The second is from AHRGS, *lata* 428, off. let. from cs of Quarai and Livramento to pp on January 7, 1865.

43. For this latter case, see note 41 above. For the commission to buy horses, see AHRGS, *lata* 422, off. lets. from cs of Cruz Alta to pp on May 29, 1866, May 30, 1866, and August 13, 1866.

44. AHRGS, *caixa* 210, *maço* 3, off. let. from cs to pp on July 8, 1834.

45. The source for the disbanded contingents is AHRGS, *lata* 435, off. let. from cs of the Comarca of Missões to pp on January 2, 1849.

For instructions given to the com. of Cruz Alta, AHRGS, see *lata* 448, off. let. from the said com. to pp on December 15, 1850.

46. AHRGS, *lata* 435, off. let. from the cs of São Borja to pp on June 18, 1869. For other illustrative cases, see AHRGS, *lata* 428, off. let. from cs of Quarai and Livramento to pp on January 7, 1865, and *lata* 422, of cs [?] of Cruz Alta to pp on May 4, 1865. Also, AN, IG[13] 674, off. let. from cs of the Comarca of Rio Pardo to pp on August 12, 1884.

47. See AHRGS, *lata* 435, off. let. from cs of Missões to pp on July 4, 1849.

48. AN, *caixa* 783, *pac.* 1, off. let. from cs of Missões to pp on February 16, 1850.

Chapter 7

1. Durkheim performed the extraordinary exploit of discussing morality scientifically without a disenchanting attitude. Parsons did not. Weber's "probabilistic" method reduced its significance.
Kant's reflections may be found in the *Conclusion* to his *Critique of Practical Reason*.
The sublimity evoked by the representation of the moral universe is discussed in his *Critique of Judgement,* first part, second book, "Analytic of the Sublime."
For information on the Luddites, see Elpídio de Almeida, *História de Campina Grande* and Horácio de Almeida, *Brejo de Areia: Memórias de um município.*
The quotation above was drawn from Elpídio de Almeida, *História,* pp. 147–148.

2. Ibid., pp. 149–150.

3. The source of the invasion of public lands is in AN, IJ¹ 661, off. let. from pp of Minas Gerais to MJ on March 21, 1842.
The statement of the court judge may be found in AN, IJ¹ 771, off. let. from the Juiz de Direito da Comarca do R. Grande to pp. of Minas Gerais on September 26, 1853.
The statement about security conditions comes from AN, IJ¹ 410, official letter from Chief of Police of Bahia to MJ on March 31, 1855.

4. The above quotations were all drawn from dispatches from the pp of Sergipe to MJ on, respectively, December 3, 1851, September 3, 1851, and February 3, 1851.

5. AN, Seção de Doc. Hrica, *caixa* 823, *pac.* 2, off. let. from pp. of Rio Grande do Norte to MJ on May 11, 1850.

6. Ibid. For another illustrative case with regard to the synchronized action between elections and political reassertiveness, see AN, *caixa* 783, *pac.* 2, letters from Antonio Joaquim da Silva Gomes [pp of Goyaz] to MJ on May 11, 1851, June 11, 1851, and July 11, 1851.

7. This affair was reconstructed from the following sources: AN, IJ¹ 709, off. let. from pp of Bahia to MJ on July 1, 1843; AN, IJ¹ 400, off. let. from cs of Pilão Arcado to pp on December 31, 1843; and pp of Bahia to MJ on September 30, 1844; AEB, G.N.: *maço* 355, off. let. from act. cs of Pilão Arcado to pp on February 4, 1845; let. from cs of Joazeiro to pp on July 3, 1845; and let. from Manuel da Costa to cs of Joazeiro on September 29, 1845; AN, IJ¹ 709, off. let. from pp of Bahia to MJ on September 23, 1845; off. let. from major com. of detachment to pp in Rio das Contas, September 10, 1845; off. let. from court judge of Rio das Contas to pp on September 10, 1845; off. let. from pp of Bahia to MJ on December 10, 1845; January 10, 1846; August 27,

1846; AN, IJ¹ 710, off. let. from pp of Bahia to MJ on February 10, 1848; May 18, 1848; July 12, 1848; August 31, 1848; off. let. of court judge of Sento Se to pp on June 13, 1848; and Municipal Camara of Sento Se to pp on April 17, 1848; off. let. from the police chief of Bahia to pp on October 15, 1848; and let. from pp (very probably to a senator at the Court) on August 16, 1848 from which the last quotation was drawn.

8. The official envoy's report, written by the Col. Francisco Feliz da Fonseca and addressed to the Field Marshall and Com. of the Army in Rio Grande do Sul on February 3, 1851, may be found in AN, Sec. de Doc. Hrica, *caixa* 823, *pac.* 2.

The rebellion of the Barão de Jacuhy is partially documented in same *caixa* and in AN, IG¹³ 671, off. no. 1095 from the commander-in-chief of the Army to pp of Rio Grande do Sul on November 29, 1853.

9. For the concepts of penalty and revenge, see Hegel, "Droit naturel e droit politique," par. 110 in his *La societé bourgeoise,* and *Philosophy of Right,* par. 102 and par. 220.

For the ambush episode, see AN, IJ¹ 765, off. let. from pp of Minas Gerais to MJ on August 10, 1835. Another very illustrative case may be found in AN, IJ¹ 866, let. from the *fazendeiro* Felicio Augusto Lacerda [to MJ?], Vera Cruz, Pati do Alferes, November 10, 1855.

For the last quotation, see AN, IJ¹ 612, off. let. from pp of Minas Gerais to MJ on December 10, 1843.

10. See, for instance, L.A. Costa Pinto, *Lutas de famílias no Brasil: Introdução ao seu estudo.* It was also a family vendetta that gave rise to the extraordinary rebellion of Antonio Conselheiro at the end of the century, and to the equally extraordinary work that recreated it, *Rebellion in the Backlands,* by Euclides da Cunha.

11. AN, *caixa* 783, *pac.* 2, off. let. from pp of Paraíba do Norte to MJ on July 21, 1851. Four months later, this recently incumbent president had been caught in the described whirlwind: "I have staged a frontal war against criminals, etc." AN, *caixa* 783, *pac.* 2 on November 5, 1851.

12. Max Horkheimer quotes a text by Kierkegaard that illustrates the discussed proposition that the traditional foundation of the Brazilian patrimonial state was no longer sufficient to build a legal and valid order. "When Christ says: 'there is eternal life' and when Petersen, a doctoral candidate in theology, says: 'there is eternal life,' both say the same thing; there is no more deduction, development, profundity, richness of thought in the first statement than in the second; aesthetically appreciated, both statements are equally good. And yet, there is an eternal, qualitative difference! Christ, as man-God, has the specific quality of authority. . . . To demand whether Christ is profound is a blasphemy and an insidious attempt to annihilate him (whether consciously or unconsciously) because the question contains a doubt about his authority . . . as if he were there to submit a test and he had to give a lesson." Kierkegaard, *Der Begriff des Auserwählten, apud* Max Horkheimer, "Autoridad y familia," in *Teoría crítica,* p. 129. A systematic exposition of Kierkegaard's basic thesis behind the above quoted text—the idea that truth is subjectivity—may be found in his *Concluding Unscientific Postscript,* book two, part two, particularly chap. II. We are not claiming, of

course, that traditional authority is always established with the transcendental legitimacy that is quoted above. All we mean is that bureaucratic authority is more of the Petersen kind—persuasively grounded on argument, rationalization, discourse, logos, or even "affection," as desired by the inexperienced president of the previous note.

13. AN, IJ⁶ 418, off. let. from the justice of the peace of the 3rd district of Sacramento [Court] to the court judge and police chief on December 17, 1835.

14. Kant's distinction may be found in his *Critique of Practical Reason*, book I, chap. 3. Parson's position is stated in his *The Social System*, particularly in "The institutional integration of action elements," of chap. 2. Weber's may be found in *Economy and Society*, vol. 1, chap. 1.

15. AEB, G.N.: *maço* 3535, off. let. from cs of the Capital of Bahia [to pp?] on November 19, 1839.

16. AEB, G.N.: *maço* 3344, off. let. from cs of the Capital of Bahia to pp on June 23, 1873.

17. These were the most common versions.

18. These were the most common formulas, but they could also take elaborate forms such as: "Your Excellency will, however, order that which in your wisdom you think best."

19. AEB, G.N.: *maço* 3528; off. let. from cs of Villa do Caetité to pp on September 10, 1833. For a significant incident in Rio Grande do Sul, see AHRGS, G.N.: *lata* 432, off. let. from cs of Rio Pardo to pp on January 10, 1861.

20. BPER [G.N.: Niterói, 1870], off. let. from com. of 1st. bat. of the reserve service of Niterói to the chief of police of the province on January 21, 1870.

21. The first quotation is from BPER [G.N.: Avulsos sem classificação], off. let. from cs of Itaguahy to pp on July 1, 1870. The case of Bahia is from AEB, G.N.: *maço* 3612, proposals for the appointment of officers of Ilheus in off. let. form cs of the Capital to pp on August 26, 1867.

22. These are literal translations.

23. AN, IJ⁶ 464, decree of dismissal of April 15, 1871; off. let. from pp of Rio Grande do Sul to MJ on November 15, 1869; and Imperial dispatch: R.G.S.—Guarda Nacional: dismissal on January 13, 1870, wherefrom I draw the quotations.

24. For another illustrative case, see AHRGS, *lata* 428, annexed comments of mandarins to proposals for appointment of officers of corps no. 55 on April 8, 1882, and July 2, 1882 of the G.N. of Quarai and Livramento.

25. AHRGS, *lata* 422, off. let. from cs of Cruz Alta to pp of Rio Grande do Sul on October 20, 1860.

26. Ibid., off. let. of December 4, 1860.

27. AEB, G.N.: *maço* 3582, manuscript comment annexed to off. let. of cs of Jaguaripe to pp of Bahia on July 5, 1854. Another interesting illustration on the discussion above is AN, IJ⁶ 443, off. let. from ch. of leg. of Valença to MJ on August 10, 1833.

28. AHRGS, G.N.; *lata* 432, off. let. from the inspector of the *Guarda Nacional* in Porto Alegre to pp on January 21, 1851.

29. AN, IJ¹ 661, off. let. from pp of Minas Gerais to MJ on February 4, 1842. See also the approbatory remarks of this same authority to MJ with regard to the legal change indicated above in AN, IJ¹ 661, off. let. on March 31, 1842.

30. The archival evidence on this topic is vast. For the references in this paragraph as well as others of striking character, see AN, IJ⁶ 443, off. let. from com. of Praia Grande, Rio de Janeiro, to MJ on October 14, 1833 and the bureaucratic comment at the margin; the same to the same on November 26, 1833; and off. let. from com. of Mangaratiba to MJ on December 23, 1832. See also AN, IJ⁶ 422, off. let. from cs at the Court to MJ on August 21, 1839; IJ⁶ 423, off. let. from cs at the Court to MJ on November 6, 1840; AN, IJ⁶ 414, off. let. from act. cs at the Court to MJ on February 26, 1834; IJ⁶ 429, off. let. from cs at the Court to MJ on October 28, 1857; and IJ¹ 466, off. let. from cs of Magé, Estrella, and Petrópolis to pp relayed by the latter to MJ on February 5, 1864, particularly the comments of the mandarin.

31. The Rio Pardo case may be found in AHRGS, *lata* 128–129, Camara Municipal de Rio Pardo: Correspondência.

32. With regard to the demands for autonomy regarding garrisoning, discussed above, see AN, IJ¹ 412, off. let. from pp of Bahia to MJ on June 20, 1861.

For the president's personal decision about enlistment and approval by the Ministry, see BPER [G.N. Avulsos sem classificação], off. let. from MJ to pp of Rio de Janeiro on June 8, 1865.

For consciousness of the provisional character of the prerogative, see AN, IJ¹ 423, off. let. from pp of Bahia to MJ on February 18, 1874.

33. A very illustrative instance may be found in AN, IJ⁶ 414, off. let. from act. cs of the G.N. [at the Court] to MJ on March 14, 1834. Significantly, the commander suggested the adoption of the administrative patterns of the professional army.

34. Relevant sources for this topic may be found in AN, IJ⁶ 423, off. let. from cs [at the Court] to MJ on March 21, 1840; IJ⁶ 425, off. let. from cs [at the Court] to MJ on February 13, 1845; and documents in IJ⁶ 427 for 1849. It seems that the innovation of the standard forms came from Marshall Caldwell, a prominent professional military man.

35. See, for instance, the model of convocation for enlistment into active service in AN, IJ⁶ 427 annexed to off. let. from cs [at the Court] to MJ on September 9, 1851. See also the model of report of conduct for officers in AN, IJ⁶ 429 annexed to off. let. from cs [at the Court] to MJ on March 27, 1857.

36. The first Imperial decree found to this effect was issued on July 27, 1865.

37. The full series may be found in BPER [G.N.: Avulsos sem classificação], circular form MJ to pp on October 17, 1873; January 19, 1874; April 21, 1874; April 8, 1876; January 15, 1877; July 7, 1877; December 11, 1877, and May 15, 1878.

It is very likely that some circulars with the same request for the period of 1875 were also sent. They could not be found, however.

Sources

I. General Bibliography

Aron, Raymond. "Social Class, Political Class, Ruling Class," in Reinhard Bendix and Seymour Martin Lipset, eds., *Class, Status, and Power: Social Stratification in Comparative Perspective*. London: Routledge & Kegan Paul, 1967, pp. 201–210.

Bendix, Reinhard. *Nation-Building and Citizenship: Studies of Our Changing Social Order*. Garden City, New York: Anchor Books, 1969.

Bergson, Henri. *Les deux sources de la morale et de la religion*. Paris: Presses Universitaires de France, 1973.

Blum, Jerome. *Lord and Peasant in Russia: From the Ninth to the Nineteenth Century*. Princeton, New Jersey: Princeton University Press, 1961.

Couturat, Louis. "On Leibniz's Metaphysics," in Harry G. Frankfurt, ed., *Leibniz: A Collection of Critical Essays*. Garden City, New York: Anchor Books, 1972.

Geertz, Clifford. *Islam Observed: Religious Development in Morocco and Indonesia*. New Haven, Conn: Yale University Press, 1968.

_____ . *Peddlers and Princes: Social Change and Economic Modernization in Two Indonesian Towns*. Chicago: University of Chicago Press, 1963.

Goffman, Erving. *Asylums: Essays on the Social Situation of Mental Patients and Other Inmates*. Garden City, New York: Anchor Books, 1961.

Elisenstadt, S. N. *Traditional Patrimonialism and Modern Neopatrimonialism*. Beverly Hills, Ca: Sage Publications, 1973.

Hegel, G. W. F. *La société bourgeoise*. Paris: François Maspero, 1975.

————. *Logic: Being Part One of The Encyclopaedia of the Philosophical Sciences (1830)*. Translated by William Wallace. Oxford: Clarendon Press, 1975.

————. *The Phenomenology of Mind*. Translated by G. B. Baillie. London: George Allen & Unwin, 1949.

————. *The Philosophy of History*. Translated by J. Sibree. New York: Dover Publications, 1956.

————. *The Philosophy of Right*. New York: Oxford University Press, 1967.

Homans, George Caspar. *English Villagers of the Thirteenth Century*. New York: Harper Torchbooks, 1970.

————. "The Rural Sociology of Medieval England," in G. C. Homans, *Sentiments and Activities: Essays in Social Science*. New York: The Free Press of Glencoe, 1962.

Horkheimer, Max. *Teoría Crítica*. Buenos Aires: Amorrortu Editores, 1974.

Kant, Immanuel. *Critique of Judgement*. Translated by J. H. Bernard. New York: Hafner Press, 1951.

————. *Critique of Practical Reason*. Translated by Lewis White Beck. New York: The Bobbs-Merrill Co., 1956.

————. *Critique of Pure Reason*. Translated by Norman Kemp Smith. London: Macmillan, 1929.

Kierkegaard, Søren. *Concluding Unscientific Postscript* [*to the Philosophical Fragments*]. Edited by Walter Lowrie. Princeton: Princeton University Press, 1968.

Lukács, Georg. *History and Class Consciousness: Studies in Marxist Dialectics*. Cambridge, Mass.: MIT Press, 1971.

Macpherson, C. B. *The Political Theory of Possessive Individualism: Hobbes to Locke*. New York: Oxford University Press, 1964.

Marshall, T. H. *Sociology at the Crossroads and Other Essays*. London: Heinemann, 1963.

Marx, Karl. *Contribution à la Critique de l' Économie Politique*. Paris: Editions Sociales, 1957.

Murvar, Vatro. "Patrimonial-Feudal Dichotomy and Political Structure in Pre-Revolutionary Russia: One Aspect of the Dialogue between the Ghost of Marx and Weber," *The Sociological Quarterly* 12 (1971): 4.

Parsons, Talcott. *The Social System*. New York: The Free Press, 1964.

Pirenne, Henri. "Stages in the Social History of Capitalism," in Bendix and Lipset, eds., *Class, Status, and Power*, pp. 97–107.

Plumb, J. H. *The Growth of Political Stability in England: 1675–1725*. Baltimore: Penguin Books, 1969.

Rosenberg, Hans. *Bureaucracy, Aristocracy and Autocracy: The Prussian Experience, 1660–1815*. Boston: Beacon Press, 1958.

Stinchcombe, Arthur L. "Some Empirical Consequences of the Davis-Moore Theory of Stratification," in Bendix and Lipset, eds., *Class, Status, and Power*, pp. 69–72.

Stone, Lawrence. *The Crisis of the Aristocracy: 1558–1641*. New York: Oxford University Press, 1967.

Swanson, Guy E. *The Birth of the Gods: The Origin of Primitive Beliefs*. Ann Arbor: University of Michigan Press, 1964.

Vagts, Alfred. *A History of Militarism: Civilian and Military*. New York: The Free Press, 1959.

Weber, Max. *Ancient Judaism*. New York: The Free Press, 1967.

―――. *Economy and Society: An Outline of Interpretive Sociology*, 3 vols. Edited by Guenther Roth and Claus Wittich. New York: Bedminster Press, 1968.

―――. *From Max Weber: Essays in Sociology*. Edited by H. H. Gerth and C. Wright Mills. New York: Oxford University Press, 1958.

―――. *The Methodology of the Social Sciences*. Edited by Edward A. Shils and Henry A. Finch. New York: The Free Press, 1949.

―――. *The Religion of China: Confucianism and Taoism*. New York: The Free Press, 1951.

―――. *The Religion of India: The Sociology of Hinduism and Buddhism*. New York: The Free Press, 1967.

II. Specialized Bibliography on Brazil and Latin America

Abreu e Silva, Florêncio C. de. *O gado bovino e sua influência na antropogeografia do Rio Grande do Sul*. Rio de Janeiro: Empresa Gráfica Mandarino & Molinari, 1942.

―――. "Retrospecto econômico e financeiro do Estado do Rio Grande do Sul: 1822–1922." *Revista do Archivo Público do Rio Grande do Sul* 8 (1922).

Almeida, Elpídio de. *História de Campina Grande*. Campina Grande, Paraíba: Edições da Livraria Pedrosa, n.d.

Almeida, Horácio de. *Brejo de Areia: Memórias de um município*. Rio de Janeiro: Ministério da Educação e Cultura, 1958.

Antonil, André João [João Antônio Adreoni]. *Cultura e opulencia do Brasil*. São Paulo: Companhia Editora Nacional, 1967. (Introduction by A. P. Canabrava to the edition of 1711).

Barman, Roderick James. "Brazil at Mid-Empire: Political Accommodation and the Pursuit of Progress under the Conciliação Ministry, 1853– 1857." Ph.D. dissertation, University of California, 1970.

————. "Uma nobreza no novo mundo: a função dos títulos no Brasil Imperial." *Mensário do Arquivo Nacional* iv, 6 (1973): 4–21.

Barretto, Vicente. *A ideologia liberal no processo da independência do Brasil.* Brasília: Centro da Documentação e Informação, 1973.

Barroso, Gustavo. *História militar do Brasil.* Rio de Janeiro: Companhia Editora Nacional, 1938.

Bello, José Maria. *Memórias de um senhor de engenho.* Rio de Janeiro: Livraria José Olympio Editora, 1938.

Boxer, C. R. *Four Centuries of Portuguese Expansion, 1451–1825: A Succinct Survey.* Johannesburg: Witwatersrand University Press, 1963.

————. *Salvador de Sá and the Struggle for Brazil and Angola: 1602–1686.* London: Athlone Press, 1952.

————. *The Golden Age of Brazil: 1695–1750: Growing Pains of a Colonial Society.* Berkeley: University of California Press, 1969.

[Brazil, Ministério da Fazenda]. *Balanço da receita e despesa do Império.* Rio de Janeiro: Typographia Nacional, various years.

[Brazil, Ministério da Fazenda]. *Exposição do estado da Fazenda Pública.* Rio de Janeiro na Typographia Nacional, 1823.

Buarque de Holanda, Sérgio. *Raízes do Brasil.* Rio de Janeiro: José Olympio, 1969.

Buescu, Mircea. *História econômica: Pesquisas e análises.* Rio de Janeiro: Apec, 1970.

Calogeras, João Pandia. *A History of Brazil.* Translated and edited by Percy Alvin Martin. New York: Russell & Russell, 1963.

Camargo, Antonio Eleutherio de. *Quadro estatístico e geographico da Província de S. Pedro do Rio Grande do Sul.* Porto Alegre: Typographia do Jornal do Commércio, 1868.

Camargo, Aspásia Alcântara de. "Autoritarismo e populismo, bipolaridade no sistema político brasileiro." *Dados* 12 (1976): 22–45.

Cardoso, Fernando Henrique. *Capitalismo e escravidão no Brasil meridional: O Negro na sociedade escravocrata do Rio Grande do Sul.* São Paulo: Difusão Européia do Livro, 1962.

Carvalho, José Murilo de. "As forças armadas na Primeira República: O poder desestabilizador." *Cadernos do Departamento de Ciência Política* (1974) 1.

————. "Elite and State-Building in Imperial Brazil." Ph.D. dissertation, Stanford University, 1974.

Castro, Jeanne Berrance de. "O povo em armas: Guarda Nacional, 1831–1850." Tese de Doutoramento, São Paulo: Faculdade de Filosofia, Ciências e Letras da Universidade de São Paulo, 1968.

Chevalier, François. *Land and Society in Colonial Mexico: The Great Hacienda.* Berkeley: University of California Press, 1970.

Cintra, Antonio Octavio. "A integração do processo político do Brasil: algumas hipóteses inspiradas na literatura." *Revista Brasileira de Administração Pública* 5 (1971): 2.

[Colombia, Congreso Nacional]. *Leyes i Decretos espedidos por el Congreso Constitucional de la Nueva Granada en el año 1850*. Bogotá: Imprenta del Neogranadino, 1850.

Conrad, Robert. *The Destruction of Brazilian Slavery: 1850–1888*. Berkeley: University of California Press, 1972.

Costa Pinto, L. A. *Lutas de famílias no Brasil: Introdução ao seu estudo*. São Paulo: Companhia Editora Nacional, 1949.

Cunha, Euclides da. *À margem da história*. Porto: Lello & Irmão, 1941.

――――. *Rebellion in the Backlands: Os Sertões*. Translated by Samuel Putnam. Chicago: University of Chicago Press, 1944.

Duarte, Nestor. *A ordem privada e a organização política nacional*. São Paulo: Companhia Editora Nacional, 1966.

Faoro, Raymundo. *Os donos do poder: Formação do patronato político brasileiro*. Rio de Janeiro: Editora Globo, 1958.

Fleiuss, Max. *História administrativa do Brasil*. São Paulo: Companhia Melhoramentos, 1922[?].

Franco, Maria Sylvia Carvalho. *Homens livres na ordem escravocrata*. São Paulo: Editora Ática, 1974.

Freyre, Gilberto. "Social life in Brazil in the Middle of the Nineteenth Century," in Lewis Hanke, ed., *Readings in Latin American History*, vol. 2. New York: Thomas Y. Crowell, 1966.

Graham, Richard. *Britain and the Onset of Modernization in Brazil: 1850– 1914*. Cambridge: Cambridge University Press, 1968.

Guimarães, Alberto Passos. *Quatro séculos de latifúndio*. Rio de Janeiro: Editora Paz e Terra, n.d.

Gurfield, Mitchel. "Class Structure and Political Power in Colonial Brazil: An Interpretative Essay in Historical Sociology." Ph.D. dissertation, New York: New School for Social Research, 1975.

Halperin Donghi, Tulio. *Politics, Economics and Society in Argentina in the Revolutionary Period*. London: Cambridge University Press, 1975.

Haring, C. H. *The Spanish Empire in America*. New York: Harbinger Books, 1963.

Iglesias, Francisco. *Política econômica do governo provincial mineiro: 1835– 1889*. Rio de Janeiro: Instituto Nacional do Livro, 1958.

Kennedy, John Norman. "Bahian Elites, 1750–1822." *Hispanic-American Historical Review* 53 (1973): 415–439.

Leal, Victor Nunes. *Coronelismo, enxada e voto: O município e o regime representativo no Brasil*. Rio de Janeiro, 1948.

Lins do Rego, José. *Menino de engenho*. Rio de Janeiro: Livraria José Olympio Editora, 1969.

Lobo, Eulália Maria Lahmayer. "Conflict and Continuity in Brazilian History," in Henry H. Keith and S. G. Edwards, eds., *Conflict and Continuity in Brazilian Society*. Columbia, South Carolina: University of South Carolina Press, 1969.

Love, Joseph L. *Rio Grande do Sul and Brazilian Regionalism: 1882–1930*. Stanford: Stanford University Press, 1971.

Lyra, Heitor. *História de Dom Pedro II: 1825–1891*. 3 vols. Rio de Janeiro: Cia. Editora Nacional, 1938–1940.

Machado, Alcântara. *Vida e morte do bandeirante*. São Paulo: Livraria Martins Editora, 1943.

Magalhães, João Batista. "História e evolução militar do Brasil." Anais [do] IV Congresso de história nacional, Rio de Janeiro, IHGB, 1950: 6.

Morner, Magnus. "La hacienda hispanoamericana en la historia: Un esquema de reciente investigación y debate." *Desarrollo Económico* 13 (1974): 52.

Morton, F. W. O. "The Military and Society in Bahia, 1820–1821." *Journal of Latin American Studies* 7, 2: 249–269.

Ots Capdequi, José Maria. *Instituciones de gobierno del Nuevo Reino de Granada durante el siglo xviii*. Bogotá: Universidad Nacional de Columbia, 1950.

_____. *Nuevos aspectos del siglo xviii español en América*. Bogotá: Editorial Centro, 1946.

Palmeira, Moacyr. "Latifundium et Capitalisme au Brésil: Lecture Critique d'un Débat." These 3e. cycle, Paris, 1971.

Pang, Eul-Soo and Ron L. Seckinger. "The Mandarins of Imperial Brazil." *Comparative Studies in Society and History* 9, 2 (1971): 215–244.

Pereira de Queiróz, Maria Isaura. "O mandonismo local na vida política brasileira." *Anhembi* 6: 24, nos. 71–76.

Prado Jr. Caio. *The Colonial Background of Modern Brazil*. Translated by Suzette Machado. Berkeley: University of California Press, 1971.

Reis, Fabio Wanderley. "Brasil: 'Estado e Sociedade' em perspectiva." *Cadernos do Departamento de Ciência Política* (1974): 2.

Rocha, Justiniano José da. "Ação, reação, transação: Duas palavras acerca da atualidade política do Brasil," in Raimundo Magalhães Junior, *Três Panfletários do Segundo Reinado*. São Paulo: Cia. Editora Nacional, 1956, pp. 161–218.

Saint-Hilaire, Auguste de. *Segunda Viagem do Rio de Janeiro a Minas Gerais e a São Paulo: 1822*. Belo Horizonte: Livraria Itatiaia Editora, 1974.

Santos, Wanderley Guilherme dos. "Liberal Praxis in Brasil." Paper presented to the Seminar on Ideology and Inter-American Relations, University of South Carolina, February 1974.

Schwartz, Stuart B. "Free Labor in a Slave Economy: The Lavradores de Cana of Colonial Bahia," in Dauril Alden, ed., *Colonial Roots of Modern Brazil*. Berkeley: University of California Press, 1973.

————. *Sovereignty and Society in Colonial Brazil: The High Court and its Judges. 1609–1751*. Berkeley: University of California Press, 1973.

Schwartzman, Simon. "Representação e cooptação política no Brasil." *Dados* (1970): 7.

————. *São Paulo e o estado nacional*. São Paulo: Difel, 1975.

Sodré, Nelson Werneck. *Formação histórica do Brasil*. São Paulo: Editora Brasiliense, 1962.

Stein, Stanley J. *Vassouras: A Brazilian Coffee County, 1850–1900*. Cambridge, Mass.: Harvard University Press, 1970.

Stein, Stanley J., and Barbara H. Stein. *The Colonial Heritage of Latin America: Essays on Economic Dependence in Perspective*. New York: Oxford University Press, 1969.

Torres, João Camilo de Oliveira. *A democracia coroada: Teoria política do Império do Brasil*. Rio de Janeiro: Livraria José Olympio Editora, 1957.

Uricoechea, Fernando. *Patrimonialism, Electoral Patterns and Social Stratification in Imperial Brazil*. Rio de Janeiro: IUPERJ, 1977.

Vianna, [Francisco José de] Oliveira. *Evolução do povo brasileiro*. Rio de Janeiro: José Olympio Editora, 1956.

————. *Instituições políticas brasileiras*. Vol. 1. Rio de Janeiro: Livraria José Olympio Editora, 1955.

————. *Populações meridionais do Brasil*. Rio de Janeiro: Paz e Terra, 1973.

Vieira da Cunha, Rui. *Estudo da nobreza brasileira: I-Cadetes*. Rio de Janeiro: Ministério da Justiça e Negócios Interiores, Arquivo Nacional, 1966.

III. Archival Sources

Arquivo Nacional

General Entry: *Guarda Nacional*

Section: *Seção de Documentação Histórica*

Códices: 112, vols. 5, 6, 7 (1814–1848); 430, vol. 1 (1867–1868); 502, vol. 1 (1822–1874); 594, vols. 1 and 2 (1852–1883); 606, vol. 1 (1522–1882); 707, (1853–1903); 718 (1814–1845).

Caixas:

1. *Ministério da Justiça*: 771 *Pacotilha* 2 (n.d.); 771 *Pacotilha* 4 (n.d.); 777 *Pacotilha* 1 (1831–1862); 778 *Pacotilha* 1 (n.d.); 778 *Pacotilha* 2

(n.d.); 778 *Pacotilha* 3 (n.d.); 781 *Pacotilha* 1 (1849–1850); 781 *Pacotilha* 2 (1872); 783 *Pacotilha* 1 and 2 (1849–1851).
2. *Ministério do Império: caixa* 503 (n.d.).
3. *Coleção Caxias: caixa* 823 Pacotilha 1 (1806–1822); *caixa* 823 Pacotilha 2 (1822–1824); *caixa* 823 Pacotilha 3 (1860–1885).

Section: *Seção dos Ministérios: Ministério da Justiça*
Caixas: IJ^6 10 (1858–59); IJ^6 14 (1854–57); IJ^6 17 (1859–60); IJ^6 29 (1835–38); IJ^6 31 (1865–67); IJ^6 413 (1831–33); IJ^6 414 (1834); IJ^6 415 (1832); IJ^6 416 (1835); IJ^6 417 (1835); IJ^6 418 (1836); IJ^6 419 (1836); IJ^6 420 (1837); IJ^6 421 (1838); IJ^6 422 (1839); IJ^6 423 (1840–41); IJ^6 424 (1842–43); IJ^6 425 (1844–46); IJ^6 426 (1847–48); IJ^6 427 (1849–51); IJ^6 428 (1852–54); IJ^6 429 (1855–57); IJ^6 430 (1858–63); IJ^6 431 (1864–70); IJ^6 432 (1871); IJ^6 433 (1871 e um processo de 1919); IJ^6 442 (1832–34); IJ^6 443 (1831–33); IJ^6 444 (1834–68); IJ^6 445 (1832–79); IJ^6 446 (1834–79); IJ^6 447 (1833–68); IJ^6 448 (1837–71); IJ^6 449 (1832–35); IJ^6 450 (1836–64); IJ^6 451 (1865–78); IJ^6 452 (1879); IJ^6 453 (1879); IJ^6 454 (1854–75); IJ^6 455 (1875); IJ^6 456 (1876); IJ^6 457 (1876); IJ^6 458 (1877); IJ^6 459 (1878); IJ^6 460 (1879); IJ^6 461 (1879); IJ^6 462 (1833–67); IJ^6 463 (1833–79); IJ^6 464 (1878–79); IJ^6 465 (1853–79); IJ^6 466 (1857–68).
IJ^1 489 (1865–67).

Section: *Seção dos Ministérios: Ministério da Guerra: Estado do Rio Grande do Sul*
Caixas: IG^{13} 661 (1888); IG^{13} 695 (1870–1891); IG^{13} 717 (1872–1918); IG^{13} 721 (1858–68); IG^{13} 725 (1874–75); IG^{13} 726 (1861); IG^{13} 736 (1887–88); IG^{13} 728 (1854–55); IG^{13} 729 (1867–95); IG^{13} 730 (1879); IG^{13} 731 (1880–88); IG^{13} 732 (1887); IG^{13} 733 (1887); IG^{13} 741 (1858–96); IG^{13} 742 (1867–97); IG^{13} 395 (1868–93); IG^{13} 396 (1878–1911); IG^{13} 397 (1880–96); IG^{13} 398 (1881–96); IG^{13} 399 (1881–98); IG^{13} 400 (1881–1902); IG^{13} 512 (1860–75); IG^{13} 513 (1888); IG^{13} 759 (n.d.); IG^{13} 670 (1850–61); IG^{13} 671 (1853); IG^{13} 672 (1853–59); IG^{13} 673 (1864–65); IG^{13} 674 (1870–89); IG^{13} 675 (1871–1920); IG^{13} 676 (1872–98); IG^{13} 677 (1882–94); IG^{13} 700 (1874–95); IG^{13} 720 (1881); IG^{13} 724 (1872–74); IG^{13} 740 (1856–59); IG^{13} 764 (1884–1907); IG^{13} 758 (n.d.); IG^{13} 759 (n.d.); IG^{13} 760 (n.d.); IG^{13} 659 (1871); IG^{13} 660 (1871–72); IG^{13} 697 (1865–72); IG^{13} 698 (1873–95); IG^{13} 699 (1873–95); IG^{13} 701 (1887); IG^{13} 686 (1858–97); IG^{13} 687 (1859–81); IG^{13} 689 (1868–70); IG^{13} 690 (1871–81); IG^{13} 691 (1880–8?); IG^{13} 692 (1881–90); IG^{13} 693 (1885–1912); IG^{13} 669 (1858); IG^{13} 688 (1868–70); IG^{13} 722 (1868–98); IG^{13} 723 (1876).

Section: *Seção dos Ministérios: Ministério da Guerra: Diversas Províncias*
Caixas: IG^{13} 87 (1873–92); IG^{13} 88 (1879–94); IG^{13} 106 (1869–99); IG^{13} 136 (1855–95); IG^{13} 170 (n.d.); IG^{13} 172 (n.d.); IG^{13} 173 (1873); IG^{13} 290 (1867–69); IG^{13} 291 (1886–88); IG^{13} 696 (n.d.); IG^{13} 769 (1865–

67); IG¹³ 770 (n.d.); IG¹³ 771 (1918); IG¹³ 780 (n.d.); IG¹³ 783 (n.d.); IG¹³ 793 (1894); IG¹³ 1187 (1839–71).

Section: *Seção dos Ministérios: Ofícios dos Presidentes de Província ao Ministro da Justiça*

Caixas: I. *Rio de Janeiro:* IJ¹ 859 (1823, 1832–37); IJ¹ 935 (1824–67); IJ¹ 860 (1838); IJ¹ 447 (1842–43); IJ¹ 450 (1847–48); IJ¹ 456 (1854); IJ¹ 866 (1854–56); IJ¹ 873 (1864); IJ¹ 466 (1864); IJ¹ 484 (1874); IJ¹ 485 (1874); IJ¹ 879 (1880, 1885–87). II. *Bahia:* IJ¹ 707 (1831–35); IJ¹ 708 (1836–42); IJ¹ 400 (1842–44); IJ¹ 709 (1843–47); IJ¹ 710 (1848–51); IJ¹ 410 (1855–56); IJ¹ 412 (1860–62); IJ¹ 418 (1869); IJ¹ 423 (1874); IJ¹ 718 (1886). III. *Minas Gerais:* IJ¹ 763 (1831–33); IJ¹ 764 (1834); IJ¹ 765 (1835); IJ¹ 766 (1836); IJ¹ 769 (1839); IJ¹ 770 (1840–48); IJ¹ 611 (1841–42); IJ¹ 612 (1843); IJ¹ 616 (1847–48); IJ¹ 771 (1850–53); IJ¹ 772 (1854–56); IJ¹ 620 (1854–55); IJ¹ 774 (1860); IJ¹ 775 (1861); IJ¹ 632 (1867); IJ¹ 633 (1867); IJ¹ 660 (1879); IJ¹ 661 (1879).

General Entry: *Apurações Eleitorais*

Section: *Seção dos Ministérios*

Caixas: IJJ⁵ 12 (1846–48); IJJ⁵ 1 (1846–48); IJJ⁵ 2 (1848–50); IJJ⁵ 8 (1858–60); IJJ⁵ 11 (1838); IJJ⁵ 13 (1838); IJJ⁵ 45 (1838); IJJ⁵ 36 (1843–69); IJJ⁵ 43 (1859–61); IJJ⁵ 38 (1881); IJJ⁵ 44 (1822–73); IJJ⁵ 43 (1860); IJJ⁵ 27 (1828–34); IJJ⁵ 28 (1835–37); IJJ⁵ 23 (1838–41); IJJ⁵ 24 (1842–47); IJJ⁵ 25 (1848–81); IJJ⁵ 43 (1861); IJJ⁵ 43 (1860–61); IJJ⁵ 43 (1860–61); IJJ⁵ 43 (1860–63); IJJ⁵ 43 (1860–61); IJJ⁵ 43 (1861); IJJ⁵ 43 (1860); IJJ⁵ 43 (1860–61); IJJ⁵ 43 (1860); IJJ⁵ 43 (1860–61); IJJ⁵ 43 (1860–61); IJJ⁵ 40 (1822–37); IJJ⁵ 31 (1834–63); IJJ⁵ 41 (1840–49); IJJ⁵ 17 (1821–49); IJJ⁵ 17 (1823–67); IJJ⁵ 19 (1823–43); IJJ⁵ 20 (1844–49); IJJ⁵ 34 (1833–63); IJJ⁵ 18 (1824–49); IJJ⁵ 22 (1822–59); IJJ⁵ 42 (1822–49); IJJ⁵ 32 (1872); IJJ⁵ 21 (1822–49); IJJ⁵ 15 (1821–49); IJJ⁵ 29 (1862–66); IJJ⁵ 14 (1822–49); IJJ⁵ 30 (1824–73).

Arquivo Histórico do Rio Grande do Sul

General Entry: *Guarda Nacional*

Ofícios dos Comandantes Superiores ao Presidente da Província
Códices: 80 (n.d.); 89 (n.d.).
Latas: 448 (n.d.); 435 (1849–82); 428 (1853–95); 431 (1848–49); 422 (1850–84); 441 (n.d.); 432 (1850–86).
Caixas: 210, *maço* 3 (1834); 432 (n.d.).
Conselhos de Qualificação
Códices: 84.

Latas: 442 (1861–62); 428 (1835–95); 443 (1861); 444 (1874); 445 (1874–83); 448 (1850); 439 (1849); 435 (1849–82); 444 (1874).

Promoções

Códices: 82 (1870); 83 (1858–78); 84 (1859–78); 88 (1879–89).

Latas: 439 (1859–74); 440 (1857–1872); 441 (1863–73); 437 (1868–86); 435 (1849–82); 428 (1853–95); 446 (1857–70); 447 (1858–74).

Caixas: 88/doc. 353 (1840–63).

General Entry: *Apurações Eleitorais*

Section: *Grupo 9*

Latas: 154 (1833–72); 110 (1834–89); 128 (1832–47); 129 (1848–58).

Unclassified Material: Assorted Electoral Documents ranging from 1835–1883.

Arquivo Público do Estado da Bahia

General Entry: *Guarda Nacional*

Section: *Presidencia da Província:*
   Militares, Guarda Nacional
   Ofícios dos Comandantes Superiores ao Presidente da Província

Maços: 3528 (1832–34); 3564 (1832–49); 3529 (1833–35); 3535 (1835–39); 3534 (1838); 3562 (1840–48); 3563 (1840–48); 3554 (1845); 3582 (1853–55); 3586 (1853–57); 3651 (1860–79); 3612 (1862–67); 3605 (1864–65); 3637 (1870); 3646 (1870–76); 3650 (1870–78); 3638 (1871); 3644 (1871–75); 3663 (1880–89).

Conselhos de Qualificação

Maços 3510 (1843–69); 3514 (1850); 3515 (1850); 3516 (1850); 3513 (1850–87); 3500 (1851–58); 3501 (1851–73); 3502 (1851–73); 3511 (1857–87); 3509 (1859–88); 3505 (1860–69); 3506 (1860–69); 3507 (1862–78); 3503 (1865); 3504 (1865); 3508 (1871–87); 3512 (1875).

Promoções

Maços: 3587 (1832–58); 3653 (1836–83); 3584 (1841–57); 3640 (1843–73); 3588 (1846–58); 3573 (1849–51); 3574 (1850–51); 3575 (1850–52); 3577 (1850–53); 3579 (1850–55); 3580 (1850–55); 3590 (1850–59); 3591 (1850–59); 3592 (1850–59); 3606 (1850–61); 3617 (1850–68); 3576 (1852); 3581 (1852–55); 3585 (1852–57); 3578 (1853–54); 3593 (1853–59); 3583 (1855–56); 3594 (1855–59); 3595 (1856–59); 3596 (1856–59); 3662 (1856–89); 3623 (1857–69); 3597 (1857–59); 3589 (1858); 3598 (1860); 3601 (1860–64); 3607 (1860–66); 3616 (1860–68); 3624 (1860–69); 3625 (1860–69); 3651 (1860–79); 3599 (1861); 3602 (1861–64); 3603 (1861–65); 3660 (1861–68); 3618 (1861–68); 3600 (1862); 3604 (1862–65); 3612 (1862–67); 3626 (1862–69); 3608 (1863–66); 3609 (1863–66); 3627 (1863–69);

3628 (1863–69); 3629 (1863–69); 3605 (1864–65); 3610 (1864–66); 3611
(1864–66); 3630 (1864–69); 3631 (1864–69); 3613 (1865–67); 3614 (1866–
67); 3632 (1866–69); 3654 (1866–83); 3615 (1867); 3619 (1867–68); 3620
(1867–68); 3621 (1867–68); 3633 (1867–69); 3622 (1868); 3634 (1868–
69); 3635 (1869); 3636 (1869); 3637 (1870); 3639 (1870–72); 3641 (1870–
74); 3648 (1870–78); 3649 (1870–78); 3650 (1870–78); 3638 (1871); 3642
(1871–74); 3643 (1872–74); 3647 (1872–76).

General Entry: *Eleições*
Section: *Presidencia da Província*
    Série Judiciário-Eleições
Maços: 2798 (1821–78); 2797 (1824–76); 2794 (1832–56); 2796 (1832–
74); 2802 (1850–69); 2801 (1854–89); 2795 (1856–69); 2799 (1858–85);
2803 (1875–89); 2804 (1878–89); 2800 (1880–86); 2805 (1880–89); 2806
(1885–89).

Arquivo Público do Estado de Minas Gerais

General Entry: *Guarda Nacional*
Section: *2a. Seção: 1702–1870*
Ofícios dos Comandantes da Guarda Nacional ao Governo
Códices: 228 (1839); 229 (1839); 230 (1839); 231 (1839); 286 (1840–42);
321 (1842–49); 391 (1846–48); 768 (1859).

Promoções e Matrículas
Códices: 427 (1849–50); 486 (1853); 515 (1854); 578 (1855); 579 (1855);
614 (1856); 615 (1856); 643 (1856–63); 671 (1857–63); 672 (1857); 721
(1858); 722 (1858); 723 (1858); 769 (1859); 782 (1859); 828 (1860); 829
(1860); 830 (1860); 883 (1861); 884 (1861); 885 (1861); 904 (1861–62);
942 (1862); 943 (1862); 944 (1862); 993 (1863); 994 (1863); 995 (1863);
996 (1863); 1051 (1864); 1052 (1864); 1053 (1864); 1107 (1865); 1108
(1865); 1109 (1865); 1110 (1865); 1147 (1866); 1148 (1866); 1149 (1866);
1150 (1866); 1195 (1867); 1196 (1867); 1197 (1867); 1258 (1868); 1259
(1868); 1260 (1868); 1261 (1868); 1315 (1869); 1316 (1869); 1317 (1869);
1318 (1869); 1319 (1869); 1367 (1870); 1368 (1870); 1369 (1870); 224 (2
vols.) (1880–89); 224 (1880–92); 11 (1880–92); 12 (1883–92); 6 (1879–
91); 15 (1880–92); 8 (1880–88); 1 (1880–92); 14 (1880–91); 2 (1880–92);
10 (1880–88); 4 (1880–87); 3 (1880–87); 13 (1880–92); 9 (1880–91); 16
(1880–89).

General Entry: *Eleições*
Apurações Eleitorais
1. Catálogo da Câmara de Ouro Preto, 1712–1886: no. 226 (1828–32);
233 (1829–44); 239 (1829–56); 585 (n.d.); 355 (1841–44); 305 (1836–41);
503 (1855).

2. Catálogo da Câmara Municipal de Paracatu, 1744–1838: 9 (1821–47); 12 (1824–38).

3. *Livros Manuscritos*, 1702–1870 S2: 575 (1855); 907 (1861–64); 951 (n.d.); 1071 (1862–67); 603 (1856); 604 (1856); 605 (1856); 606 (1856); 997 (1863); 999 (1863); 1155 (1866); 1156 (1866); 1059 (1864); 1060 (1864); 1156 (1866); 1264 (1868); 1265 (1868); 1266 (1868); 1267 (1868); 1270 (1868); 1269 (1868); 1268 (1868); 1267 (1868); 266 (n.d.).

Arquivo da Biblioteca Pública do Estado do Rio de Janeiro
All the entries corresponding to this Archive are provisional. They are referred to in brackets because the Archive has still not officially classified that material. The bracketed classification was suggested by the author and is the provisional one adopted by the Archive.

Arquivo da Prefeitura de Valença (Rio de Janeiro)
Codice: Vol. 147 (1865–1867).

Index

Administrative centralization, 174–179

Administrative order: conditions under patrimonialism, 3; and dilettantes, 4, 75, 123, 125–126, 153–154; and partisan institutions, 58, 171–172; and *bachareis,* 59; role played by dominant groups, 80; obstacles to its erection, 170–179

Bachareis: administrative career of, 23, 58–59; mentioned, 161, 164

Bahia, province of: cattle-breeding in the hinterland, 10; and the *governo-geral,* 13; public expenditures, 40–49 *passim;* militia organization, 107, 108, 137, 143–144; value system predominant in, 125, 136–138, 168, 204*n10,* 208*n11,* 209*n14;* mentioned, 41, 53, 119, 135, 189*n40,* 202*n5*

Bergson, Henri, 39, 193*n8*

Bureaucracy. *See* Bureaucratic organization; Patrimonial bureaucracy

Bureauacratic organization: stimulated by patrimonial administration, 14, 180–184 *passim;* and professionalization, 14, 15, 187*n16;* impact on prebendal administration, 15; structural conditions for its development, 15, 155, 180–184 *passim;* and ra-

Bureauacratic organization (continued) tionalization, 15–16; analysis of, 39–50; prevailing salaried conditions, 80–82. *See also* Rationality; Values

Bureaucratic principle. *See* Status principle

Class consciousness. *See* Corporative consciousness

Coroneis, mentioned, 58, 195*n41*

Corporate. *See* Corporative association; Corporative consciousness

Corporative association: and patrimonialism, 22; and status orientations, 25, 189*n37;* and aristocratic developments, 30–31; among *bachareis,* 59

Corporative consciousness: weak development in colonial society, 14, 187*n16;* historical development of, 23–36 *passim;* and economic integration of agrarian society, 24; and life stylization, 24; determinants of its development in the patrimonial militias, 87–96 *passim,* 136

Duarte, Nestor, 11, 198*n9*

Durkheim, Émile, 39, 131, 156, 213*n1*

Electoral principle. *See* Status principle

229

Compositor: Chapman's Phototypesetting
Printer: Thomson-Shore, Inc.
Binder: Thomson-Shore, Inc.
Text: VIP Palatino
Display: VIP Palatino Semibold
Cloth: Holliston Roxite B 53575
Paper: 50 lb. P & S Offset